MW01621087

בס"ד

THE Wasome ITCHE KADOOZY SHOW

WRITTEN BY
Dovid Taub
and Jono Goorvich

Chabad.ORG

ALL the Greatest
Episode Scripts
Are Inside!

HDTV

DISCLAIMER
s Rabbi Kadoozy's legal
presentative I hereby
orm you that this book
xtremely addicting! HA!

THE
The Wasome
ITCHE
KADOOZY
SHOW

THE WASOME ITCHE KADOOZY SHOW
ALL THE GREATEST EPISODE SCRIPTS

FIRST PRINTING

Book layout and design © Copyright 2019
Zalman Goldstein

Published by

Reprinted with permission from

and the show's creators
Dovid Taub and Jonathan Goorvich

ISBN 978-1-891293-61-0

For Information & Orders
The Jewish Learning Group
1-(888)-56-LEARN
www.JewishLearningGroup.com

ALL RIGHTS RESERVED

All rights reserved under international and pan-American copyright conventions. No part of this book may be reproduced in any form or by any means without written permission from the publisher, except for brief passages included in a review in a newspaper or magazine.

DEDICATION

To Dovid Taub and Jonathan Goorvitch
for blending so much Torah education
with equal parts joy and laughter!

ACKNOWLEDGEMENTS

Putting this book together to capture for posterity the much beloved wit and wisdom of "The Itche Kadoozy Show," was an incredibly fun and rewarding experience. Without the generous cooperation and assistance of show creators Dovid Taub and Jonathan Goorvitch, as well as Rabbi Meir Simcha Kogan and the entire team at Chabad.org, this book would have never materialized. Thank you all for helping make it happen!

Thank you Aryeh Friedman and Ginny Westcott for creative input, and to my children for introducing me to this awesome educational show!

Zalman Goldstein
Zalman@JewishLearningGroup.com

Show Creators and Writers **Dovid Taub** (l)
and **Jonathan Goorvitch** (r)

ABOUT THE SHOW CREATORS

Dovid Taub and Jonathan Goorvich grew up a block away from each other in the northwest suburbs of Chicago, Illinois. Together they drew comics and made videos they thought were hilarious, but in retrospect they thought were probably pretty awful.

In 2000, Dovid went to Rabbinical school and Jonathan went to film school. A few years later they both landed in Chicago again and despite now being full grown adults, they immediately started creating funny videos together again, this time with puppets, and thus “The Itche Kadoozy Show” was born and lives to this day on Chabad.org.

TABLE OF CONTENTS

The Cast

The Show

WASDMEI

The Parsha Report

The Quest for Fish

THE CAST

RABBI ITCHE KADOOZY

AGE: 63
OCCUPATION: Rabbi
FAVORITE MUSIC: Nigun L'Shabbat V'YomTov #372

Rabbi Itche is the Rabbi of the Ira and Edna Bernstein Jewish Center. He's been married to his wife, Mrs. Kadoozy, for 40 years and has 8 children and 57 grandchildren. Rabbi Kadoozy enjoys helping others, finding a way to learn something from every situation in which he finds himself and eating rice-cakes with peanut butter.

JONO

AGE: 23
OCCUPATION: Film Student
FAVORITE MUSIC: Anything you hear when you're on hold with a bank

Jonathan Weinsteinstein was Rabbi Kadoozy's neighbor, but then moved into the Rabbi's basement because he ran out of food. While he often has difficulty paying attention to the Rabbi's lessons, he enjoys living in a Jewish environment. Particularly because he has unlimited access to the Yarmulke Box which, in his words, is "like an archeological dig of weddings and Bar Mitzvahs.

G-FISH

AGE: 704
OCCUPATION: Serial entrepreneur, cereal entrepreneur, freelance alchemist
FAVORITE MUSIC: The sound you hear when you accidentally call a fax machine

Gefilte P. Fish is a rare, semi-aquatic creature. G-Fish was originally purchased as a pet by Jono, but has come to be considered as an equal (although he considers himself far superior.) He enjoys playing board games, posting on social media and running counter-scams on telemarketers.

CAST INTERVIEW

RABBI: Yeah, my name is Rabbi Itche Kadoozy. I am the rabbi of the Ira and Edna Bernstein Jewish Center.

JONO: The first time I actually met the rabbi was before I even knew he was going to be my rabbi. He moved into my apartment building with his wife and I went over there to ask for a cup of sugar and a hot meal. So he sat me down at his table and he gave it to me. And then, I never really wanted to eat my food or in my house anymore.

RABBI: My father was a rabbi and his father was a rabbi and his father was a tailor. So I was going to be a tailor, but it didn't work out.

JONO: If I could be trapped on a desert island with just one rabbi, that rabbi would probably be Jackie Mason if he had a rabbinical degree, but he doesn't have a rabbinical degree. So my next choice; well, that would be Rabbi Kadoozy if he had a rabbinical degree.

RABBI: I make a weekly community access cable show called Is It Holy. My wacky neighbor, Jonathan, really should help me out seeing how he's a film student and all, but I don't know. He's not interested.

JONO: Rabbi Kadoozy, is he a strong man? No. Is he a brave man? Probably not. Is he an intelligent man? I don't even know. One thing I do know is that he feeds me dinner all the time and that's something that I can depend on.

JONO: Well, I'm Jonathan. I'm a student at the Jay Shandimonieh (Ph) Academy of Moving Pictures. My concentration there is film producing, directing, writing, editing, starring, writing, lighting, catering, microphoning.

RABBI: Jonathan is my wacky neighbor and he's a great guy and a wonderful film student.

JONO: Filmmaking, storyboarding, pre-productioning, post-productioning, productioning. I'm well-rounded.

RABBI: I'll tell you, he eats a lot of kosher food. He eats all of my kosher food. Everything I have, basically, he eats. He must only eat kosher food because I don't have any left.

JONO: I started eating at the Rabbi's. It started off, he just would invite me over for Shabbat, but it turned into an every night occasion because I didn't want to go grocery shopping or cook, and I don't have enough money to order out.

RABBI: I have to hide stuff in my glove compartment. I have a bag of circus peanuts hidden in my glove compartment and he doesn't get to those.

JONO: I say I want to own a pet store because I really wouldn't have to do anything. I mean, I'd hire guys who would just clean up after all the animals. I wouldn't have to watch them all get old and sick. The animals, that is. The guys who clean up after them, I'd probably have to watch get old and sick, mostly sick. That would kind of be sad, so forget that. I'd rather own a candy store because you don't have to clean up after candies.

G-FISH: I'm a Gefilte Fish.

RABBI: The Gefilte Fish is my wacky neighbor Jonathan's pet. He's sort of a strange pet.

G-FISH: What?

RABBI: He is the first talking Gefilte Fish I've ever seen and he's the largest Gefilte Fish I've ever—he's only Gefilte Fish I've ever seen.

JONO: The Gefilte Fish is my pet and he's also a very good friend of mine. We play board games together.

G-FISH: Well, on Monday nights, we play Monopoly. On Tuesday nights, we play Connect Four. Wednesday nights, we play Scrabble.

JONO: He sort of picky when it comes to board games. He wouldn't let me be the thimble or the top hat and we weren't even playing Monopoly, so it's not like it makes a difference anyways.

G-FISH: On Thursday nights, we play Connect Four again.

JONO: When it comes to board games, the Gefilte Fish a tricky opponent; a tricky, slimy, moist, smelly sort of opponent. Come to think of it, he's pretty slimy, moist and smelly most of the time.

RABBI: He's a nice guy. He sometimes leaves a jelly-broth residue on my sofa. I don't like that.

JONO: I wonder sometimes about the origins of the Gefilte Fish. Is he some sort of government experiment gone terribly horribly, terribly wrong or is he just some sort of junior high school science-fair experiment gone terribly horribly, terribly wrong?

RABBI: He's a symbol of Jewish culture, but it's not like I have a talking Latke in my house.

JONO: The Gefilte Fish to me is sort of like a symbol of my Jewish identity; a giant talking symbol of my Jewish identity that I can play board games with.

RABBI: I don't have a giant talking matzah in my house or a giant talking Kugel. I don't have one of those, but I don't want to give Jonathan ideas because he might go find those things.

JONO: A giant talking Kugel? That sounds awesome. Maybe he won't beat me at board games all the time.

###

THE SHOW

The original website Homepage promoting "The Itche Kadoozy Show"

INTRO & BEHIND-THE-SCENES

"The Show" seems like an oddly authoritative name for a seemingly random handful of videos, but it makes a little more sense with a bit of background. In 2003 my friend **Jono** and **I** started "The Itche Kadoozy Show" with a few goofy videos that we made in my parent's kitchen, which we then attempted to sell to real people for actual legal tender. Turns out, not a lot of people wanted to spend $12 on a 15-minute Video CD-ROM. But we weren't deterred.

We built a tiny website on a computer in a closet in my parent's basement to promote our little brand. One site section was "The Show" which encouraged people to spend their hard earned monies on the 15-minute Video CD-ROM, and then there were a couple of Flash games and some short videos in which Rabbi Itche answered questions sent in by the twelve real people who knew about the site.

When **Itche Kadoozy** and his friends moved to Chabad.org about a year or so later, I kept some of the design elements from the original site and "The Show" became the place where all of the videos went. Those videos were mostly sitcom style stories with a few one-off episodes experimenting with various genres.

As long as "The Show" was the name of the section with all of the videos in it, it made sense, but once I started creating other "Itche Kadoozy" videos with their own sections, "The Show" just became the place for standalone episodes that didn't fit anywhere else.

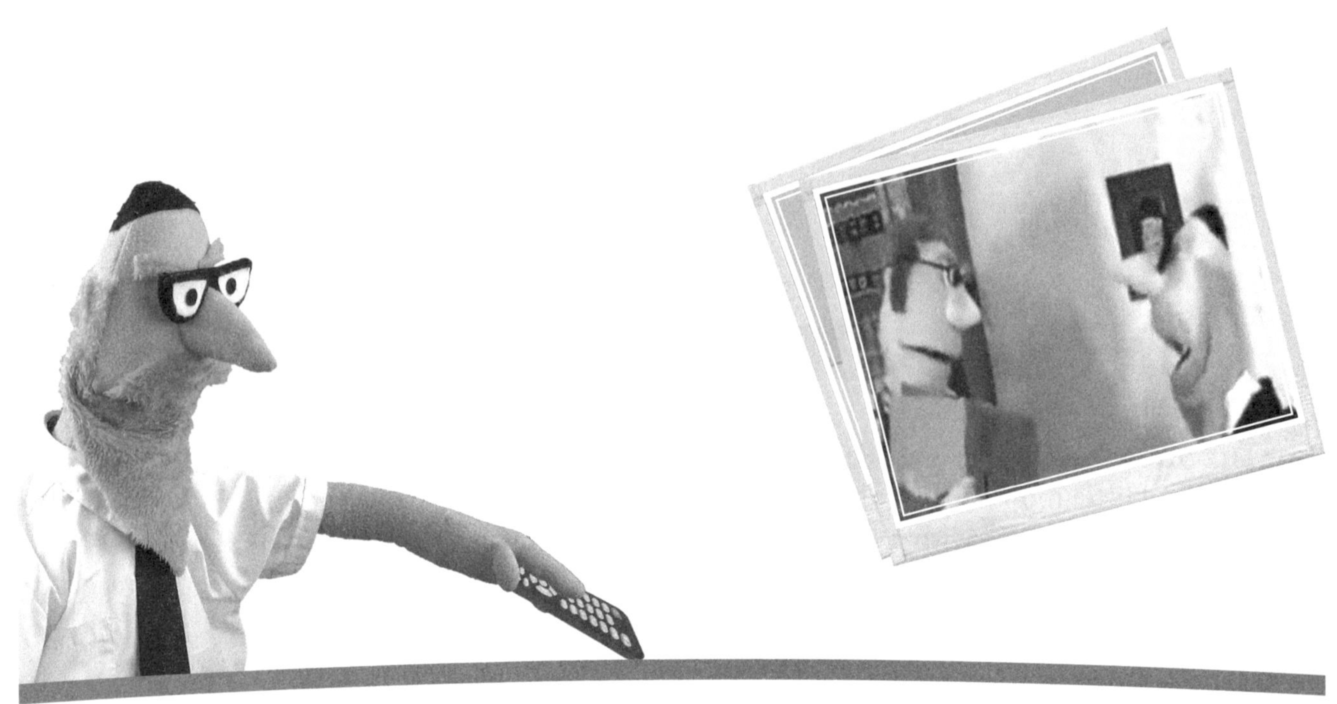

FEELIN' AT HOME

SCENE: Rabbi Itche is at home, reading a booklet

JONO: Rabbi, Rabbi, Rabbi, Rabbi, Rabbi. What is a twelve-letter word that begins with a double "S" and ends with a "4"?

RABBI: Ends with a "4?" Jonathan, are you sure you're doing that crossword puzzle right?

JONO: Are you sure you're doing that right?

(Bell rings)

JONO: Ah, ah, oh my StairMaster's here!

RABBI: StairMaster?

JONO: Yeah.

RABBI: Jonathan, I don't mind you staying in my home for a while, but, but—

JONO: Indefinitely.

RABBI: Yeah, but I still think that you should really check with me first before having large machinery delivered to my home.

JONO: Rabbi, I—you—uh—you just don't understand...uh, I'll be right back (Jono leaves and returns after a minute with a small box).

RABBI: Oh, that's it? That's a StairMaster? That's not so big.

JONO: (Laughs) No, Rabbi. The StairMaster is ginormous, this isn't a StairMaster. It's just a bunch of other junk I ordered. You know, tiki torches, pineapple cups, grass table skirts, 12 plastic bowling sets—for $9.95—and about 120 noisemakers.

RABBI: (Incredulous) Bowling sets, Tiki torches, pineapple cups —— what's going on here, Jonathan?

JONO: It's for a luau.

(Fade to invitation: "Rabbi Itche and Jono's Luau" during every night in August at the Rabbi's house.)

RABBI: Now, hold on one moment, Jonathan. Now, I like to make you feel at home in my home. But I like to feel at home in my home also. And when you do things in my house with my furniture and my toothbrush without thinking about how I feel about it, it makes me feel very uncomfortable. It makes it very difficult for me to feel at home. In my own home! (Pauses) You know, Jonathan, we can take this opportunity to learn about a Dira B'tachtonim, making the world a dwelling place, a home for Hashem.

JONO: Hold on, hold on, hold on. You keep talking...I'm just going to go put this box in the china cabinet (walks out with box).

RABBI: Oh, okay. Jonathan, our job in this world is to make a dwelling place for Hashem. And when everyone just does what they want without

thinking about what Hashem wants with the world He created, that doesn't make Hashem feel too homey.

(Loud crash in the background)

JONO: Oops, that must have been, like, 100 years old!

RABBI: Jonathan, are you listening?

JONO: Yes.

RABBI: But if we can use everything in this world the way Hashem wants us to, then this shows that He's really the only One and that this is His home.

JONO: (Jono returns) Rabbi, I've been thinking while you've been talking and I've decided that I want to make you feel more at home here in your home. I'll start by fixing that plate thing. You won't even know it's broken, like you didn't even know your grandfather clock is broken.

RABBI: My grandfather clock is broken? Oy!

[THE END]

THE FISH

SCENE: Rabbi Itche is fast asleep in his favorite recliner, while Jono is sneaking up from behind, in an effort to snatch a lollipop from the Rabbi's shirt-pocket without waking him.

RABBI: (Wakened, shouts in surprise) Ah!!!

JONO: (Startled by the noise) AH!!!!!!

RABBI: Ahhhh!!!!!

JONO: AHHHHHH!!!!!

(Both catching breath…calming down)

RABBI: Jonathan?

JONO: (Cough…cough) Yeah?

RABBI: What are you doing here?

JONO: I'm sorry.

RABBI: Ah!!.

JONO: What?

RABBI: You scared me!

JONO: I'm sorry.

RABBI: I'm just trying to learn a little bit here.

JONO: You were fast asleep, Rabbi.

RABBI: Yeah.

JONO: Look, the thing is I'm kind of ashamed of myself. I was trying to get your lollipop.

RABBI: You could've just asked me for the lollipop.

JONO: Yeah, I know that, but it was either that or bug you for money because I got to feed my Gefilte Fish.

RABBI: What, you need money to buy some Gefilte Fish? Is that what you're saying?

JONO: No, that's not what I said. I said I need to feed my pet Gefilte Fish.

RABBI: Look, I don't know what you're saying but there's no such thing as a Gefilte Fish, Jonathan.

JONO: Then, what was I just playing Scrabble with?

(New voice in the background:)

G-FISH: Meshugas isn't an English word, Jonathan.

JONO: Sure it is, Fish. The Rabbi uses it all the time. For example, when I started tap dancing on the dining room table, he said, "Hey, what's this meshugas?" Or like, when I had the marching band practice

in the living room for over a month, he said, "I'm tired of this meshugas."

RABBI: Or like that time when you made those radish latkes for my annual Hanukah luncheon and I said, "Radish latkes? What sort of meshugas is this?"

JONO: Those were good.

G-FISH: Fine, but no triple-word score.

RABBI: Really, Jonathan, what are you playing Scrabble with?

JONO: I told you…my pet Gefilte Fish, and he gets super cranky when he hasn't eaten.

(A large Gefilte Fish enters the scene)

G-FISH: (Moaning…) Oh, so huuungry!

JONO: You know, I've been wondering this for a while now. Why can't you just eat that carrot on your head?

G-FISH: What? My carrot? Is that a joke? No, I think he's serious. I wear this carrot as a reminder. It's a reminder of my Gefilte Fish heritage. Do you know what it's like growing up in an ocean and being the only fish in school with a carrot on his head? No, you don't have any idea. It was hard. Stares. Questions. They even made up songs about me. Where do you get off asking me that?

JONO: (Turns to Rabbi) Sheesh…I told you he gets cranky.

RABBI: I understand where he's coming from. He's clearly been through some hard times, but what I don't understand is what is what is he? (Turning to the fish) what ARE you?

G-FISH: I'm a Gefilte Fish!

RABBI: (Looks at Jono) Look, I've learned a lot of Torah and even some Kabbalah and I've seen some strange things, but I've never seen anything that explains this. But uh, I got a lot of questions but the one I'm going to ask you is, why do you have a pet Gefilte Fish?

JONO: Well, why do you buy a mezuzah and put it on your door? Why do you have matzah on Passover?

RABBI: Look, those are mitzvot. The Torah says we have to do those things.

JONO: So? It isn't written in any book that you have to have a pet Gefilte Fish, but I like to. It sort of makes me feel more Jewish.

RABBI: So what you're saying is that sometimes it's the little things that we don't necessarily have to do but that we want to do because they make us feel more connected to who we are as Jews that make the biggest impact?

JONO: I guess. I mean, I remember how my grandmother always had Gefilte Fish, so when I saw this crazy little guy in a spooky shop in Chinatown, I just felt like I had to get him. Oh, now I understand why you're so touchy about that carrot on your head.

G-FISH: (Crankily...) I am so hungry and weak now.

JONO: Come on, Gefilte Fish...let's go get some bagels and some lox.

G-FISH: I cannot believe he just said that...uuuuuhhh.

[THE END]

THE PIGEON

SCENE: A large pigeon is standing in a park, talking to the camera

PIGEON: I like to think of myself as a people person, a pigeon pigeon, a people pigeon.

RABBI: (At home, commenting…) He looks more like a duck.

PIGEON: Whatever. I get along with people is the point. Most pigeons don't. Most pigeons just sort of flap their arms and you know they run away. Not me, I like people. (Cut to Pigeon sitting in a swing, talking to someone at the park) How are you doing? What's your name? Please don't touch me. What's your name? (Looks off to the horizon) Sometimes I feel like I want more out of life, like there could be something bigger. (A kid reaches for his mouth) No, don't touch my beak! (Cut to Rabbi)

RABBI: I like to go to the park every so often and feed the birds, to relax. And um, well, he became one of the regulars. Then, one day, he just sort of walked up to me and then he said—(Cut back to Pigeon)

The Show

PIGEON: Hey, Rabbi, what should I do to make myself a better person, a better pigeon? (Cut back to Rabbi)

RABBI: I guess he was searching for something. He was looking something, something greater in life, something better.

PIGEON: (Cut back to Pigeon) I've thought about karate lessons maybe, some martial arts; a lot of discipline. You can learn some valuable skills there—self-discipline. (Cut back to Rabbi)

RABBI: So I suggested maybe piano lessons, maybe learn a foreign language. (Cut back to Pigeon who's on the phone, looking at a phone book)

PIGEON: Yeah, hello? Yeah, I'm looking for piano lessons. (Pause) Uh-huh. Yeah, I don't have fingers. I have wings...(pause)...a pigeon. Yes, I'm a pigeon. (Talking to camera) sometimes I like to hang out on the swings; watch kids playing in the park here. (Cut back to Rabbi)

RABBI: You know, it's interesting, Jewish mysticism compares human intellect to a bird. Just like a bird soars up higher and higher and flies into the sky, so too, the human intellect desires and yearns to go beyond where it's at. With the right kind of discipline, this desire can lead a person to a deeper and greater level of commitment to Judaism.

PIGEON: (Back to Pigeon on swing) The great thing about a swing is you could just swing up higher and higher. You know, you're not stuck on the ground. I'm a pigeon, I could just fly, but...I don't know...I like to swing.

(Fade to black)

[THE END]

KOSHERMENTARY

SCENE: Jono is walking down the street

JONO: Hello. Have you ever wondered what makes kosher food kosher? I haven't. But I've made a film for you in which I pretend that I have.

(Cut to Rabbi Itche Kadoozy who is sitting in his beloved recliner)

RABBI: Kashrus is really something that you could trace it all the way back to when Hashem gave the Jews the Torah, and not really the moment in which we become—(Rabbi's voice begins to fade...)

JONO: As Rabbi Kadoozy continued to speak—for several hours—I decided to leave the camera running to go make some phone calls. (Cut to Jono on the phone) Yeah. Rabbi Moskowitz? It's Jonathan. Grab your koshering stick because we're about to do a whole lot of koshering. Yeah. All right. Then just grab a clipboard. I'll see you in an hour.

(Cut to Jono standing in front of a large building)

JONO: Here we are at a cookie factory. Let's go inside. (Enters. Lots of activity is evident; huge machines are mixing cookie dough) Bear with me as we go make some cookies. (Jono spots a rope next to a sign that reads "Fire Extinguisher") I don't know what this rope is but I better not pull it. (Looks at a clipboard hanging on the wall) Everything here is set out. (Enters another room, sees large grinder) What would happen if I stuck my face in here?

(Cut to Jono standing next to Rabbi Moskowitz)

JONO: Here I am with Rabbi Moskowitz in a dough factory, and um, Rabbi, tell me exactly what it is you do here.

RABBI MOSKOWITZ: I am the supervisor of kosher for this wonderful company here called Bear Stewart in Chicago, and basically, what they do is, they provide batter for many of the food services here in Chicago.

JONO: Uh, Rabbi, if the batter is made here, where is the pitcher ring?

RABBI MOSKOWITZ: No…you've got it wrong.

(Cut to Rabbi Itche Kadoozy, at home in his recliner)

RABBI: Now uh, I believe many people are under the impression that the supervising rabbi actually lives on the premises of the facility —

(Cut back to Jono at the factor, standing in front of an indoor shed)

JONO: So this is the shed where I believe the rabbi stays to make sure everything is kosher in the plant. I don't want to disturb him because it's nap time now.

(Cut back to Rabbi Itche Kadoozy)

RABBI: — and, uh, that's just not true.

(Cut back to Rabbi Moscowitz at the factory)

RABBI MOSKOWITZ: I come into this factory without telling anyone that I'm going to come here.

(Cut to Rabbi Itche Kadoozy)

RABBI: The rabbi actually comes to the facility, uh, unannounced so that he can get a, sort of, candid look at what is going on in the facility.

(Cut to Rabbi Moscowitz at the factory)

RABBI MOSKOWITZ: I have to make sure that all the ingredients here are kosher and they have the proper symbol of that.

JONO: So how do you go about doing that? You say a prayer over everything?

RABBI MOSKOWITZ: (Laughs) You know what? That's what many, many people think. When I go to a company, at first, they say "Rabbi, when are you going to bless the company?" That's not what it's all about.

(Cut to Rabbi Itche Kadoozy)

RABBI: Well, uh, anytime a factory decides to make a new line, a new product line, so if they have new ingredients or if they have a new formula they give the list of ingredients to the mashgi'ach, the kosher supervisor.

(Cut to factory. A baker is talking with Rabbi Moscowitz)

BAKER: We've come up with a couple of new formulas. I'd like to submit one now to you for your approval.

(Cut back to Rabbi Itche Kadoozy)

RABBI: And, uh, he checks all the ingredients listed on the list to make sure that they're all certified.

(Cut to factory. Rabbi Moscowitz is checking the label on a box of ingredients)

RABBI MOSKOWITZ: Okay. Let me check over here. I see you've got this from Waxon...and it has a CRC pareve...cappuccino flavor...(Looks at clipboard) matches to this...looks okay over here.

(Cut back to Rabbi Itche Kadoozy)

RABBI: Then, when the mashgi'ach goes to visit the plant itself, then he has to look at the raw ingredients that are in the inventory of the factory...look at what's actually going into the product to see that that matches up to the list that they gave him.

(Cut to factory. Jono is looking at a huge sack of cake mix)

JONO: Devil's food cake mix, pareve. Check. (Moves on to next one) Cream cake base, pareve. Check. (Moves on to next one) Bakery mix, yep, pareve. Check. (Tuns to man driving a forklift) One last question for you...

BAKER: Yeah?

JONO: What will it take to give me a ride on this thing?

BAKER: Well, go ahead. Feel free.

JONO: Really?

BAKER: Yeah.

(Jono riding on the forklift, whimpering in fear which slowly gives way to laughter and excitement)

JONO: Hey, what do you think of this? (Jono singing out loud as he's being driven around.

(Fade to black. Fade in. Jono is at a juice factory)

JONO: Can I lick the spoon? (Laughter. Jono is walking around the factory watching the different stations. He spots a vat with a huge bag of Kiwi Limeade concentrate and lays down on it) Ahhh! Thank goodness for the water-bed department!

(Cut to Jono in the office of the factory. Jono shakes hand of the foreman.)

JONO: Good afternoon…Jonathan.

PHIL: Hi Jonathan! Phil. Glad to meet you.

JONO: Glad to meet you, Phil. Now we're here in Juice Time?

PHIL: That's correct.

JONO: What do you do here in Juice Time?

PHIL: Well, we manufacture juice for food service operations.

JONO: Did you say Jews?

PHIL: Juice (laughs)

JONO: Juice.

PHIL: Yes. We manufacture juice.

JONO: Oh, juice. Oh, orange juice, apple juice.

PHIL: Orange juice, apple juice. That's correct.

JONO: I myself might be a banana-strawberry Jew. (Laughter)

(Cut to Jono continuing his tour of the factory)

MATT: So now you're entering the Juice Time production facility so I'd like everyone to put on a hair net and also a beard net if you don't mind. (Turning to Jono) Do you want me to put it on there for you?

JONO: If you could.

MATT: Sure. How's that? I'll say make sure you cover your hair and your sideburns. We covered this up real good for you. (Puts hair net on Jono; Rabbi Itche Kadoozy shows up and gets a hair net too)

RABBI: Thank you. Makes sure the yarmulke doesn't fall in the juice! Thank you.

MATT: Perfect. Very good. All right? You're ready. Let's go. Let's roll it.

(Cut to Rabbi Itche Kadoozy, at home in his recliner)

RABBI: If you look at the ingredients on a food product, you'll see natural flavorings. There are artificial flavors and there are natural flavors. Now, natural doesn't necessarily mean fruits and vegetables.

(Cut back to factory)

MATT: How about meat, is meat natural?

JONO: Yeh, sure! I could throw a pig in here!

(Cut back to Rabbi Itche Kadoozy)

RABBI: Natural means anything not made out of chemicals in a lab.

(Cut back to factory. Rabbi Moscowitz looks at huge sacks of flavorings)

RABBI MOSCOWITZ: Grape concentrate.

JONO: Check.

RABBI MOSCOWITZ: Natural and artificial flavors.

JONO: Check.

RABBI MOSCOWITZ: But it doesn't tell us what flavor!

JONO: Uh, uh…um, I could put anything in there!

(Cut to Rabbi Itche Kadoozy)

RABBI: They take a close look at every specific ingredient, every particular ingredient, to make sure that it's also kosher.

(Cut back to factory. The factory foreman is standing next to Jono)

PHIL: Jonathan, I hope you enjoyed your tour here today at Juice Time.

JONO: I certainly did!

PHIL: We hope you come back again very soon!

JONO: Absolutely!

PHIL: Have a good day!

JONO: You too…thanks.

(Cut to Jono at home looking inside the fridge)

JONO: Any kosher food in here? (Turns to camera) Oh, my video camera! Well, I guess this is a good time to draw this whole documentary to a close. So in conclusion, there's a whole lot of stuff that goes into making foods kosher (pause) but I don't remember any of it. Good night! (Fridge door closes. Credits roll. Fade to black.)

(Fade in, Jono and Rabbi Itche are sitting at a picnic table in a park. They are looking at a laptop that is playing the credit roll of the same documentary. Last line of credits reads "In Loving Memory of Rabbi Itche Kadoozy").

JONO: So rabbi, what did you think?

RABBI: (Incredulous) In loving memory?

JONO: Yeah.

RABBI: Do you know what that means, Jonathan?

JONO: Yeah. It means that I dedicated it to you, rabbi.

RABBI: I'm a little bit uncomfortable with that, could you change it?

JONO: I'm hungry. I think Mrs. Kadoozy is whipping up some Kugel. Let's go! (Jono runs off)

[THE END]

YARMULKE

SCENE: Rabbi Itche is reading a question someone submitted.

RABBI: Okay. "Dear Rabbi Kadoozy. Could you please explain the importance of wearing a yarmulke? Maybe if you were to explain it, Jonathan would begin wearing one, too. Inspired by Mendel F., 4-years old."

(Rabbi Itche turns to the camera:) You should know, by the way, that Jono does wear a kippah sometimes. Whenever he comes to synagogue he wears one and for some reason whenever he eats bagels. As for the importance of wearing a yarmulke, I once did a television commercial for yarmulkes a few years back. Originally, it was supposed to be about some kosher breakfast cereal I think...but I didn't really keep to the script. Here, I'll show it to you.

(Cut to an old commercial featuring Rabbi Itche:) Hey, kids. Try new fantastic Kosher Sugar Os, Sugar Coated Sugar Cereal. (Singing:) Sugar Os are tasty and Sugar Os are yummy.

Sugar Os are crunchy and 50-percent fat-free.

Sugar Os are frosty, so…wear it on your head when you're playing ball and even in your bed.

Wear a kippah on your head to help you keep in mind that even higher than you head there is a G-d that's strong and kind.

Everywhere you go and everything you do you can remember that G-d's always there and you will always be a Jew.

(Rabbi Itche abruptly stops singing and turns to the camera:) Wait a second! I think I was supposed to be doing a breakfast cereal commercial.…um…buy the cereal!

[THE END]

KIDDUSH

SCENE: Rabbi Itche is reading a question someone submitted.

RABBI: Okay, here's an interesting one: "Dear Rabbi Kadoozy. Why do Jewish people drink wine for Kiddush on Shabbat? From Sarah H. of Los Angeles, California."

(Rabbi Itche turns to the camera:) Well, Sarah, first we'll start by understanding what Kiddush is. Kiddush is the blessing we say to thank G-d for giving us this special day of Shabbat. (Jono enters…)

JONO: Rabbi, Rabbi, Rabbi, Rabbi, Rabbi…

RABBI: Yes, Jonathan? (Rabbi Itche is not happy to be interrupted)

JONO: What?

RABBI: You want to tell me something?

JONO: I just want to say "Hello."

RABBI: So, say "Hello."

JONO: I did!

RABBI: No, you said, "Rabbi, Rabbi, Rabbi."

JONO: (Fumbling for words…) Wha…wha…what am I supposed to say?

RABBI: How about "Hello?"

JONO: (Sighs) Fine. "Uh…Hello!"

RABBI: (Notices Jono's feet) Jonathan? Why are your feet purple?

JONO: Hmm, that's a really good question, but I think a better question might be, "Why do I have grapes stuck between my toes?" The answer to both of those questions is because I was stomping grapes with my feet.

RABBI: Why were you stomping grapes with your feet?

JONO: To make wine!

RABBI: Why are you making wine, Jonathan?

JONO: I need wine for Kiddush tonight.

RABBI: Tonight is Tuesday, Jonathan. Why do you need wine for Kiddush?

JONO: Because I've had a really long, hard day stomping grapes.

RABBI: Jonathan, the reason why we drink wine for Kiddush on Shabbat is because wine is something we don't usually drink. So when we say the blessing to thank G-d for giving us the day of Shabbat, it's customary for the leader of the household to drink a little bit of wine or grape juice to remind us that Shabbat is special and different from the rest of the week.

JONO: Hmm, well, then I guess I'm not making Kiddush tonight. That's probably better anyway because my wine tastes like feet. Get it?

[THE END]

BRACHOT

SCENE: Rabbi Itche is reading a question someone submitted.

RABBI: (Looks up to camera:) Oh, hello. You've come just in time to watch me check this email I got from Benny R. of Chicago, Illinois. He says, (looks at email) "Dear Rabbi Kadoozy, I learned in Hebrew school about saying the blessing 'Hamotzi Lechem Min Ha'aretz' when we eat bread. Are there other blessings to say on other stuff? Benny.

(Rabbi Itche turns to the camera:) Well, Benny, actually there's a blessing we say before we eat anything. (Jono enters…)

JONO: Wait on. Wait there. Hold on. Hey there. Hold on. Stop a second, Rabbi. Did you say you could make a blessing on anything?

RABBI: Yes. There are about six different blessings to say on different types of food. They all start with "Boruch Atah Hashem Elokeinu Melech Ho'olam," and they each end differently to thank G-d for the specific type of food you are about to eat.

JONO: What blessing do you say on a grape?

RABBI: "Boruch Atah Hashem Elokeinu Melech Ho'olam, Borei Pri Ho'eitz," Creator of fruit of the tree.

JONO: What about a cracker?

RABBI: Crackers and cakes and cookies are a separate category. The blessing to say before eating those ends with "Borei Minei Mezonot," the creator of types of nourishment.

JONO: What about an index card?

RABBI: An index card? You can't eat an index card, Jono.

JONO: Well then what about an orange?

RABBI: An orange grows on a tree. So the blessing would end with "Borei Pri Ha'eitz."

JONO: Well what about an orange index card? (Rabbi Itche gives him a stern look)...Okay. Okay, okay. Well then, what about a potato?

RABBI: A potato grows in the ground so the blessing to say on it ends with "Borei Pri Ho'adamah," creator of fruit of the ground. That's the blessing we make on most vegetables.

JONO: Grape Juice?

RABBI: "Borei Pri Hagofen," creator of fruit of the vine.

JONO: Oh, that's right. I knew that one. Then what about a muffin tin?

RABBI: A muffin?

JONO: No. A muffin tin.

RABBI: You can't eat a muffin tin, Jonathan.

JONO: What about a sponge?

RABBI: Eating a sponge sounds dangerous, Jonathan.

JONO: Wait, wait. Dangerous like I should call a doctor right away and get to the hospital dangerous? Or I just shouldn't do it again dangerous? In any case, (Jono holds his stomach...) I'm not feeling too well. I'm going to excuse myself.

RABBI: (Rabbi Itche turns to the camera:) So in conclusion, every time we eat something we can thank G-d for it. This helps us to remember to use the energy we get from eating each and every thing we eat to go do a mitzvah. Okay, zai gezunt. Remember to email me. Maybe I'll answer it to you right here on the web. Zai gezunt. See you next time!

[THE END]

HEBREW LESSON

SCENE: Rabbi Itche is standing in his kitchen; Jono enters.

JONO: Rabbi, rabbi, rabbi…rabbi!

RABBI: Oh, a fourth Rabbi. This must be important!

JONO: Yeah, it is. I've decided I'm going to do something important with my life. So I've decided to go into foreign policy.

RABBI: I thought you were going to be a fireman?

JONO: No, I was going to be a fireman yesterday. Today, I want to go into foreign policy.

RABBI: And tomorrow you'll want to be an astronaut?

JONO: No, tomorrow I'm going to want to be a roller-coaster designer. That sounds awesome. But today, I want to be a foreign policy guy. And to do that, I need to know a foreign language. So I was thinking, maybe you can teach me some Hebrew?

RABBI: Sure. Hebrew is a wonderful language to learn. Our holy Torah is written in Hebrew, and Hebrew is the language with which G-d created the world. He said *"vayehi ohr"* which means let there be light, and He created light. Really, those same Hebrew words He used to create the world in the beginning, G-d uses to keep the world and all of its creations in existence every single second. I'm delighted that you're interested in learning Hebrew!

JONO: Look, Rabbi, with all due respect, my attention span lasts about a minute these days. So…let's make the best of the…43 seconds we've got left.

RABBI: Okay, let's start with he.

JONO: Who?

RABBI: Exactly.

JONO: What?

RABBI: *"Hu"* is he.

JONO: That's what I want to know, Rabbi!

RABBI: What?

JONO: Who is he?

RABBI: That's right. Now you're catching on!

JONO: I am?

RABBI: Yes, you are. Now, *"hee"* is she.

JONO: Whoa…hang on a second, Rabbi. I don't even know who he is! And now you're telling me that he's a she?

RABBI: She, in Hebrew, is *"hee."*

JONO: Who?

RABBI: No, *"Hu"* is he.

JONO: (Exasperated) That's what I want to know!

RABBI: Maybe we'll move on to animals.

JONO: Okay. That's better. I'm sure that'll come in handy at the U.N..

RABBI: *"Dag"* is fish.

JONO: What? This is a crazy language, Rabbi. First you tell me that he's a she, which really caught me by surprise. And now you tell me that a dog is a fish? Couldn't G-d have chosen an easier language, something more universal? Like Esperanto, perhaps?

RABBI: Maybe I started off too advanced. Let's begin with something more familiar, your own name: Jonathan—

JONO: Yes, Rabbi.

RABBI: I'm going to translate your name into Hebrew.

JONO: Oh, okay.

RABBI: Jonathan...

JONO: Yeah, what's up?

RABBI: Let me finish. Jono, in Hebrew, is Yonatan.

JONO: My Hebrew name is Yonatan?

RABBI: Yes.

JONO: No, it's not.

RABBI: What?

JONO: My Hebrew name is Naftali.

RABBI: Why is your Hebrew name Naftali?

JONO: My mother wanted to name me after her grandfather.

The Show

RABBI: So your great-grandfather's name was Naftali?

JONO: No, my great-grandfather's name was Moishe.

RABBI: So where does the name Naftali come from?

JONO: From the Torah, I think. Come on, Rabbi, you should know that.

RABBI: No, I mean where does it come from in your family?

JONO: I said my mother *wanted* to name me after her grandfather. But my father's Hebrew name was Moishe. So they named me Naftali instead. (Looks at his watch) Oh, there goes my attention span. See you later, alligator! (Exits scene).

RABBI: After a while, Naftali!

[THE END]

A WORD FROM JONO

SCENE: Jono is in his room

JONO: Oh! Hello, friends. Welcome to my bedroom, or as the Rabbi calls it—his basement. I called you down here today to share a little Judaism fun-fact that would only take a cool dude like myself to interpret from the text. This exploration began when Rabbi Kadoozy gave me a Siddur for my birthday. I immediately put it on my shelf with my chemistry set, Rubik's Cube and doll collection. In other words, the stuff I play with when I got nothing better to do.

Little did I know that in the not-so-distant future I *was* going to have nothing better to do. You see, the Rabbi took away my comic books after I set the kitchen counter on fire to protect myself from zombies. That was a bad move for two reasons. One: There is no such thing as zombies. And two: Protecting myself from something that doesn't exist cost the Rabbi $2,500 in damages. So he did what any responsible rabbi whose house you moved into would do. He took away my comic books. I pretended not to let it bother me. I

angrily grabbed the Siddur and started reading. But you know what I learned? I learned that those ancient dudes who wrote the Siddur were thinking the same thing I've been telling people for years. And that is that G-d is *awesome!*

(Jono takes a Siddur) Let me read you a quote: "The name of the Almighty G-d, the great powerful and awesome King, holy is He." You hear that? They called him *awesome!*

Here's another quote: "He is awesome and praised, Master of wonders." (Wowed)…I mean, come on!

Okay. Here's one from the Amidah: "Blessed are You, Lord our G-d and G-d of our fathers, G-d of Abraham, G-d of Isaac and G-d of Jacob, the great, mighty and awesome G-d."

You hear that? *"Awesome!"* G-d is *awesome!* I guess I really was created in His image…*boo-ya!*

Anyway friends, I just wanted to share my findings with you. If you were like me and thought that Jewish texts were out of date, think again. Because a holy assembly of ancient rabbis, hundred years ago, shared my more modern opinions of awesomeness.

You can get back to surfing the web now. I am going to find the part in here where they call Moses a righteous guy.

See you later!

[THE END]

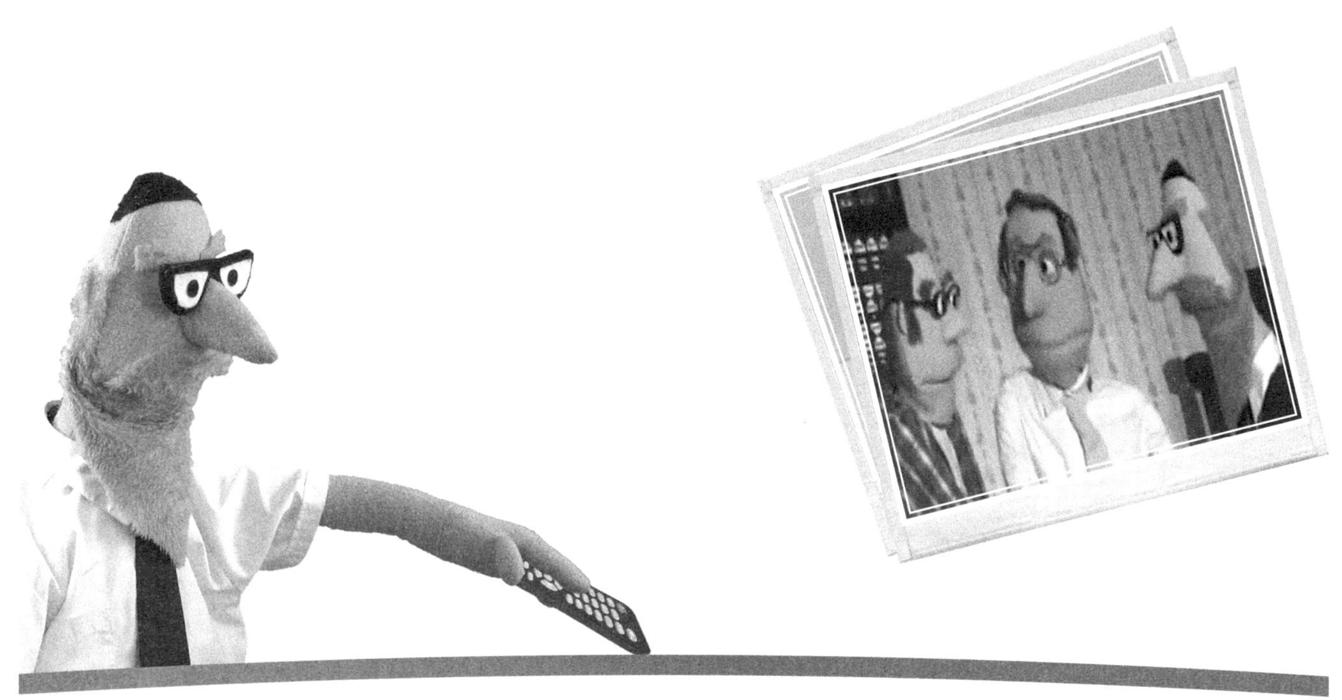

JONO AND THE WHALE

SCENE: Rabbi Itche and Jono are sitting in the living room

JONO: (Jono enters) Rabbi, which of the following magazines should I subscribe to, "Horse Owners Monthly," "Senior Citizens Weekly," or some medical journal devoted entirely to poor dental hygiene?

RABBI: Why are you interested in subscribing to *any* of those publications?

JONO: Well, sir, I received an official looking document today that says, quote: "You have already been chosen as the grand-prize winner of the super grand-prize sweepstakes. All you have to do to redeem your prize is purchase 75 magazine subscriptions. And then there was an asterisk, which I chose to ignore.

RABBI: Jonathan, don't you know that these things are scams? They just want your money! I hope you didn't give them your Social Security number.

The Show

JONO: Ummmm...(Phone rings)...Phew!

RABBI: (Rabbi Itche picks up the phone) Hello? Yes...yes...what? Hold on a moment please. (Turns to Jono) Jonathan, I don't believe this, but apparently you have actually won a prize.

JONO: See, rabbi, I told you so! I probably won a bazillion dollars!

RABBI: You mean a bajillion dollars.

JONO: No...if I meant a bajillion a would have said bajillion, but I didn't mean bajillion I meant bazillion, so I said bazillion.

RABBI: Bazillion isn't a word. Bajillion is a word.

JONO: Bazillion isn't a word?! Bajillion isn't a word! When I type bajillion and bazillion on the computer, bajillion has a red squiggly-line under it and bazillion doesn't! That means that bazillion is a word and bajillion isn't a word!

RABBI: What?

JONO: Look, can we discuss this later, I want to find out what I won!

RABBI: (Returns phone to his ear) Hello? Yes...yes...a what? A whale?

JONO: A whale?! I won a whale?!

RABBI: Jonathan, you're not keeping a whale here!

JONO: I'll put it in the bath tub.

RABBI: Do you know how big a whale is?

JONO: So...I'll put in 2 bath tubs.

RABBI: (Glares at Jono...)

JONO: Six bath-tubs?

RABBI: (Back on the phone) What? Yes?...I understand. Ok. (To Jono) They said that whether I want it here or not, you are the legal owner of the whale. Which means that until I figure out something else to do with it, it's staying here.

JONO: Oh boy! My vary own whale! My childhood dream has finally come true!

RABBI: Your childhood dream was to own a whale?

JONO: Well…not quite. My childhood dream was to be an astronaut…but this is as close as I'm gonna get.

(Cut to the following day. Rabbi Itche is in the living room. Doorbell rings. Rabbi goes to the door and then returns)

RABBI: Jonathan?! The UPS man is here with a very large cardboard box for you!

JONO: (Enters) *Oh boy! My whale!*

RABBI: You have someplace to keep him? I don't want this to turn out like the time you kept that tarantula in my medicine chest.

JONO: For your information, I just inflated a kiddie pool for my whale. It took me six hours and my lungs are aching something awful, but I'd do anything for little Whaley.

RABBI: Whaley?

JONO: What am I supposed to name it, Cowy? Ok, I'm gonna get Cowy settled in (Exits)

RABBI: Don't get him too comfortable, my lawyer Larry Goldstein, is coming over to see if there's something we can do to get rid of it.

(Jone walks out. Doorbell rings…)

RABBI ITCHE: Come in.

(Larry Goldstein enters)

LARRY: Rabbi, how ya doin'?

RABBI: Baruch Hashem, thank G-d I'm doing alright. Thanks for helping me out.

LARRY: Anything for you rabbi. Now what's the issue?

The Show

RABBI: I've got a whale in my house!

LARRY: Maybe you should call an exterminator…just kidding. But seriously I don't think there's anything I can do. Once you accept that whale onto your property, you've pretty much accepted responsibility for it.

RABBI: So if I want to get rid of it, I have to pay the shipping fees myself?

LARRY: I'm afraid so, Rabbi. Ha!

RABBI: That's going to cost me a bajillion dollars.

LARRY: More like a bazillion, Rabbi. Ha!

(Sounds of a whale moaning)

JONO: (Enters) Rabbi, what do you do to stop a whale from moaning?

RABBI: Jonathan, that whale *cannot* stay here! It's not healthy; a whale has to live in water to survive.

JONO: But, I bought it a case of bottled spring water, rabbi. What else can it ask for. (Under breath:) greedy whale.

RABBI: Jonathan, pouring a bottle of water over its back is not going to help…Whaley. He needs to live in water and be surrounded by it constantly. Everything he does has to be in the water. Eating, drinking, swimming, and playing—all in the water.

JONO: It even has to play tennis in the water?

RABBI: If it could play tennis…yes. You see, we can learn a lot from whaley. A Jew needs Torah and mitzvot like a fish or sea mammal, for that matter, needs water. We can't just learn a little bit of Torah here an there and go to shul once a year. We have to incorporate our Judaism and Jewish identity into every part of our life.

JONO: So, you're saying I should give my whale a kippah?

LARRY: Rabbi, that was beautiful. Tell you what, I'm going to donate the cost of the shipping fee. Let's overnight this guy and by tomorrow he'll be back at the aquarium.

JONO AND RABBI: Hooray!

[THE END]

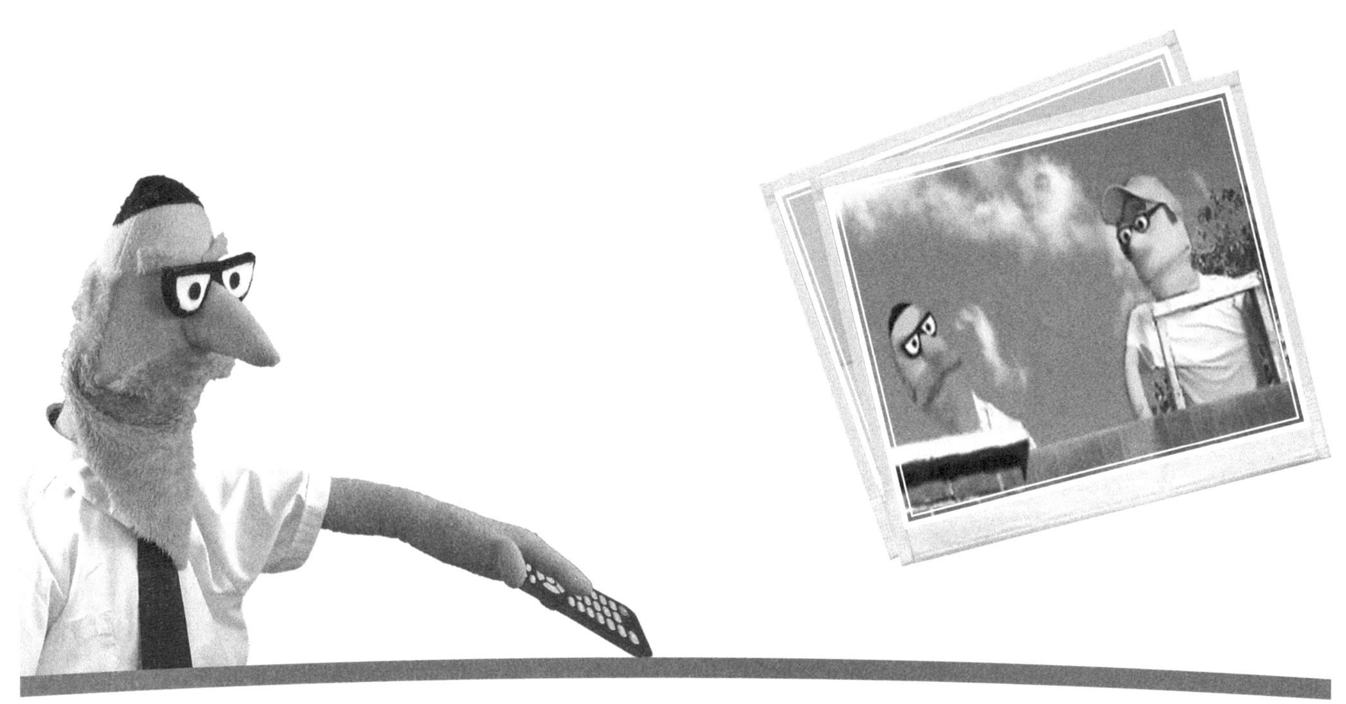

THE BURGLARY

SCENE: Rabbi Itche is standing in the middle of the living room in pajamas Everything is in disarray.

RABBI: Jono! Jono! Jono! Come up here *right away!*

JONO: (Enters) Rabbi, what's going on? I heard a crash and then I heard you yell, and then I heard a crunch because I stepped on an egg.

RABBI: I don't have time for this, somebody broke into the house and…you stepped on an egg?

JONO: I always keep an egg with a little face drawn on it next to my bed.

RABBI: Whatever. The point is, an intruder came into the house through the window and…an egg with a face drawn on it?

JONO: So I don't get scared at night. And it worked. Apparently their was an intruder in the house and I didn't even realize! Did he take anything?

RABBI: Well, he tried to steal my mailing list, probably to solicit donations from my congregants. But he ended up taking my list of Yahrtzeits instead. He won't get very much money from those people...

JONO: Is he still here? You hold him down and I'll get a nerf bat.

RABBI: No, he escaped. I already called the police and...a nerf bat?

JONO: Rabbi, what this house needs is a security system. First thing in the morning, you and I should install one.

RABBI: That sounds like a good idea. (Fade to black)

(The next morning...Fade in, Rabbi Itche and Jono climb a ladder onto the roof of the house. Rabbi Itche is wearing gloves, ready for work.)

RABBI: Ok, all we've gotta do is staple these wires up here. (Bends down. staple, staple. Tries to stand up, but he can't) Oh no, I've stapled my glove to the roof. (Tries a few more times to stand up but still can't.)

JONO: Rabbi, could you pass the stapler?

RABBI: I can't...I'm stapled to the roof! (Tries to reach over with the other hand to pass the stapler but can't reach)

JONO: Come on rabbi, reach just a little bit further!

RABBI: I can't reach, Jono! Here's I'll toss it to you. (Tosses stapler. Jono Tries to catch it and ends up leaning the ladder back, it starts to fall and then stops in mid-air, held in place by the wire Jono is holding onto)

RABBI: Jono!

JONO: I'm okay rabbi! This wire is holding me. (Starts pulling himself forward with the wire yet the ladder falls forward again and hits the roof) *Ooomph!* (Jono gets off the ladder. Meanwhile, Rabbi Itche is trying to pull his hand loose and succeeds, but falls backward into Jono pushing him off the roof.)

RABBI: Jono! (Bounce noise is heard. Jono pops back up.)

JONO: Hey Rabbi! (Falls back down) *Oomph!*

RABBI: Jono, I'll be down in a minute, I just have to attach this last wire... (Picks up wire and electrocutes himself. Fade to black.)

(Later that day...Fade in, Rabbi Itche and Jono are both wrapped in towels and drinking hot cocoa.)

MRS. K: Are you two alright?

RABBI: I'm fine, Boruch hashem

JONO: I'm doin' ok. Thanks for the Hot Cocoa, Mrs. K.!

MRS. K: Oh, Gefilte Fish made the Hot Cocoa. I was too busy fixing the car. So did you at least finish installing the security system?

RABBI: Yeah, but there's one more very important part of the security system we still have to make sure is working.

JONO: What's that? I thought we've checked everything.

RABBI: The mezuzah. (Doorbell) Oh, that must be the Sofer, the scribe.

MRS. K: I'll go let him in (Exits)

JONO: What does the mezuzah have to do with home security? Did you put a hidden camera in it? Or a laser-shooter? Or a hidden camera that shoots lasers?

RABBI: Having kosher Mezuzot on the doorposts of your house is a declaration of the spirituality of the home and the recognition of G-d. In turn, the mezuzah symbolizes G d's recognition of us and those who dwell in the home, keeping us safer and healthier...G-d willing.

SOFER: (Enters) Well, Rabbi, I checked all of the Mezuzot and each one is written correctly, with all the letters formed properly. 100% kosher!

RABBI ITCHE AND JONO AND SOFER: Hooray!

[THE END]

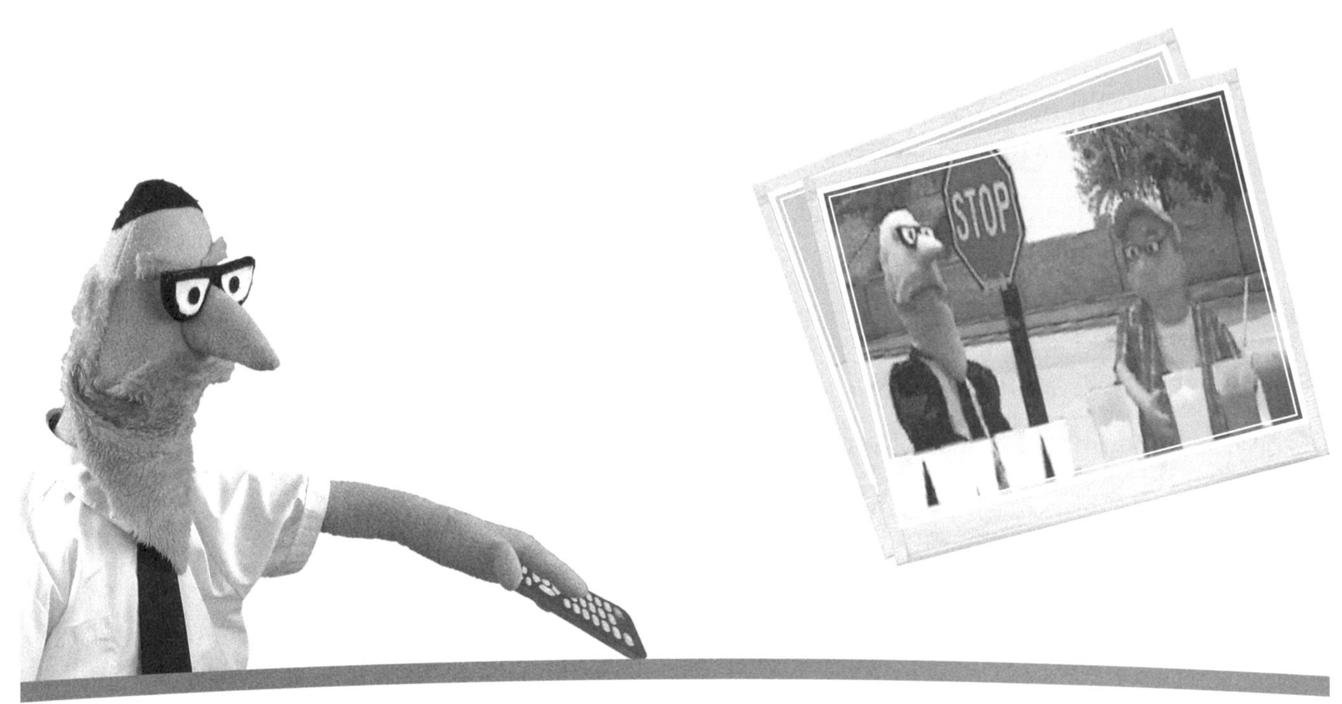

JONO'S LEMONADE STAND

SCENE: Jono is on the phone

JONO: My credit card number? Sure. 1-7-3-5-eleventeen-Q-stick figure-tilda—yes. Yes, that's exactly as is written on the card. No, no it's not a real card. I made it myself. Is that a problem?...Hello?...Hello?

RABBI: Jono, did you just try to buy something with a homemade credit card?

JONO: No, I've already discovered the hard way that that doesn't work. So I just tried to donate money to a Jewish website with a homemade credit card. Which apparently doesn't work either...

RABBI: Jonathan, I'm glad you were trying to do the mitzvah of giving Tzedakah, but the whole point of the mitzvah is that you're actually giving up real money that you could have used to buy things for yourself.

JONO: But I don't have any real money. I don't even have any Monopoly money…wait, I have an idea! (Fade out)

(Fade in. Jono is standing in front of their house at table with a huge sign on front saying, "Garage Sale." Displayed are all of Rabbi Itche's prized tools.)

RABBI: (Approaches) So Jono, what are you up to? (Notices the items on the table) *My calculator! My AC adaptors! My transistor radio! Jono, what are you doing with this stuff!?*

JONO: Selling it! Mrs. K. told me that I could sell all this old junk in the garage sale and split the profit with you guys.

RABBI: You can't get rid of this stuff. This radio, I heard about Watergate on this radio.

JONO: Well, I guess you could call this the "Jono-Gate Scandal."

RABBI: You already used that name for when I caught you recording my phone calls. Anyway, Jono, this isn't exactly what I meant by using your own money to give Tzedakah. How about working and earning some money the hard way?

JONO: I usually don't like doing anything the hard way. I usually like doing things the easy way. Or the lazy way. Or the have-somebody-else-do-it-for-me-lazy-easy way.

RABBI: You could do some odd jobs around the shul. Get a part-time job at a bookstore…

JONO: Start a lemonade stand…

RABBI: Lemonade stand. That's usually something nine-year-olds do.

JONO: And a nine-year-old is definitely no match for a 19-year-old. Sounds like a plan!

(Cut to Jono standing in front of a Lemonade stand. Rabbi Itche approaches.)

RABBI: So, Jono, how's the lemonade stand coming?

JONO: Great! So far I made a whopping grand total of $1.75. And some guy gave me a food stamp.

RABBI: Do you mind if I try some?

JONO: Go ahead. Free lemonade for members of the clergy.

RABBI: (Tries some and gags from its taste) *What is this?*

JONO: Oh, that's the garlic-flavored lemonade.

RABBI: *Garlic* lemonade?

JONO: Yeah, I'm providing the masses with a variety of lemonade flavors, including Savory Garlic Lemonade, Soy Sauce Lemonade, Chocolate Lemonade, and my crowning achievement—Organic Soil Lemonade. That was a hard one to get past the FDA but my lawyer is working hard on it even as we speak.

(Cut to G-Fish who is in a courtroom talking to a Judge.)

G-FISH: Your Honor, Organic Soil Lemonade? My client is *clearly* insane. I rest my case!

JONO: (Back to Jono) And of course, there's Classic Lemonade for folks who don't want to live on the edge. And apparently that isn't such a popular place to live anymore, 'cause Classic Lemonade is all I've sold so far.

RABBI: So you're doing well.

JONO: Definitely better than that nine-year-old across the street. I doubt he'll last another hour out here. But I'll tell you, Rabbi. Being a lemonade entrepreneur isn't easy. It's a lot of hard work.

RABBI: And when you give Tzedakah with the money you earned from your hard work, all of that time and energy you invested to earn that money becomes part of the mitzvah, too.

JONO: Rabbi, I think it's time for me to present the Ira and Edna Bernstein Jewish Community Center with a brand new fluorescent light-bulb.

(Cut to image of a fluorescent fixture with one working light and a dedication plaque with an arrow to the working one.)

[THE END]

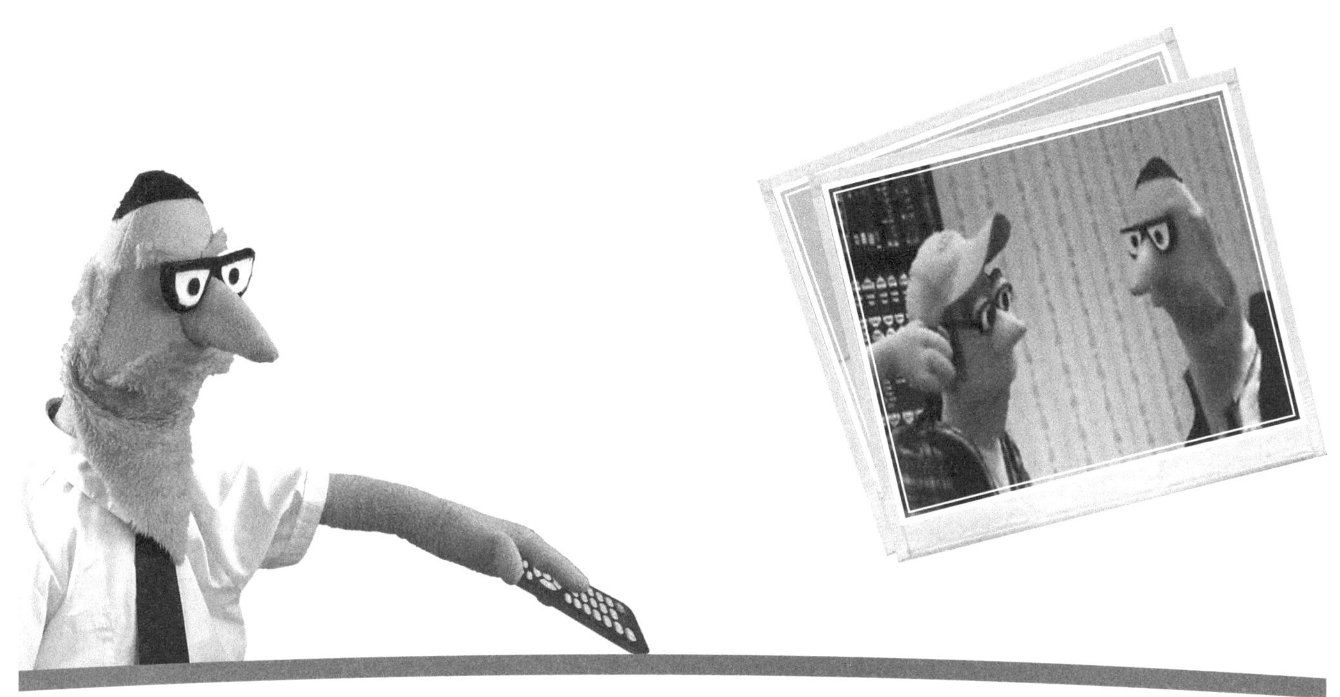

JONO'S CELLPHONE

SCENE: Jono enters with a large backpack, with a cord connected to his cell-phone

JONO: Rabbi, Rabbi, Rabbi!

RABBI: Yes, Jono?

JONO: Hang on a second I'm on the phone… (Pause) ok, I'm on hold. What do you want, Rabbi?

RABBI: Jono, why is your cell-phone connected to your back-pack?

JONO: I was tired of running out of battery, so I hooked this guy up to a ginormous car battery. This battery can give me up to 48 hours of consecutive talk time, plus two years standby time!

RABBI: Why would you ever need to stay on the phone for 48 hours? And what kind of cell-phone plan do you have? Isn't 48 hours of consecutive use going to cost a small fortune?

JONO: I can answer both of those questions in one shot. I called the cell-phone company to find out how many minutes I have left and they put me on hold for 48 hours!

RABBI: What do you need a cell-phone for anyways?

JONO: For games, mostly. What do you use your cell-phone for?

RABBI: I try to use my cell-phone as often as possible to talk about Torah and Judaism.

JONO: You mean…you just call people up and talk about Judaism?

RABBI: Yeah.

JONO: I'm not sure I completely understand this. Let's act this out. I'll be me and you'll be…. you.

RABBI: Jonathan I don't…

JONO: (Ring ring) Hello?

RABBI: (Forcing himself) Hello, Jonathan.

JONO: Oh Rabbi, How did you know it was me?

RABBI: I looked on the imaginary caller-ID… Jonathan, what am I supposed to say?

JONO: So Rabbi, what's on your mind?

RABBI: I This week's Torah portion…

JONO: Hang on…Rabbi, I really don't have many minutes left on my imaginary cell-phone, could you call me back on my imaginary land-line?

RABBI: Jonathan, this is ridiculous! The point is, that when we say words of Torah over the phone, the radio waves that transmit the sound travel through the air all over the world, filling the entire world with words of Torah!

JONO: There are words of Torah in the air? (He ducks) *Phew* that was a close one. I almost got hit by an invisible Gimmel.

[THE END]

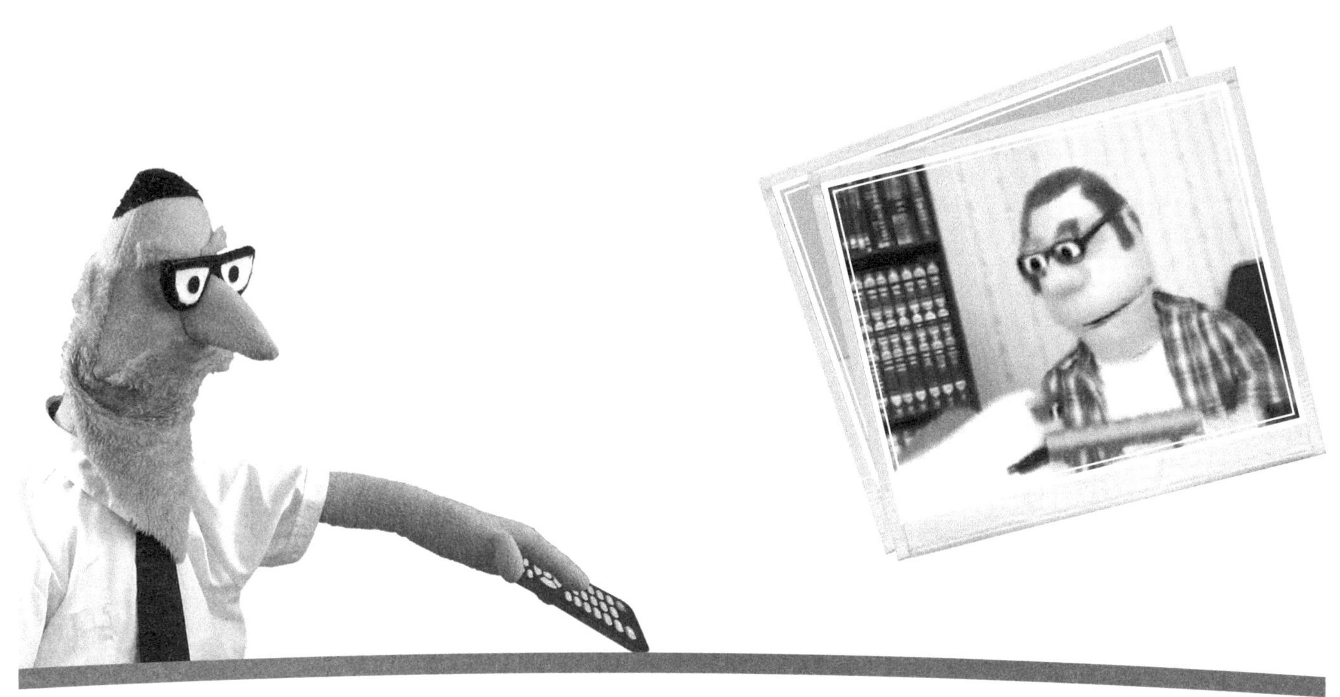

PRAYER

SCENE: Rabbi Itche is sitting at his desk

RABBI: Okay. It's been 10 minutes since I last checked my e-mail; maybe I have a new one! (Types away on the keyboard) Oh, a new one! "Dear Rabbi Kadoozy. Why do we pray? From, Mendel L." Well, Mendel, it's interesting that you asked that because I think Jonathan is praying right now.

JONO: (Cut to Jono) Hey, G-d, what's up? It's me, Jono. You probably already know this, but I have a 30-page term paper due tomorrow and I sat in front of my computer for three hours, but I didn't accomplish anything. Well, I did accomplish something. I got to the highest level in Ms. Pac-Man. But my report is going nowhere, so that's where you come in. If you could please deliver a finished term paper under my pillow by 6:00 a.m. I'd appreciate it. It doesn't even have to be that good. You can double-space it and make the margins real big if you want.

The Show

G-FISH: (G-Fish slowly appears but remains just out of Jono's view) Ooooh, wooooo…Jo-nnnna-tttthan…

JONO: Oh boy, I'm having a revelation or going completely insane. But either way, I might as well take advantage of this situation. Please write my term paper for me and make it appear underneath my pillow. And while you're at it, a hot-fudge sundae wouldn't hurt none. Not under my pillow, though. That might hurt some.

G-FISH: That's a lot to ask from me. Who do you think I am, G-d?

JONO: What? Hey, it was you the whole time?

G-FISH: Silence or I will smite you. I've smitten before and I'll smite again, by golly.

JONO: Cut it out. You hijacked my prayer! Now, what am I going to do about my term paper and my sundae?

G-FISH: I don't know, maybe you could write your term paper yourself.

JONO: I'm getting tired of your attitude G-Fish.

RABBI: (Rabbi Itche enters) Hold it, hold it, hold it. Jono, the point of prayer is to ask G-d for what we need. And when we ask G-d to help us with the things that are important to us, we bring G-d into those parts of our lives.

JONO: So, do I have to write my term paper or not?

RABBI: You write your term paper, but ask G-d to help you do it even better than you could ever do on your own. (Turning to camera) Well, Mendel, I guess you got your answer.

JONO: And I'm going to get a hot-fudge sundae.

RABBI: Everybody, thanks for all your questions. Keep on watching, learning and having fun.

[THE END]

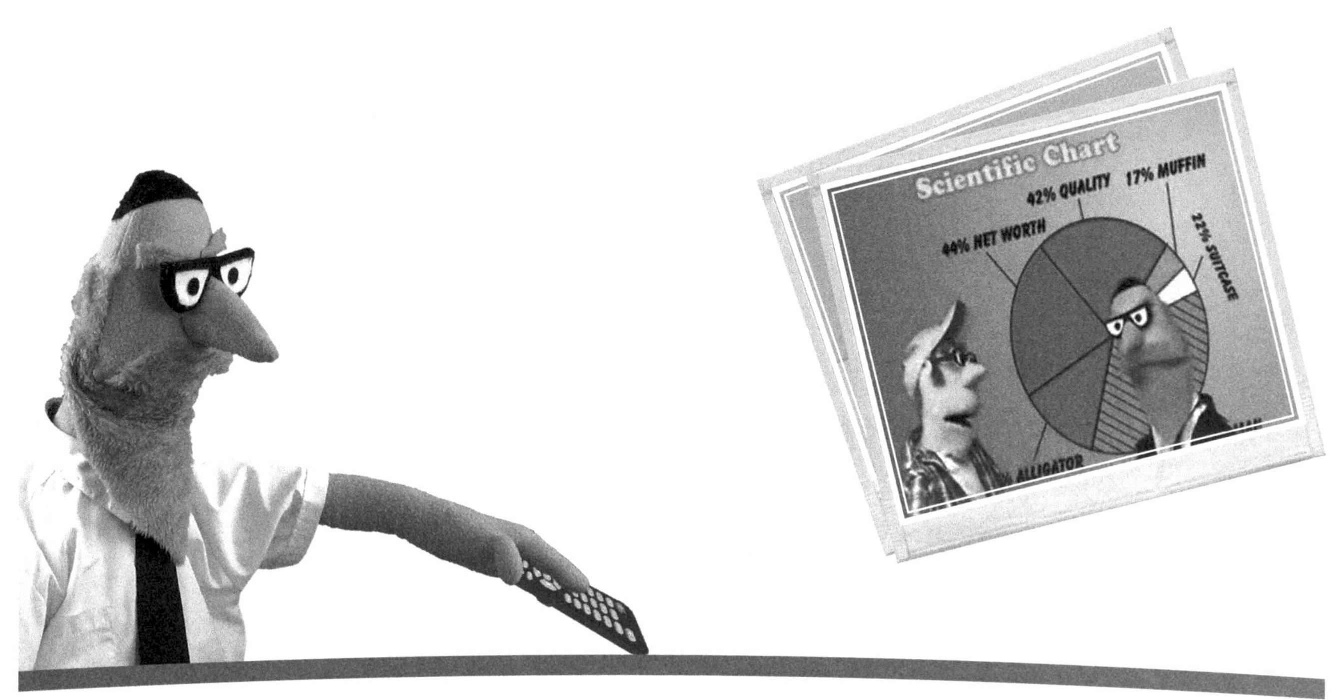

PERSONALITY CLASH

SCENE: Rabbi Itche is entering his basement

RABBI: Jonathan? Jonathan? I'm looking for some light-bulbs…

JONO: (Pops up from behind couch:) Rabbi, Rabbi, Rabbi!

RABBI: AHHHHH!

JONO: AHHHHH!

RABBI: What's going on here, Jono? Why were you on the floor?

JONO: I slept on the floor last night, Rabbi.

RABBI: Why?

JONO: For very scientific reasons. Reasons so scientific that I'd need a scientific chart to explain it. (Cut to ridiculous pie chart. Jono walks on in front of it.) You see, what we're dealing with here is 44% Net Worth 42: Quality Control, 17% muffin, 22% suitcase 78% Mailman, and 37 % alligator.

RABBI: (Enters. He is clearly getting nervous) Jonathan, this all adds up to 240%!

JONO: I know, we exceeded our expectations by 140%!

RABBI: What does any of this have to do with why you slept on the floor?

JONO: Nothing.

RABBI: (Very nervous) Then what does this chart mean?!

JONO: It tells us the percentages of each of these things.

RABBI: Percentage what?!

JONO: Of the chart.

RABBI: But what does the chart represent?!

JONO: How much percentage there is uf muffin and mailman and net worth! Rabbi, I think this chart is remarkably simple! Frankly, I'm a little bit offended that you insist on misunderstanding it!

RABBI: Jono, none of this makes any sense (Walks off. Cut back to basement. Rabbi Itche and Jono walk back in)

JONO: Rabbi, I think maybe we need to give ourselves a little bit of time away from each other. After a little a few days apart, we'll be back to being the best of friends.

RABBI: Maybe that's a good idea.

JONO: Good, I'll pack your bags.

RABBI: This is my house! Jonathan, this is ridiculous, I'm going to go study in my office.

(SCENE 2: Jono is putting tape on the wall. Rabbi Itche enters)

JONO: AH…Don't cross that line Rabbi.

RABBI: What? Why? What's going on here, Jonathan? WHat are you doing?

JONO: Rabbi, it's no secret that we haven't been getting along as of late. Even the neighbors complained about the noise we've been making screaming at each other.

RABBI: Jonathan, we haven't been screaming at each other. The neighbors were complaining the hammering you've been doing at all hours of the night.

JONO: You mean the work I've been doing on my pinewood derby racer? Anyway, the point is, that to help us keep a healthy distance for a while, I put a masking tape line across the each room of the house. You stay on your side, and I'll stay on mine.

RABBI: How are you planning on getting to the door?

JONO: Oh. Good point. I've sort of cornered myself in here, haven't I. Well…I guess I could use the window…or a rocket-pack…or I could rocket-pack myself through the window.

RABBI: Jonathan, I don't think this is necessary (Starts to walk toward Jono)

JONO: AH…stay on your side. Oh, and could you toss me my remote control car?

RABBI: It's three feet away from you, Can't you get it yourself?

JONO: No. It's on your side. If I cross that line I'll be breaking my own rules. And nobody likes a guy who breaks his own rules…unless of course those rules are ridiculous…but my rule is completely un-ridiculous Oh, and if you could pass me a soda too…oh wait (Looks around at his trappedness) I'd better not, the bathroom is on your side.

RABBI: Jonathan, I'm sorry I've gotten a little bit upset with you lately. We're two very different people, but letting those difference stop us from enjoying each other's friendship is not the solution.

JONO: Good, because it would be really annoying to have to toss stuff back and forth all the time. However, I may continue throwing stuff across the room just for fun.

RABBI: You see, Jono, one of the most important mitzvot in the entire Torah is Ahavas Yisroel—to love your fellow Jew. On the outside we may seem very different, but on the inside we both have a completely G-dly soul. So no matter how different we are, there's a part of both of us that is completely beyond these differences.

JONO: Rabbi, if I was paying attention to what you just said, I would probably be very touched.

RABBI: Well…you must have been paying attention well enough to realize THAT.

JONO: Yeah, I guess I was. Rabbi, I'm going to leave this tape up to remind me never to let this happen again. And because if I take it down your wall paper will probably come with it.

(They both exit)

[THE END]

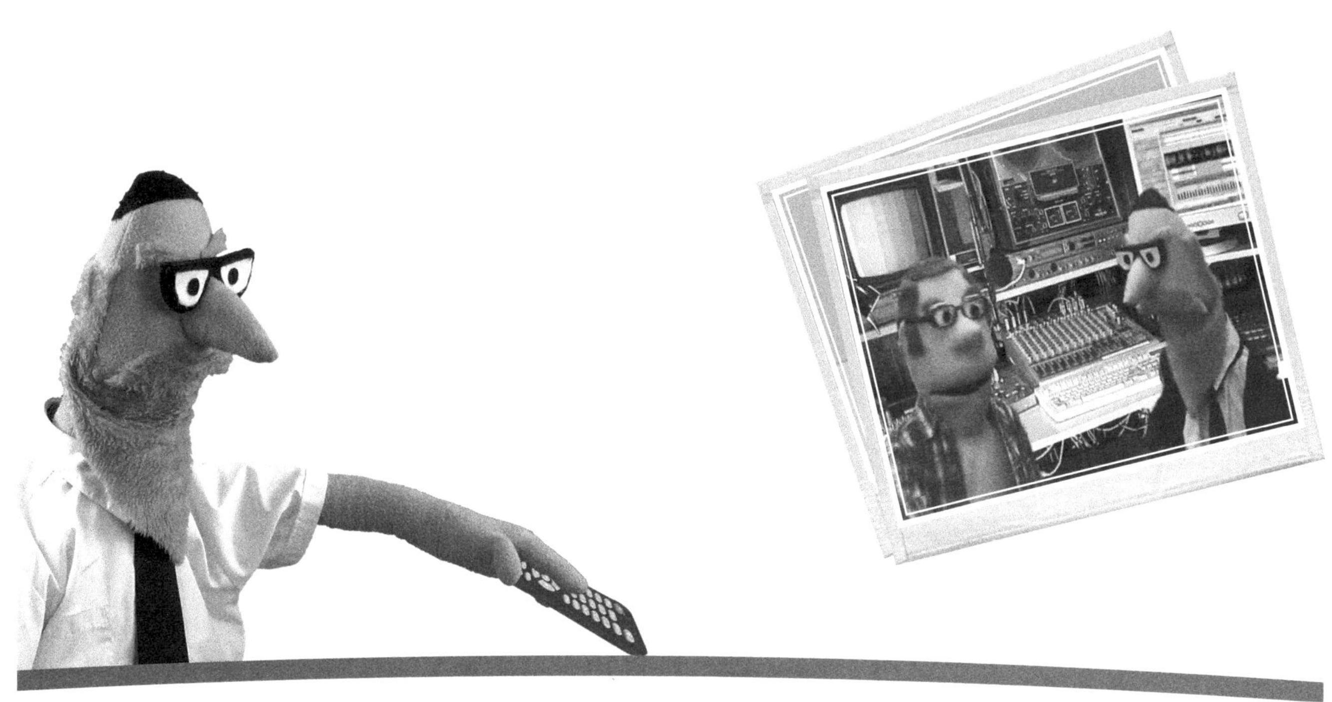

NEW AND IMPROVED?

SCENE: Rabbi Itche is standing on an empty sound-stage; Jono enters.

JONO: Rabbi, Rabbi Ra…whoa! What happened to your house?

RABBI: The producers of the show feel that we might need to…renovate our appearance, make it more hip, and cool—something that the kids can relate to.

JONO: And therefore they stole your house?

RABBI: Basically. So I was thinking maybe something along the lines of a cartoon Kiddush Cup with sun-glasses riding a skate-board.

JONO: You mean something like…this (Snaps his fingers and the screen cuts to a cartoon environment with the aforementioned kiddush cup.)

KIDDUSH CUP: Hey, Kids, I'm the Kiddush Cup man, and I'm rad! I love Shabbat! It's the COOLEST day of the week!

RABBI: (Back to Rabbi Itche and Jono) Yeah! That's exactly what I was thinking. And no information would actually be incorporated into the script. Any and all information would just pop up on the screen in fun-fact form.

(Fun fact pops out on the screen. "Did you know? The celebration and observance of Shabbat gives life to and set's the spiritual tone for the upcoming weekdays!)

JONO: And every episode should end with a rock and roll musical number!

(Back to cartoon, a bunch of Kiddush cups are playing various musical instruments.

MAIN KIDDUSH CUP: I'm the Kiddush Cup Man, Yeah Yeah Yeah, I've got a Kiddush Cup Band, Yeah yeah Yeah. And I ride on a skateboard 'cause I'm totally rad!

(Back to Rabbi Itche and Jono)

RABBI: So, what do you think?

JONO: I think I want your house back. Where am I supposed to eat supper tonight?

RABBI: Good Point!

[THE END]

JONO'S TIME MACHINE

SCENE: Rabbi Itche is learning when he suddenly hears an explosion

JONO: (Off screen) Rabbi, are you upstairs? Is there still an upstairs?

RABBI: (Gets up) I gotta see what's going on down there! (Cut to basement) Jonathan, what's going on down here?

JONO: Rabbi, if you're able to look past all the stuff I just exploded, you'd be looking at the future winner of the time machine award!

RABBI: What's the time machine award?

JONO: It's the award I'm going to win for building this time machine! I made it out of a refrigerator box, twelve rolls of aluminum foil, some duct-tape a calculator and six explosions. I call it "the time machine-o-tron 2000."

RABBI: A time machine? You mean it let's you travel through time?

JONO: That's right rabbi, all you have to do is punch some numbers on the control panel...

RABBI: The calculator duct-taped to the refrigerator box?

JONO: Yes, a calculator duct-taped to the refrigerator box! what else was I supposed to duct-tape it to?

RABBI: Well, how does that work?

JONO: After you're done punching in some numbers....

RABBI: What numbers?

JONO: Doesn't matter. Now after you're done punching in some numbers, you step inside the time machine. After six hours, the time machine will have transported you precisely six hours into the future!

RABBI: You mean, you go into the box and come out six hours later?

JONO: Exactly! Six hours into the future! I haven't quite figured out how to go into the past yet, but I'm pretty sure it has something to do with sitting in an aluminum foil covered refrigerator box for negative six hours.

RABBI: I hate to be critical Jonathan, but it seems like all you've done is figured out how to waste time.

JONO: Waste time?! You call scientific discovery a waste of time?! You call the furtherment of time travel experimentation a waste of time?! You call sitting in a cardboard box for six hours reading comic books and eating cookies a waste of time?! Fine...be that way. (Steps into box) I'm going to move forward with science and technology and I guess you're just going to have to lag six hours behind. Could you hand me that comic book over there? Thanks. I'll send you a postcard, Rabbi. From the future! (Fade out)

(Fade in. Living room. Rabbi is learning again.)

JONO: (Runs in wearing goggles and an aluminum foil suit and holding an American flag) People of the future, I mean you no harm. Do not be alarmed by my old fashioned appearance. I understand not your futuristic customs and nuances. I am a simple man, from a simpler time…a time six hours before yours.

RABBI: Jonathan?

JONO: Oh, Rabbi! You're not extinct! Thank G-d. Everything is so strange to me here, in the future. It's good to know there's at least one familiar face here. What did they do, freeze you?

RABBI: Jonathan, sitting in a cardboard box for six hours reading comic books, doesn't equal time travel.

JONO: Well according to my calculations it does. (Show a page of jonathan's "scientific" calculations.) All sorts of math symbols and stuff and at the bottom "sitting in a box for six hours reading comic books equals time travel.) Look rabbi, why is this so hard for you to understand? (Sigh) I didn't want to have to resort to this but let me present to you the following proof of my time travel journey (Pulls out a bottle of milk and holds it under the Rabbi's nose).

RABBI: Ugh!! This milk is sour! Get it away from me!

JONO: That's absolutely right rabbi. You see, the expiration date on this bottle of milk is July 16. When I entered the time machine on July 15 at 6:30 pm, with this bottle of milk, it was still fresh. Now, six hours in the future, July 16 12: 30 am, this milk is sour. This is most obviously the effect of traveling past the time of the expiration date during my expedition through the time-space continuum.

RABBI: Jonathan, during the time you were in that box, I davened the afternoon prayer, learned two pages of talmud with commentary, gave tzedakah, drove a friend to the airport, learned classic chassidic texts, helped somebody with a personal dilemma, picked the guy up from the airport, and prayed the evening prayer.

JONO: So much has happened in these six hours. It's amazing!

The Show

RABBI: So much has happened because there's a lot we can accomplish, and are responsible to accomplish, in a short period of time!

JONO: I accomplished a lot; I read three whole comic books! And I filled out the little subscription card inside. (Show subscription card) But I guess I could have done a lot more.

RABBI: That's right. Every moment can be used to do another mitzvah!

JONO: If only there was a way to reverse time, to go back before I started sitting in my time-machine, so I could stop myself from sitting in my time-machine so I could get more done than just sitting in my time-machine. Wait! I know! I'll go sit in my time-machine! for negative six hours! Transition. Basement. Jono is sitting at the computer,

RABBI: (Enters) What are you doing now, calculating how to sit in a box for negative six hours?

JONO: Psh, No. I'm making a video game simulator of how to manage my time. Watch. I gotta run around and jump up and catch all the mitzvahs before the time runs out.

RABBI: What are those little mushroom guys for?

JONO: Just for good measure.

RABBI: And why the red overalls?

JONO: Are you going to watch or not?

[THE END]

G-FISH 'TOON

NARRATOR: The following is the pilot episode for an animated spin-off of the Rabbi Itche Kadoozy show, depicting G-Fish's life in the ocean, before he came to live with Jono. Just in case you don't know, a spin-off is an often poorly thought out new series guaranteed instant success based solely on the popularity of a character from an existing series. Anyway, enjoy.

G-FISH 1: Oh boy, I'm having so much fun in the ocean while it's there.

G-FISH 2: Hey son, why don't you sign up for the potato sack race?

G-FISH 1: Do you really think I could win?

G-FISH 2: Sure I do. And besides, it's not winning that counts but having fun. Go on, give it a try.

NARRATOR: And the finalists are in the potato sack race between Seymour and G-Fish.

FROG: You don't count on winning, G-Fish, I'm the king of burlap.

The Show

G-FISH 1: Oh. I don't know about this.

G-FISH 3: Don't worry son, just go out there and have a good time.

FROG: Getting tired, G-Fish?

G-FISH 1: No. I just have a (Inaudible 00:01:35) disorder, that's all. My carrot. It's a symbol of my G-Fish heritage.

FROG: See you later, G-Fish.

G-FISH 3: Little G-Fish, I want you to know that I'm very proud of you.

G-FISH 1: But why? I lost.

G-FISH 3: You sacrificed something that was important to you just to stay true to your heritage. That's what I'm proud of and that makes you the real winner. Now go back out there and finish the race, just for fun.

FROG: Check out my fins!

ICE CREAM GUY: Seymour, shouldn't you go finish the race.

FROG: Nah. That G-Fish doesn't have a chance.

RECORDING: And the winner is G-Fish.

G-FISH 1: Hooray for me!

[THE END]

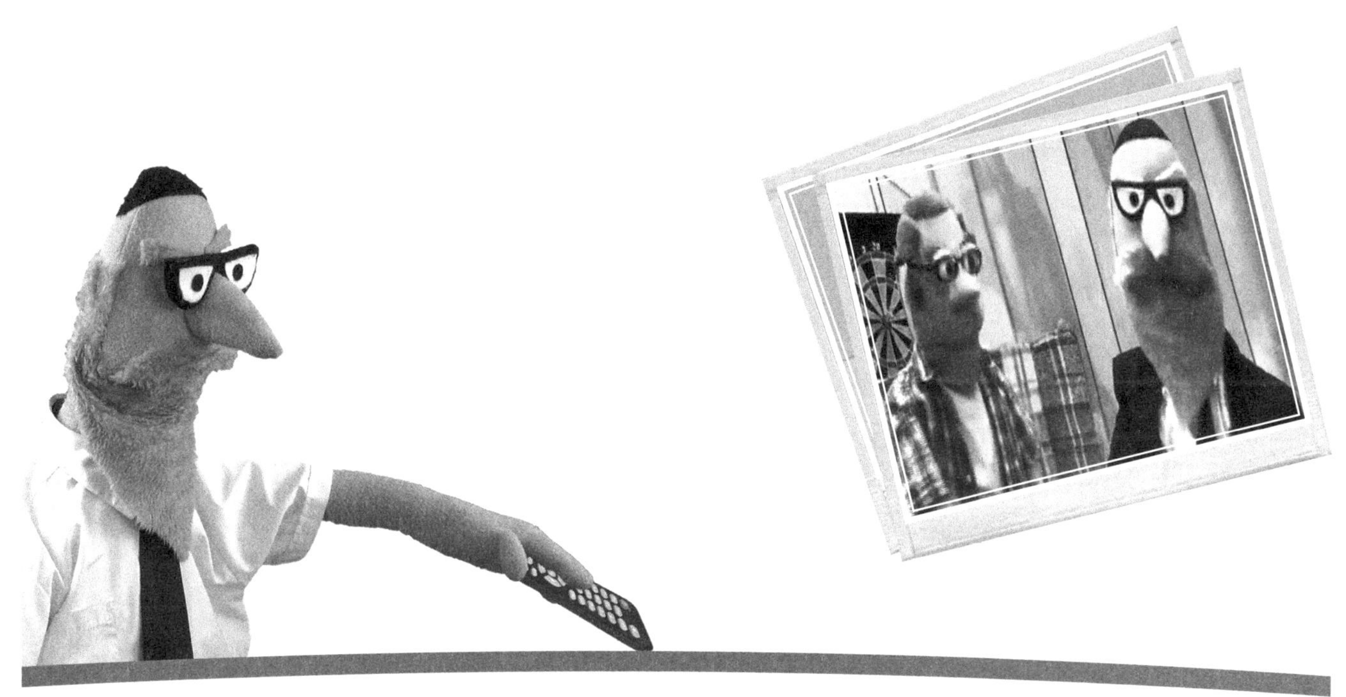

SILENT FILM

SCENE: Jono runs into the room

TITLE CARD: "Rabbi, Rabbi, Rabbi"

(Rabbi Itche looks at Jono and responds)

TITLE CARD: "Yes Jonathan?"

(Jonathan replies)

TITLE CARD: I got all of your books in your bookshelf out of order!

(Rabbi Itche gets upset and starts chasing Jono out of the room. Cut to both of them running on a repeated background. Cut to close-up of Jono running)

TITLE CARD: "You're chasing me!"

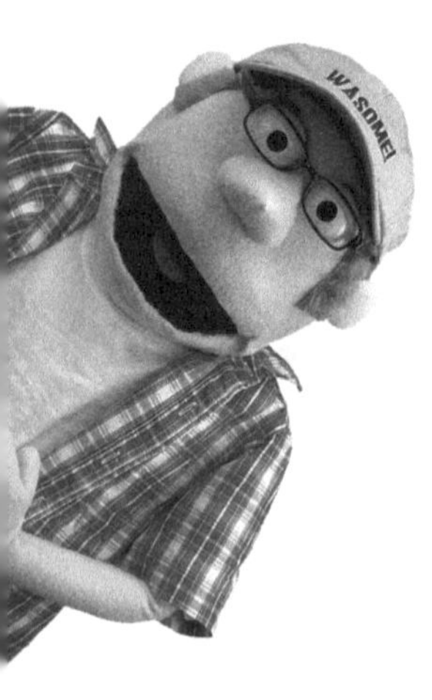

(Both of them run off screen. Pause. They run back through, this time Jono chasing Rabbi Itche. Close-up of Jono)

TITLE CARD: "Now I'm chasing you for no reason!"

(Both run off. Pause. Rabbi Itche chases Jono again. Close up of Jono running)

TITLE CARD: "Why are you chasing me?!"

(Close up of Rabbi Itche running)

TITLE CARD: "I don't know, I forgot"

(Close up of Jono running)

TITLE CARD: I think it's because I got your books all out of order!

(Close up of Rabbi Itche)

TITLE CARD: "Oh Yeah! That's right! Those books are all Torah books, and it's very important to learn Torah, and have lot's of Torah books in your house! Now I'll have to spend time putting them back in order before I can learn from them again!"

(Close up of Jono running)

TITLE CARD: "So maybe you could stop chasing me and I'll help you put them back in order)

(Both Running)

TITLE CARD: "Okay."

[THE END]

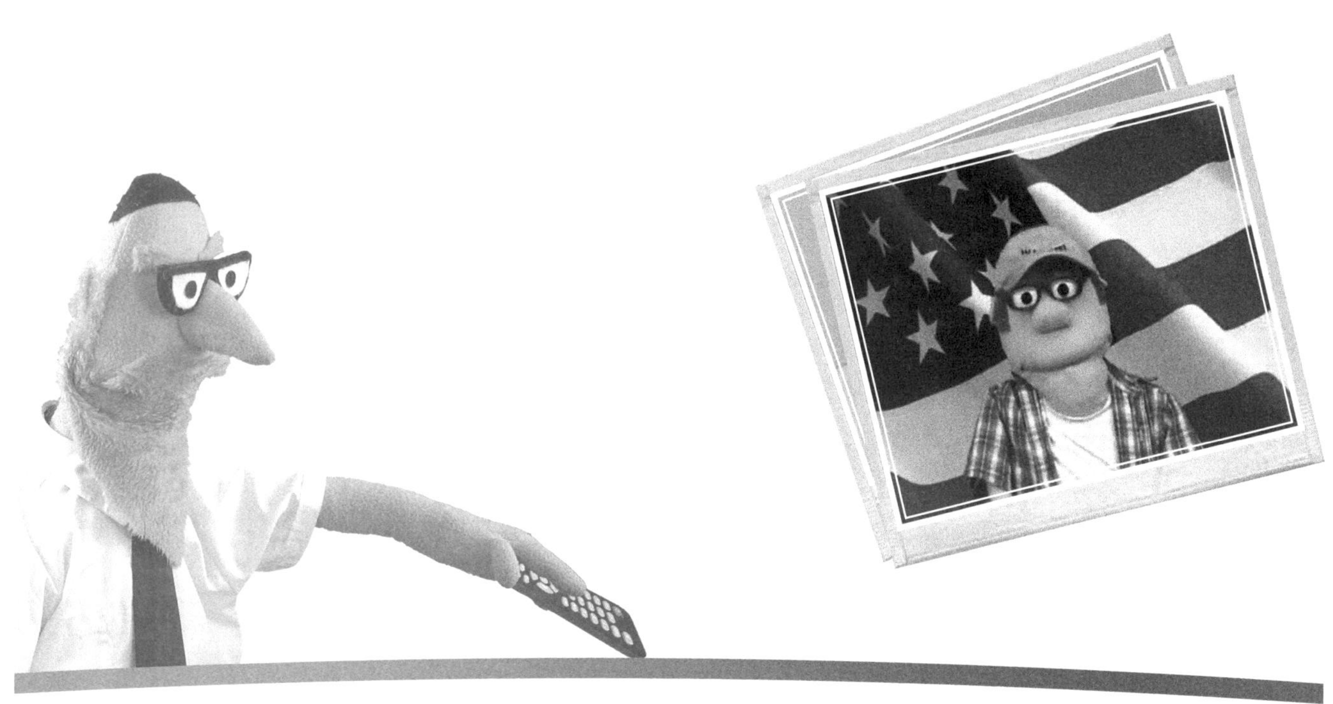

MOSES FOR PRESIDENT

SCENE: Jono standing in front of an American flag

JONO: Hello everybody, I'm Jonathan Weinsteinstein. This was supposed to be my announcement of the new Moses '08 presidential campaign. Unfortunately, however, recent developments, such as Moses having lived over 3,000 years ago, have brought this campaign to an abrupt stop, which is a real shame, because I just got these awesome posters back from the printer.

But even though you can't vote for Moses for president, you can still vote for the Moses within you, that part of each and every one of us that has an understanding of and respect for G-d and Judaism and you can cast your vote every day by taking a moment to think about how G-d created the world and gave us the Torah. We can't all speak to G-d on a daily basis like Moses did, but we can make G-d part of our daily lives.

RABBI: Jono, that was beautiful. Did you write that yourself?

JONO: If by write you mean read it off a teleprompter, then no. I'm having this said to me word for word by one of the campaign managers.

CAMPAIGN MANAGER: In conclusion —

JONO: In conclusion —

CAMPAIGN MANAGER: — I'd just like to say—oh, can I get one of those?

JONO: I'd just like to say, oh, can I get one of those. Thank you. (Sound of: glug, glug, glug, glug, glug…)

JONO: Thank you all for your continued support and remember, vote for Moses today. And, oh! This message was paid for Jonathan Weinstein. I like to talk really, really fast!

[THE END]

THE MITZVAH GUYS

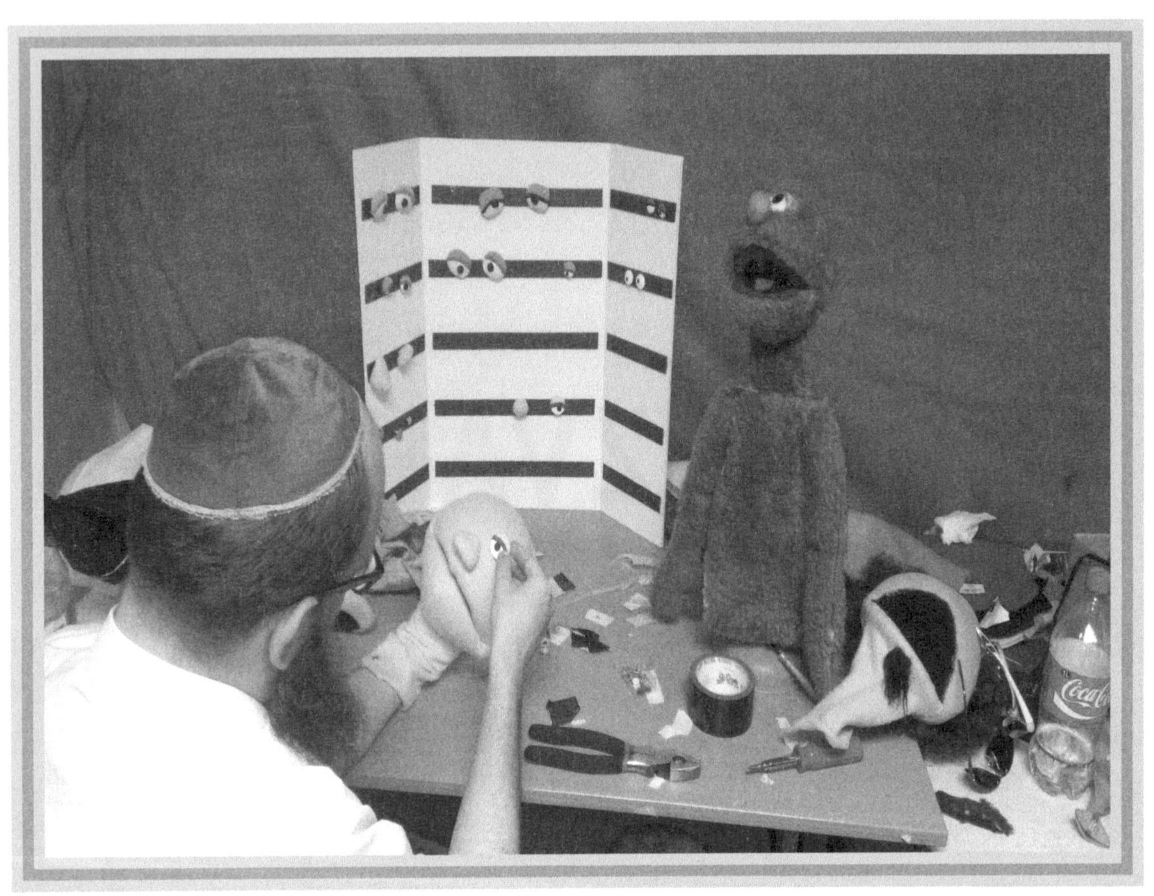

Show creator and writer **Dovid Taub** constructs a character

INTRO & BEHIND-THE-SCENES

Each "**Rabbi Itche Kadoozy Show**" series represents something I wanted to experiment with at the time. For the "**mitzvah Guys**" it was creating character-driven stories. During production of the "**Chanukah Mini-Series**" I constructed two puppets with blank faces and interchangeable facial features to account for all of the one-off characters in that script, which opened up a lot of possibilities for future episodes.

With the Parsha Report I had to be careful when I wrote the scripts because any new character meant building a new puppet. As a result, there are only a couple of episodes of that series which feature any other characters than Rabbi Itche, Jono, G-Fish, Larry and Roy. But once I had those blank puppets I could write any character I wanted.

I used those blank puppets for all of the extra characters in "The Quest" (And I built some blank Gefilte Fish puppets as well), but after that I wanted to try something different. I wanted to try writing a series in which each episode revolved around an entirely new character. I had heard about Rabbis doing mitzvah Pledge programs and it seemed like a fun way to explore different types of people with different ways of relating to their Jewishness.

Besides for the development of new characters, this series also provided some character growth for Jono—instead of always being the recipient of Rabbi Kadoozy's lessons, this time Rabbi Itche and Jono were a team, going out and helping people together.

THE MINYAN GUY

SCENE: Rabbi Itche and Jono are in the basement, going through boxes of mitzvah pledge cards.

RABBI: Over the past few weeks Jono and I have helped so many people with their mitzvah Pledges that we had to go back to the basement for more mitzvah cards. But other than that, participation at the Ira and Edna Bernstein Jewish Center is still pretty low.

JONO: I've got 2 words for you, Rabbi: Hay Rides!

RABBI: Hay Rides?

JONO: Yup. Rabbi! Yoni—the new youth director at the synagogue across town—had hey rides last week and it was wasome. And just when I thought it couldn't get any wasomer, we made our own t-shirts. Now that's how you build a congregation.

RABBI: I don't know what you're talking about, Jono, we have a very active youth group here.

(Cut to 2 guys with mustaches playing ping-pong in the youth group room)

GUY 1: (Scores a point) Oooh! And that makes me the winner. Care to play another game?

GUY 2: Neh, I gotta take my kids to a doctor's appointment tomorrow morning before work.

(Cut back to Rabbi and Jono)

JONO: Look, Rabbi—I thought the whole point of reviving this mitzvah campaign was to breath new life into this place, and quite frankly, Rabbi, I don't see or smell that happening.

RABBI: I don't know, Jono, you have to appreciate the importance of helping one person do one more mitzvah, even if it doesn't directly lead to something more.

JONO: Look, Rabbi, in about 23 seconds, my attention span is gonna reach its limit and I will no longer have any idea what we're talking about. SO let me say this quickly—First of all, what we need to do is help someone do a mitzvah that ALSO leads to building up the community here. And second…(Pause. Jono looks around, then slowly wanders off)

RABBI: (Narration) and so, Jono and I went to visit Mike Levine, who pledged to start coming to shul everyday to pray with a Minyan.

(Transition to Rabbi, Jono, and Mike Levine standing in the middle of a High School Gymnasium. Mike is wearing a t-shirt and has a whistle)

MIKE: (Whistles) Come on boys, let's see some hustle out there! (To Rabbi) Anyways, Rabbi, I'd like to help you out, but when I made that pledge I was saying Kaddish for my Mother, so I needed a Minyan. But That was 20 years ago. (Uhh…last show it was 30 years ago.. can we make up our mind?}

JONO: Oh. How's your father doing?

RABBI: JONO!

JONO: (Innocently) What? (Pause) Oh, you think...?! I would never...! That's terrible, Rabbi.

MIKE: Look, I do pray every day, I just do it home by myself, where I can concentrate better.

RABBI: I understand how you feel, Mike. If you change your mind just give me a call. (Turns to leave)

JONO: Hold on! That's it? You're just gonna let him off the hook?! {a bit harsh, That's it? No pep talk or significance speech?}

RABBI: It's his choice, Jono.

JONO: Man, I wish you woulda been this understanding when you made me promise to stop mailing sick pigeons to my old middle-school teachers.

RABBI: That was different...

JONO: Look, coach, I understand where you're coming from—I don't like going anywhere or doing anything—if I had the money I would pay somebody else to do my online shopping for me. But this is different, and it's something you should understand as a football coach.

MIKE: I don't understand.

JONO: Look at all those kids out there on the field. Each one of them is an important member of the team, right?

MIKE: Right. Well, except for him...(Blows his whistle and shouts) GET OFF THE FIELD, GLUBMAN, I CUT YOU FROM THE TEAM A MONTH AGO!

JONO: Ok, so, besides for Glubman, each one of those guys brings something special to the game. Humungo over there, and sprinty over there. Even that skrawny kid. (Jono whistles with his fingers) HEY, SCRAWNY KID, PICK OF THE PACE! (To Mike) And no matter how good a football player Humungo is, he still needs

Scrawny and sprinty and all the others to bring their talents to the game so they can win.

MIKE: So you're saying that when a group of people get together to pray, they each bring their own strengths and talents, like a team?

JONO: I hadn't thought it through to that step yet, but, yeah, that sounds like it works.

MIKE: Ok, then let's do this thing! I'll see you guys at six am tomorrow morning! (To Rabbi) HIGH FIVE! (To Jono) HIGH FIVE! YEAH! (Runs off)

(Transition to Rabbi and Jono driving)

RABBI: (Narration) So we helped Mike Levine to do his mitzvah, and we were on our way to starting up our daily Minyan Again. There was only one problem…

RABBI: Where are we going to find 10 Jewish men who will show up at 6 am tomorrow for a minyan?

JONO: I dunno. Miami?

(Fade in to Rabbi Itche in the shul making phone calls)

RABBI: Yes…yes, I understand. Well, if you can make it it would be great. Ok. Ok. Yes, I already screwed in the light bulb this morning.

(Hangs up and looks through a list of numbers)

RABBI: (Narration) After Mike Levine agreed to come to a daily prayer service, I spent the whole rest of the day making phone calls to make sure we'd have 10 people for a minyan.

JONO: (Enters) Hey, Rabbi, I just had a great idea—howsabout we make a minyan of robots! Not creepy modern Japanese androids, but cool nineteen fifties robots with light bulbs on their heads and tube arms.

RABBI: I'm sorry, Jono, but it has to be people. And what would robots need to pray for anyways?

JONO: (Pause) The ability to love. (Awkward pause) So how many people have you gotten to come so far?

RABBI: Well, I have one yes from Larry, 20 no's, and 368 maybes. So, what have you been up to all day?

JONO: Video games. And reading...video game magazines. Oh...that reminds me, I have to go play more video games!

(Jono runs off, and Rabbi Itche walks off looking at his list. Transition to Rabbi Itche in his office making phone calls. There is a clock on the wall that reads 7:30. During the following narration, the clock gets later, and Rabbi Itche get's more and more tired, until it is 9:45, and Rabbi Itche can barely hold his head up)

RABBI: (Narration) All evening long I went through my list of phone numbers and called everybody I could. I even tried calling the guy who used to be the president of the shul 25 years ago until he started a breakaway congregation because I wouldn't make a bingo night here. Finally, around 9:45, after calling nearly a thousand people, I fell asleep.

(Fade to black)

LARRY: (Voice over) Rabbi, Rabbi, wake up!

(Cut to Rabbi Itche in his office. Larry is standing next to him. Rabbi wakes up abruptly)

LARRY: Rabbi, it's 6:30 am.

RABBI: Six Thirty! It's time for the minyan! We gotta open the doors, there could be hundreds of people coming. We might even need to call a security guard!

LARRY: I'm sorry, Rabbi, but the only people here are me, Jono, and the guy you promised to have a minyan for.

(Cut to the shul. It is completely empty with the exception of Mike Levine and Jono. Rabbi and Larry Enter)

MIKE: What's going on, Rabbi? Where's the minyan?

JONO: If we had made a robot minyan like I suggested, we would be ready to start right now. Of course, there's also the possibility that we'd be fighting a robot rebellion right now. But those are the risks of progress.

RABBI: I'm sorry, Mike, I made a mistake in thinking that I could get a minyan so soon. I made a lot of calls, but it takes more than a phone call to build up a relationship with someone.

MIKE: So that's it? No minyan?

RABBI: I guess not. I'm so sorry. (Rabbi Itche hangs his head and begins to walk out. As he approaches the door, Harry Bloom, the lawnchair guy, enters) Harry? What are you doing here?

HARRY: I'm here for the Minyan, Rabbi. You helped me do my mitzvah, now I'm helping you do yours.

RABBI: That's very kind of you, harry, but I don't think we're gonna have enough people...

(Barry Rosenfeld, the string guy, enters)

BARRY: Hey, Rabbi, I'm here for the minyan! But I forgot my Tallit.

RABBI: (Flustered) Wow...ok. There are plenty here for you to borrow, but I think we're not going to be able to...

(Carl Weissman, the wilderness guy, and Mr. Frank, the blessing guy, enter)

CARL: Let's make this quick, Rabbi, I've got a bear wearing boxing gloves waiting for me at home!

RABBI: Wow, Carl, Mr. Frank, this is amazing! Out of nearly a thousand phone calls it was the people we helped with their mitzvah pledges that actually showed up.

MR. FRANK: Yeah, well, after I started doing my mitzvah, I wanted to do more, but I didn't know what to do. So when you called me about the minyan I figured this would be a good next step.

RABBI: This is really wonderful. When people get together to help one another do a mitzvah, it just leads to even more mitzvot.

LARRY: Rabbi, we have 8 guys now. All we need is 2 more and we'll be able to this after all.

(Another guy enters. his name is Doug)

DOUG: Hey, Rabbi, I'm here!

RABBI: Hey, It's Doug!

JONO: Who's Doug?

RABBI: The mezuzah guy, don't you remember?

JONO: No. I don't remember the mezuzah guy.

RABBI: Trust me, it happened.

LARRY: Well, now we're up to nine.

MIKE: Hey, Rabbi, I gotta get going soon.

RABBI: No, no! We practically have a minyan already. Everybody just start, and the tenth guy will be here in no time.

MIKE: (Hesitantly) Ok, I'll wait ten more minutes.

JONO: Hooray, ten more minutes to go play video games! (Jono runs out)

RABBI: (Narration, over a black screen) Where were we? Oh yeah…

(Cut to the shul. The mitzvah guys, Rabbi, Larry, and Jono are there.)

RABBI: Everybody just start, we'll have a minyan in 2 minutes.

RABBI: Jono, I don't have time for this now. Open your prayer books to page 27 and start reading. I'll be right back! (Runs out. Runs back in) Oh, and nobody leave! (Runs out. Runs back in) Oh yeah, and there's coffee over there. (Runs out)

RABBI: (Narrating:) After a bit of a scare we finally managed to get 9 guys for our minyan, and now the challenge was getting the tenth.

(Cut to Rabbi Itche in his office, holding a phone, frantically flipping through a phone book. Jono enters)

JONO: (Enters) Hey, Rabbi. I thought you already called everybody you knew?

RABBI: I did. That's why I'm trying an old trick I used to use when I first became a Rabbi here and didn't know anybody yet. I would open up the phone book and call any name that sounded Jewish.

(Cut to young Rabbi Itche in his office making a phone call, with a open phone book in front of him)

YOUNG RABBI: Hello, is this.... Ira Bernstein?

(Cut back to present day Rabbi Itche)

RABBI: Here's one...Alan Zeidman. (Picks up the phone. We hear the phone ringing. somebody answers)

ALAN: (Voice over) Hello?

RABBI: Hi, this is Rabbi Itche Kadoozy calling from the Ira and Edna...

ALAN: (Voice over) I don't want any, goodbye.

RABBI: No, wait...I'm not selling anything, I just wanted to know if you could come be part of a quorum of 10 Jewish men for a prayer service.

(Cut to Alan wearing a t-shirt, talking on the phone with one hand and lifting a weight with the other)

ALAN: Listen, mister. I am on the do not call list. And, see, silly me, I thought that people like you would understand that that meant DO NOT CALL ME! But I guess you didn't understand that. So let me say it again. DO NOT CALL ME! And if you call me again I'll... (Click)

RABBI: Hello? Hello? (To Jono) We must have gotten cut off. (Redials. Ring ring.)

ALAN: Hello?

RABBI: Hi, this is Rabbi Itche Kadoozy again, we must have gotten disconnected…

ALAN: That's it! I'm comin' down there!

RABBI: Terrific! I'll see you soon! (Hangs up. Cut to the shul. Rabbi runs in. Jono follows)

RABBI: Ok, everybody, the tenth guy is on his way!

JONO: Rabbi, I could hear that guy screaming through the phone. I don't think he's coming for the minyan. I think he's coming to rough you up.

RABBI: Who am I to judge people's intentions. As long as a Jew comes to shul, that's good enough for me.

(Fade to the front of the shul. Larry is Davening at the bimah. Rabbi and Jono are standing to the side)

RABBI: (Narration) A few minutes later, Alan showed up and we were able to proceed with the morning service, and say all the things that you can only say with a minyan.

(Cut to Alan standing in the doorway at the back of the shul, looking very angry, lifting his weight up and down and starring forward. Cut back to the front)

RABBI: Isn't this great!

JONO: Um…Rabbi, do you not realize that that guy back there is gonna rough you up somethin' awful?

RABBI: Honestly, Jono, I'm able to completely block that reality from my conscious thought so that I can live with a fantasy I've created in which I've pleased everybody.

JONO: Gotcha. Let me know how that works out for you.

LARRY: *Aleinu l'shabeach L'adon hakol…*

RABBI: (Narration) Eventually, we concluded our prayers and it was time for me to face reality.

(Fade to Rabbi saying goodbye to Barry Rosenfeld in front of the table full of books)

RABBI: Thank you so much for coming, Barry.

BARRY: You're welcome, Rabbi…um…Rabbi ka…um…You're welcome Rabbi. (Exits Cut to Alan standing there starring at Rabbi. Cut to Rabbi Itche. He turns and looks towards the doorway. He is now starting to realize the gravity of the moment.)

ALAN: Rabbi Itche Kadoozy? I believe we have some business to take care of. (He starts to slowly walk towards Rabbi Itche. Rabbi stands and waits for him to approach. He is scared. Eventually Alan stops and stands very close to Rabbi Itche.)

RABBI: Look, Mr. Zeidman. I know you didn't come here for the morning prayer service. I know you came down here to beat me up…or however you tough guys say it. But before you do that, I want you to know something. Even though you didn't come here to be part of our minyan, you were anyways. Just you being here completed our group of 10 so that we could pray together as a community. So even though you had your own reasons for being here, your presence alone was something special. I just wanted you to know that. Now go ahead and do what you have to do.

ALAN: (Pause) Are you going to call me again at 6:30 am?

RABBI: Probably. If I need you.

ALAN: And you know that if you do that, I'm not afraid to come down here, right?

RABBI: I'm counting on it.

(Alan turns and slowly leaves)

MIKE: Hey, Rabbi, good game, good game. I'll see you again tomorrow morning, right?

RABBI: Oy vey! (Picks up his cell-phone) Hi, this Rrabbi Kadoozy calling from the Ira and Edna Bernstein Jewish Center…

[THE END]

THE BLESSING GUY

SCENE: Fade in on Rabbi Itche in the shul going through some mitzvah card

RABBI: (Narration) One of the nice things about Jono and I helping people with their mitzvah card pledges is that it has made us much closer friends. Of course, this has come with some issues that need to be worked out.

(Jono comes wandering in wearing a pair of Rabbi's glasses. He looks very silly and he obviously can't see straight.)

JONO: Whoa, Rabbi, how do you see out of these things? Are you like…super farsighted and super nearsighted at the same time?

RABBI: Yes, I am. Jono, did I say you could borrow my spare glasses?

JONO: (Jono removes the glasses) No. But you always let me use your stuff. I thought that's our arrangement—you have stuff and I get to use it.

RABBI: No, Jono, that's not our arrangement. Of course you're welcome to use my things when you need them, but I'd appreciate it if you'd ask first.

JONO: Ok. Can I use your belt? (Looks down at his legs) Your pants are really loose on me.

RABBI: (Sigh) Come on, Jono, let's go work on this mitzvah card.

(They exit)

(Transition to Rabbi Itche and Jono in an office, talking to a guy at a desk)

RABBI: So, Mr. Frank, you filled out this mitzvah card 30 years ago and pledged to start making blessings before eating food.

MR. FRANK: Oh, yeah, I vaguely remember that.

(Mr. Frank is interrupted by the his secretary over the intercom)

INTERCOM: Mr. Frank, your two o' clock is here.

RABBI: Oh, is this a bad time?

MR. FRANK: Oh, no. I don't really have a 2 o' clock. I just have my secretary do that to make me look impressive.

JONO: That is impressive. Impressively sad.

RABBI: Anyways, Mr. Frank, here's a booklet that tells you what Bracha to make on different types of foods.

JONO: My favorite is borei pri ha-candy.

RABBI: That's not a real blessing, Jono.

JONO: Hmm, I must have read it wrong. Let me put on my reading glasses… (Puts on Rabbi Itche's spare glasses)

RABBI: (Sigh) (Cut to Rabbi Itche and Jono walking down the street)

RABBI: (Narration) With Mr. Frank's mitzvah pledge out of the way, Jono and I had some time to deal with our recent relationship issues.

JONO: By the way, Rabbi, I borrowed your toothbrush last night. I hope that's ok.

RABBI: See, Jono, this is exactly what I'm talking about!

JONO: Gee, Rabbi, I kinda thought you'd be proud of me for brushing my teeth.

RABBI: Actually, the disturbing thing about this is that I am kind of proud of you for brushing your teeth.

JONO: (Stops and looks at something on the street) Hey, Rabbi, Look at that!

(Jono is looking at a bus ad. In very large letters are the words "MR. FRANK: PROFESSIONAL FOOD BLESSER," and a picture of mr. frank with his arms spread wide in the air looking all holy. At the bottom are the words "Don't eat profane foods. Let Mr. Frank bless your food before you eat it.)

RABBI: Professional food blesser! We better go talk to this guy again.

JONO: Oh good, Maybe he can bless the melty candy bar I have in my pocket and make it edible again.

(Transition to Rabbi Itche and Jono in the waiting room of Mr. Frank's office. Mr. Frank comes out of his office with a man carrying a box of veggie burgers)

MR. FRANK: You take good care of those veggie burgers, Bill, those are holy veggie burgers now.

MAN: Thank you Mr. Frank! I don't know what I'd do without you. (Exits)

MR. FRANK: Oh, Rabbi! I'm glad you're here, I need to talk to you. You see, after we spoke yesterday about making blessings, I started up this food blessing service, and it's a huge success. I actually have a real 2 o'clock now! And all the other o'clocks as well!

JONO: Even a 37 o'clock?

INTERCOM: Mr. Frank, your 37 o'clock is here.

MR. FRANK: Business is great, but I have this strange feeling that something is not quite right about it.

RABBI: Well, actually your right. I'm sure you're just trying to help people, but you've kind of missed the the whole point of why we make Brachot before we eat. We're not blessing the food or making it holy. G-d made the whole world, so it already has a potential for holiness, just as long as we use it in a holy way.

MR. FRANK: Oh. Oops. I better go cancel my 37 o'clock. I'll be right back. (Exits)

JONO: So, Rabbi, back to what we were talking about before. Are you saying that I can't borrow your stuff anymore?

(Mr. frank enters again, but doesn't say anything. Rabbi and Jono continue their conversation)

RABBI: No, that's not what I'm saying. I actually really enjoy sharing what I have with other people—except for my toothbrush. That's kind of really gross. But generally, I have no problem with you using my things. I just want you to respect my property and ask first before you take things that don't belong to you.

MR. FRANK: Ohhhhhh. SO that's what I'm missing!

JONO: Guh?

MR. FRANK: G-d created the whole world and everything in it. Making a Bracha is a way of asking permission to use the things in G-d's world and thanking G-d for letting us use it.

RABBI: Exactly. I couldn't have said it better myself.

JONO: Hey, Rabbi, can I borrow your credit card to go buy you a new toothbrush?

RABBI: Absolutely!

[THE END]

THE STRING GUY

SCENE: Rabbi and Jono are sitting at a table in Shul, going through stacks of mitzvah pledge cards.

RABBI: (Narration) A few days ago, Jono and I decided to get people involved in my Shul again by helping them to fulfill mitzvah Pledges they had made 20 years ago.

JONO: (Reading a mitzvah card) Josh Bronstein pledged to "stop torturing animals?" Yikes. Too creepy. (Throws card off to the side) I hope this guy hasn't escalated in the past 20 years.

RABBI: Here's a simple one: "I want to start wearing a Tallit"

(Cut to Rabbi and Jono walking up to a house)

NARRATION: So, we tracked down the Tallit guy and went to visit him at home.

(Rabbi rings the doorbell. Barry Rosenfeld answers.)

BARRY: Hello?

RABBI: Hi, I'm Rabbi Itche Kadoozy from the Ira and Edna Bernstein Jewish community center. You filled out a mitzvah card...

BARRY: Hang on, hang on, stop right there. Look, I'm sorry, I'd love to help you, but you see, I've got this string tied around my finger to remind me to do something, and for the life of me I can't remember what it is! And it's been there for years! So honestly, I don't have time for you fine Bible salesmen.

RABBI: We're not selling Bibles, we're here about your mitzvah card.

BARRY: You say tomato, I say tomato. (Pronounced the same, if you choose)

JONO: (Whispers to Rabbi) This guy is nuttier than the possibly psychotic animal torture guy.

RABBI: Well, maybe we can help you figure this out and then we'll get to the mitzvah card.

BARRY: Oh, really? And are you going to bring back the years of my life I wasted trying to figure out why this BLASTED STRING IS TIED AROUND MY FINGER?!

RABBI: (Pause) We could give it a shot.

JONO: To the Rabbi-Mobile!

(Spinning background image with Jono and Rabbi's heads moving toward us and back...with Batman music...)

NARRATION: And so, we started driving around with Barry, trying to trigger his memory.

(Cut to Rabbi, Jono and Barry in Rabbi's car, driving around)

JONO: Maybe you tied the string around your finger to remind you to stop tying strings around your finger to remind you to do things.

BARRY: No, it wasn't that. That's what the one on my toe is for. This one had something to do with...history...or ancient cultures.

RABBI: There was a special Egyptology exhibit at the Museum of Natural History a few years ago. Maybe you wanted to remind yourself to go see it.

(Cut to Rabbi, Jono, and Barry at the Museum)

RABBI: So does this bring back any memories?

BARRY: Of when I used to be an ancient Egyptian?

RABBI: There's no need for Sarcasm, Barry, I'm just trying to help.

(Jono is standing by a cave man diorama, trying to offer soda to a cave man)

JONO: Hey, Guys! If I introduce Soda to these cave men, just imagine how far soda technology will have come today!

(Cut to fantasy sequence of Jono sitting on a couch. A cup of soda hovers over to him, a straw extends from the cup and inserts itself into Jono's mouth. The cup then says in a computer voice "commence drinking." Cut back to the Museum)

JONO: So practical.

BARRY: No, this isn't it. But the loin cloth on that caveman made me remember something. I think it had something to do with clothes.

JONO: When's the last time you picked up your dry cleaning?

BARRY: Oh, I don't know...what was it...laaaast Tues...no...30 years ago.

JONO: (Looks at barry from head to toe) Yeah, that seems about right.

(Cut to the three guys at the dry cleaners.)

CLEANER: Chow can I chelp you today?

BARRY: I'm here to pick up something under the name Rosenfeld?

CLEANER: (Gets excited) Rosenfeld? Barry Rosenfeld?! Svetlana, Sasha, Dimitry! Come quick! The bell-bottoms man is here! (Svetlana, Sasha and Dimitry come out from the back. They are all very excited)

SASHAH: We must celebrate with dancing! (Presses play on a tape player and Russian music starts playing)

CLEANER: That will be 4 dollars for bell-bottoms and $37,000 interest.

BARRY: Hmmmm. No, this isn't it. This is definitely not what I wanted to remember.

JONO: Great, let's get out of here. (Jono sees a dish of candy) But first…(He grabs a white and dark striped candy) Bolshaya Spaseebo! (A great big thank you!)

CLEANER: Pozhalsta. (You're welcome)

JONO: Doh Svidanya (Good-bye)

(They exit)

SASHAH: Bell Bottoms Man, come back!

(Cut to Rabbi, Jono, and Barry outside the dry cleaners)

RABBI: What now?

JONO: Now I eat this candy! Sucky sucky! (Jono holds out the candy; Barry stares at it)

BARRY: That's it! I'm remembering something—what I'm trying to remember is white with dark stripes.

JONO: The zoo! You wanted to remember to go to the zoo!

BARRY: To see the zebras?

JONO: I was gonna say stripopotamus, but sure, zebra works too.

(Cut to Rabbi, Jono and Barry at the zoo. They are walking and talking. As they walk, you see a sign in the background that reads "Please do not feed the stripopotamus." No mention of this is made.)

BARRY: No. This isn't it either. It smells here. I need to tie a string around my finger to remind myself not to go to places that smell.

JONO: Whatabout if you're at a gas station and you reaaaaaaally have to use the rest room?

RABBI: Jono, can we stay on task please?

JONO: Ok, fine. Let's go through the clues of today—It has something to do with history or ancient cultures.

BARRY: Right.

JONO: It's also an article of clothing or apparel.

BARRY: Correct.

JONO: And it's white with dark stripes.

BARRY: Yes.

JONO: Hmmmm. Can't think of anything matching that description. Sorry. Let's move on to the mitzvah card so I can get home and eat too many peaches.

RABBI: That's it!

BARRY: No, I'm allergic to peaches. They make me die.

RABBI: No, the mitzvah card! (Takes out the card) Take a look at this.

BARRY: Ooohhhhhhh! Yes! 20 years ago I wanted start wearing a Tallit!

JONO: And it was so important to you that you spent the last 20 years trying to remember it?

BARRY: Yeah. Now I remember! The strings and knots on the Tallit are supposed to remind us of the 613 mitzvot. I knew I had a terrible memory, so I wanted to do something that would remind me to do Mitzvahs. But I also knew that I'd forget to wear the Tallit too, so I tied the string around my finger!

JONO: Guuuuuuh?

BARRY: I wanted to do the mitzvah of remembering to wear something that would remind me to do even more mitzvahs!

JONO: Guuuuuuh? (Use the exact same clip of Jono doing this from before)

RABBI: Well, let's hope the strings of the Tallit do a better job of reminding you than the string around your finger did.

BARRY: What string around my finger? (Looks at his finger) Hey, what's this doing here?

RABBI: Come on, let's go to the shul and I'll get you a Tallit.

(The three guys start walking off into the distance.)

BARRY: Go to where to get me a what?

[THE END]

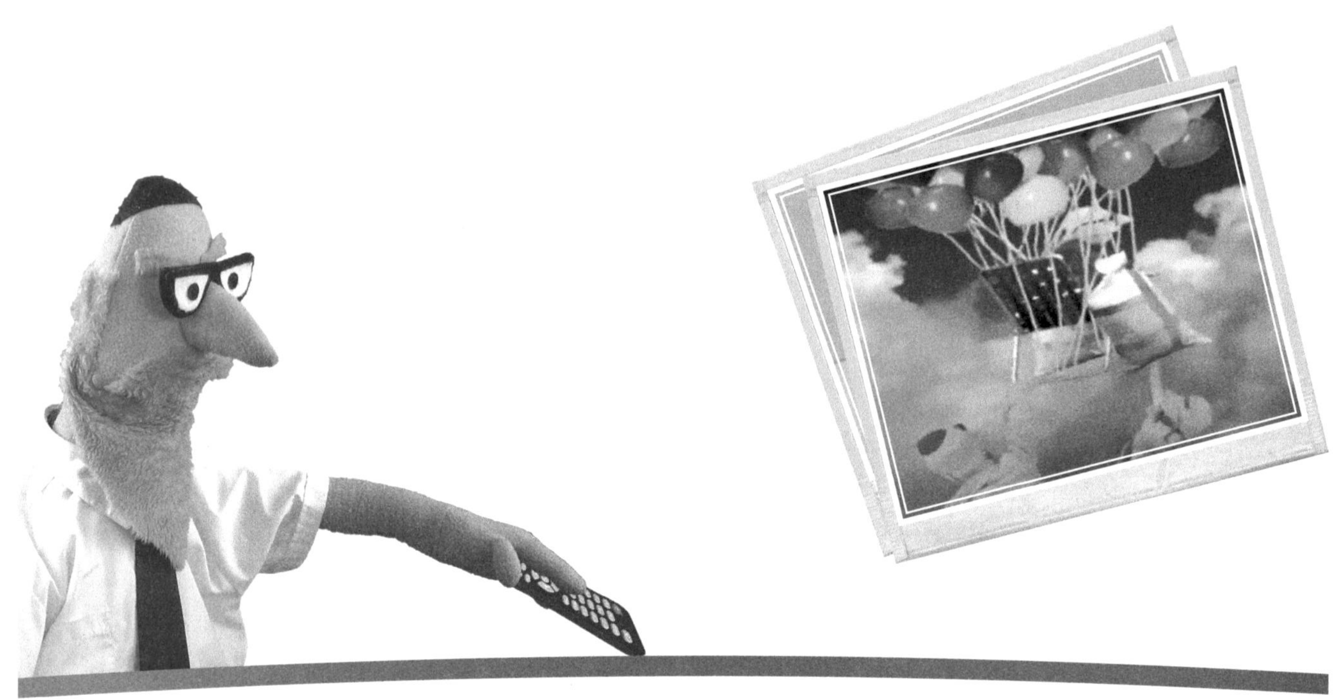

THE LAWN-CHAIR GUY

SCENE: Images of Rabbi Itche and Jono floating in coolers in the ocean

RABBI: (Narrating:) I'm Rabbi Itche Kadoozy. That's me in the Pajamas floating in a cooler. And the guy floating in the other cooler is my friend Jono who lives in my basement. I bet you're wondering why we're floating in the middle of the ocean in coolers. Well, it's kind of a long story. 5 and half minutes to be exact. It all started right before the High Holidays when Jono was helping me get the prayer books out from the basement.

(Transition to Rabbi Itche and Jono rummaging through boxes in the basement of the shul).

JONO: This is so boring. Do you think if we collect all the dust we could make a Dust Golem?

RABBI: No building a Dust Golem until you put out the Burning Bush.

(Cut to a burning bush in front of the shul)

RABBI: (Narrating:) Jono had been a little starved for adventure lately and was trying to stir up some excitement by burning bushes, putting goldfish in the water cooler.

(Cut to Larry Goldstein taking a sip from a Styrofoam cup and then choking a little, and accepting business propositions from Nigerian princes. Cut to a computer screen with an email on it that says "Think for you to have sent check for $100,000. Unfortunately, Prince Mutamba have been captured and will to be unable repay you. Ever." This is because we spent last year having a lot of adventures, (Show clips) including a high speed chase in an army jeep, and searching the globe for the family of Jono's pet Gefilte Fish. But when all that adventure was finally over, it was time for me to get back to being a Rabbi, and for Jono to get back to being a guy who lives in his Rabbi's basement.

RABBI: I'm sorry you're bored, Jono. But helping me get ready for the high holidays can be an adventure. Just pretend you're looking for buried treasure. But instead of treasure, it's box of high holiday prayer books! And instead of being buried, it's sitting right there on the floor!

JONO: Eh. I'm not convinced. (Spots some boxes) Hey, what's in those boxes?

RABBI: Those boxes? A thousand "Let my people go buttons." You want one?

JONO: Yes. But I meant those other boxes.

RABBI: (Goes over to the boxes and looks inside) Ohhhhhh. These are mitzvah cards. (Pulls one out. It has a name, phone number, and a mitzvah filled out on it. He blows some dust off of the card)

RABBI: (Narrating:) About 20 years ago the Shul started a "Million Mitzvahs" project in response to a crisis involving a little kid getting trapped in well. (Cut to a young Rabbi Itche standing outside the shul at a booth with a big "A Million Mitzvahs for Mikey" sign on it, handing out the mitzvah cards) thousands of people filled out the cards and pledged to do a mitzvah. But a week later they got Mikey out of the well, and the project was forgotten. (Dissolve to the exact

same shot but the sign on the booth now says "Donate Money For a New Bathroom Stall")

(Back to the basement)

RABBI: We were supposed to send these cards back to people with a mitzvah certificate when they completed their pledge, but I guess nobody ever followed through on it.

JONO: Rabbi, I think I know what my next adventure is going to be.

(Transition to Jono building a giant, elaborate card house in the shul. Jono is wearing a "let my people go button, which he will wear for the rest of the episode, and perhaps forever)

RABBI: It turned out that Jono's next adventure was going to be making a record braking card house modeled after the Domestic terminal at JFK out of the mitzvah cards.

RABBI: Jono, you can't build a giant card house in the middle of my shul right before Rosh Hashanah!

JONO: I can if I put my mind to it, Rabbi. Like the little engine that built a giant card house even though everybody said he couldn't.

RABBI: No, I mean, you can't do it here. There are going to be hundreds of people in this room during the high holidays. Half of them will probably be sleeping, but I don't want the other half distracted by your card house.

JONO: But, Rabbi…

RABBI: I'm sorry, Jono, you have to take it down. I know you're looking for an adventure, but I have a job to do. There is an entire congregation depending on me to be their rabbi. As it turned out, there were only about 9 guys depending on me to be their rabbi.

(Cut to an empty shul with 8 guys in it and Rabbi standing at the front.)

RABBI: (Under his breath) 7, 8…(Out loud) Ok, where did the 10th guy for the minyan go? I specifically said no bathroom breaks. (Sigh)

Apparently I had been so busy with our adventures, that I didn't realize that participation at my synagogue had dropped to an all time low, not counting the 2 weeks in 1988 that we had a family of bears living in the social hall.

(Cut to a young Rabbi Itche in the shul waving a folding chair around, bear noises are heard in the background)

RABBI: It's ok, everybody, Back to the Purim party, I got a folding chair!

RABBI: (Narration:) Needless to say, by the time the high holidays were over, I was pretty depressed. (Cut to Rabbi Itche, Jono, Larry, and Mrs. K hanging out in the shul. Rabbi is in his pajamas and has his head down on the table.)

MRS. K: Cheer up, Rabbi. It's not so bad, At least you had a minyan…some of the time. And Bernie apologized, he said the lock on the stall was jammed.

LARRY: Poor little guy. It must have been the most frightening 3 hours of his life. HA!

RABBI: It's not Bernie's fault, it's mine. I've been so busy with other things that I've let the Ira and Edna Bernstein Jewish Center deteriorate.

JONO: Hey, howsabout we have a bake sale to save the shul! But instead of baked goods we'll sell monkeys! And instead of people eating them, they'll train them to make baked goods!

RABBI: It's not an issue of money, or membership. We have thousands of members, they just don't participate any more. The only reason people even call here nowadays is to remind me to screw in a Yahrtzeit bulb. (Off screen a phone rings) I know, I know, Morris Rosenfeld. (Rabbi gets up and slowly mopes out.)

MRS. K: I'm really worried, guys. I haven't seen Rabbi Itche this upset since the time that bear ate his hat.

LARRY: In all fairness, the bear was sleeping before he was hit by that folding chair. HA!

MRS. K: Jono, please do something to cheer him up.

JONO: (Sigh) fine. But after that I'm gonna have to burn some more bushes.

RABBI: (Narrating:) So, Jono offered to take me canoeing to cheer me up, which didn't sound like such a bad plan, until I found out that Jono's idea of a canoe was a big red picnic cooler.

(Cut to Rabbi Itche and Jono standing at the river with 2 big red coolers in front of them)

JONO: Come on, Rabbi, get in your canooler!

RABBI: Absolutely not, Jono!

JONO: Come on, Rabbi, you need to cheer up, and I want to be the one to help you. You always do so much for everybody else, please let me take the opportunity to give back.

RABBI: That was beautiful, Jono. Is that really why you're doing this for me?

JONO: Kind of. The realer reason why I'm doing this is because Mrs. K won't let me go back to doing crazy slash destructive slash ethically questionable stuff until I get you out of your rut. Come on, Rabbi, hop aboard your canooler.

(Transition to Rabbi Itche and Jono floating down the river in the coolers)

RABBI: (Narrating:) So, against my better judgement, we climbed inside our picnic coolers and began floating along the Hudson river. Surprisingly, after a little while, I felt much better.

RABBI: You know, Jono, just being out here, away from everything kind of puts things in perspective.

JONO: Yup. Like how from really far away, the sun looks really really tiny even though it's actually bigger than a house.

(Rabbi Itche and Jono are both really relaxed.)

RABBI: This is really relaxing.

RABBI: (Narrating:) In fact, it was so relaxing, that we started to fall asleep.

RABBI: Thank you (Yawn) Jono.

JONO: (Snore)

(Fade to black. Fade in to Rabbi Itche and Jono in the middle of the ocean, floating in their coolers)

RABBI: (Narrating:) And I believe this is where you came in.

(Cut to Rabbi wakes up, looks around and then freaks out) JONO, JONO! Wake up!

JONO: Huh, wuh, (Wakes up slowly, then sniffs), Why do I smell like salami sandwiches and ice packs?

RABBI: Jono, snap out of it! Look where we are!

JONO: What? Where are we?

RABBI: In the middle of the ocean!

JONO: The middle of the ocean?! We're in the middle of the ocean! Coooooool! Let's call the coast guard! And all the local news stations!

RABBI: (Sighs, pulls out phone and starts making calls)

JONO: Oooh, and tell them to wait a little while, I need time to make a totally wasome card house before the camera crews get here!
(Pulls out some mitzvah cards)

RABBI: Hold on a second, Jono, (Puts down the phone) read that card to me.

JONO: Okee Dokee, Artichokee. Name: Harry Bloom. mitzvah: I built a homemade helicopter out of a lawn-chair and helium balloons for the purpose of sea rescue and have never used it. The mitzvah I pledge to do is to save a life.

RABBI: That's it, Jono! That's how we'll get people involved in the shul again!

JONO: By giving them rides on lawn-chair helicopters?

RABBI: No, by finding all those people who filled out the mitzvah cards and helping them make good on their pledges!

RABBI: (Narrating:) So we called harry bloom, who was currently a resident in a local nursing home, and it turned out that he had still never gotten around to using his homemade helicopter for sea rescue.

(Cut to Harry Bloom in the nursing home, holding the phone. He hangs up and jumps out of bed)

HARRY: I'm a-comin' Rabbi!

NURSING HOME STAFF GUY: Whoa, what's the hurry, Mr. Blum?

HARRY: I've gotta go get my lawn-chair helicopter and rescue the Rabbi from a picnic cooler!

NURSING HOME STAFF GUY: Ohhhh. Of course you do. (Turns and calls to someone off screen) Steve, I need some restraints for Mr. Blum.

HARRY: (Takes the opportunity to run away) I'm A-COMIN'!

(Transition to Harry rescuing Rabbi and Jono)

RABBI: (Narrating:) After Harry managed to escape from the nursing home, he found his helicopter and came to save our lives. While we were flying through the sky, Jono said something that helped me sort everything out.

JONO: You know, Rabbi, flying in this lawn-chair helicopter really puts things in perspective. Like, from up here, a house looks really tiny, which means that the sun must be smaller than a grape.

RABBI: (Narrating:) Maybe it was the high altitude and motion sickness that got to my head, but it was at that moment that I realized that helping people fulfill their old mitzvah pledges would also be the source of many new adventures for Jono and me.

[THE END]

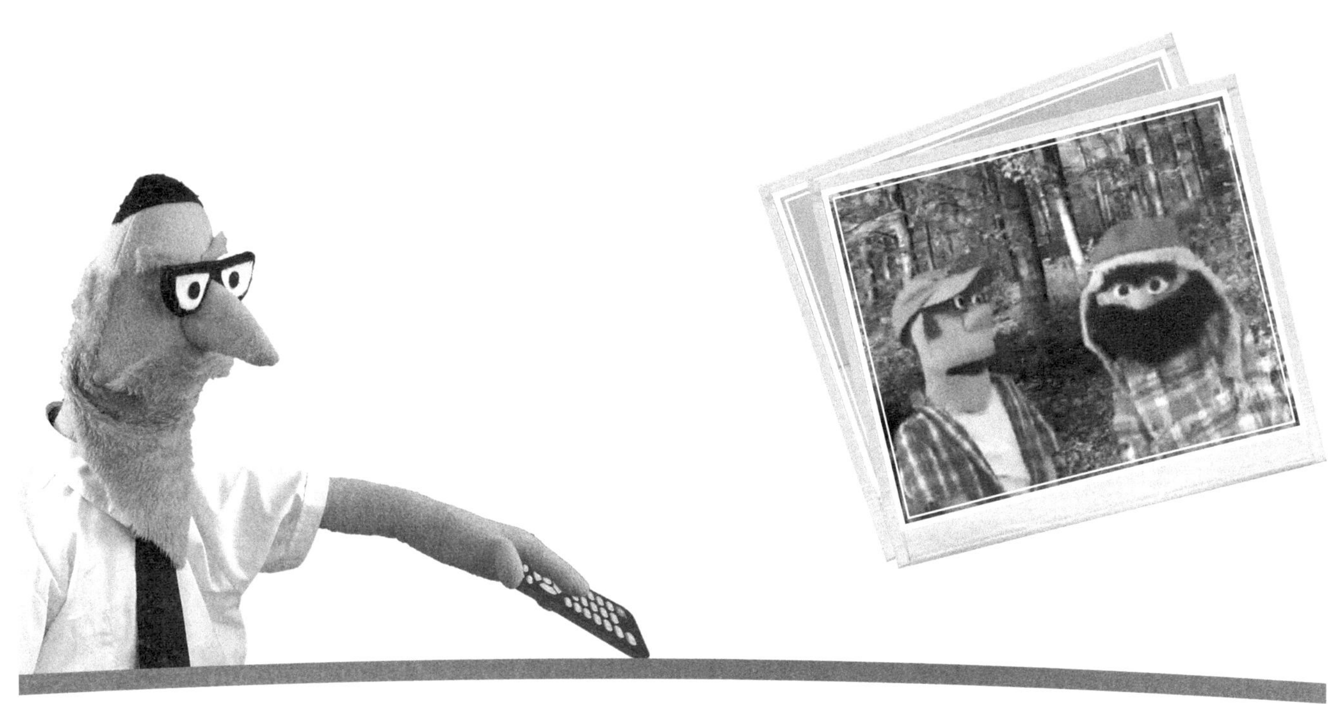

THE WILDERNESS GUY

SCENE: Rabbi Itche and Jono are driving on a dirt road

JONO: Why are we in the middle of the wilderness, Rabbi? Please tell me that a bear pledged to put on tefillin.

RABBI: Nope. (Looks at card) Carl Weissman pledged to keep kosher.

JONO: Oh. (Pause) Oh! Is Carl Weissman a bear?

RABBI: No.

JONO: A squirrel?

RABBI: No.

JONO: A half-man half-squirrel half-bear with a beaver tail and eagles eyes?

RABBI: No, he's just a guy who likes to live in a cabin in the woods.

JONO: Ohhhh, ok. He's not an animal or super-animal hybrid, he's just a creepy wilderness man. Gotcha.

(Cut to an external shot of the car approaching the cabin.)

RABBI: Narration: Jono and I have had a lot of success helping people with their mitzvah pledges. But sometimes people aren't interested anymore in the mitzvah they pledged to do 20 years ago.

(Cut to Rabbi and Jono inside the cabin with Carl. Carl is a big, hairy man with a black beard, big black bushy eyebrows, and a flannel shirt.)

RABBI: So, Mr. Weissman, 20 years ago you filled out this mitzvah card and pledged to eat kosher food. Have you already started doing that?

CARL: (Pause. Stares at them) Have you ever eaten a rabbit? Whole?

RABBI: (Narration) This was one of those times)

JONO: Ok, see, rabbit swallowing—that's probably something you're gonna want to tone down on if you want to fulfill this pledge. And if you want to not seem like a really super scary, creepy wilderness man.

CARL: Grrrrrrrr.

RABBI: Ok, I guess we're gonna be on our way now. Thank you for your time, and if you ever decide to go rabbit free, just give me a call.

(They get up and walk towards the door.)

RABBI: (Narration) Now this is where the story would have ended, if it weren't for the following challenge issued by Carl)

CARL: Hey, sideburns.

(They stop and turn around. The following is played out like a western showdown)

JONO: Who, me?

CARL: Yeah you. You're soft.

JONO: You look like a bear.

CARL: You're Soft and tiny. Like a baby marshmallow.

JONO: (Slowly and aggressively) I like marshmallows.

CARL: You're too soft. You're a disgrace! You wouldn't last a day out here in the wilderness.

(They stare each other down as Rabbi narrates)

RABBI: (Narration) If there are 2 things in this world that Jono can't say no to, it's a dare and a sleepover. This was both. (Cut to Rabbi Itche driving home by himself) And so, I drove back alone, and Jono stayed with the wilderness man.

(Cut to Jono and wilderness man sitting on logs in the middle of the forest.)

CARL: The most important thing you gotta know is that you are what you eat. If you wanna be tough, you gotta eat tough.

JONO: Like tree bark?

CARL: No, like this crowbar! (Holds up a crowbar.) Now start eatin', sideburns!

(Cut to Rabbi and Marvin in the shul)

RABBI: I hope he's ok out there.

MARVIN: Don't worry, Rabbi. If there's one guy I know who can take care of himself in the wilderness, it's Roy.

RABBI: We're talking about Jono.

MARVIN: Ohhhh, Jono. Ok, he'll definitely get eaten by raccoons.... Or maybe one of them half-man half-squirrel half-bears with a beaver tail and eagles eyes.

(Jono runs in)

JONO: RABBI, RABBI, RABBI!

RABBI: Jono! Are you alright!

JONO: No! I can't take it anymore! He told me that to be tough I had to eat tough, and then he made me eat a crowbar!

RABBI: What! That's terrible. I'm glad you didn't eat a crowbar.

JONO: Oh, I ate the crowbar, alright. But it would have been a whole lot easier if wilderness man let me use mustard.

(Carl enters)

CARL: Mustard is for the weak! We eat tools with none of them fancy fixins in the wild.

JONO: Please don't let him take me back there, Rabbi!

RABBI: OK EVERYBODY STOP! This is getting out of hand! Wilderness man, I'm ashamed of you! It's very wrong to make people eat crowbars!

CARL: (Hangs his head) Grrrrr, I know. I'm ashamed.

JONO: BUSTED!

RABBI: However...wilderness man does have a point, Jono.

CARL: I have a name you know!

RABBI: I'm sorry. Carl, you made a point that you yourself can learn from. What you eat shapes who you are.

JONO: Am I gonna turn into a crowbar?

RABBI: NO. Listen. When we eat kosher food, it brings a mitzvah right into our own bodies, and helps make Judaism part of who we are and what we do. It's really a simple way that we can be Jewish both inside and out. So maybe instead of catching and eating rabbits, Carl, you could try...catching kosher fish?

CARL: I love catchin' fish! I catch fish like a bear! (Makes a motion as if he's grabbing a fish with his hands) Catchin' fish with my paws is pretty manly anyway. Much manlier than ordering rabbits on the internet like I been doing. I think I'll give it a go.

RABBI: That's the spirit Carl!

(G-Fish floats in)

G-FISH: Um, I didn't get the memo that there's a new series, you know? What gives? I was the STAR of the last series! Stars deserve starring rolls! And here we are, almost 4 new episodes without GEFILTE FISH?

CARL: FISH! GRRRRR!!!

(Carl chases after G-Fish all around the screen – G-Fish is screaming)

CARL: I feel more Jewish already!

G-FISH: GET MY AGENT ON THE PHOOOOOOOONE!!!!

(Carl chases him off screen)

RABBI: Well, Jono, looks like we can cross this card off our list now.

JONO: Cool cool. Hey, Rabbi, I could go for some desert now. Do you have a wrench?

(Fade to black.)

(Fade back in, G-Fish is staring at the screen.)

G-FISH: That's it! I'm on strike!

ROY: (Off screen) Who cares?

G-FISH: Ohhhh…

[THE END]

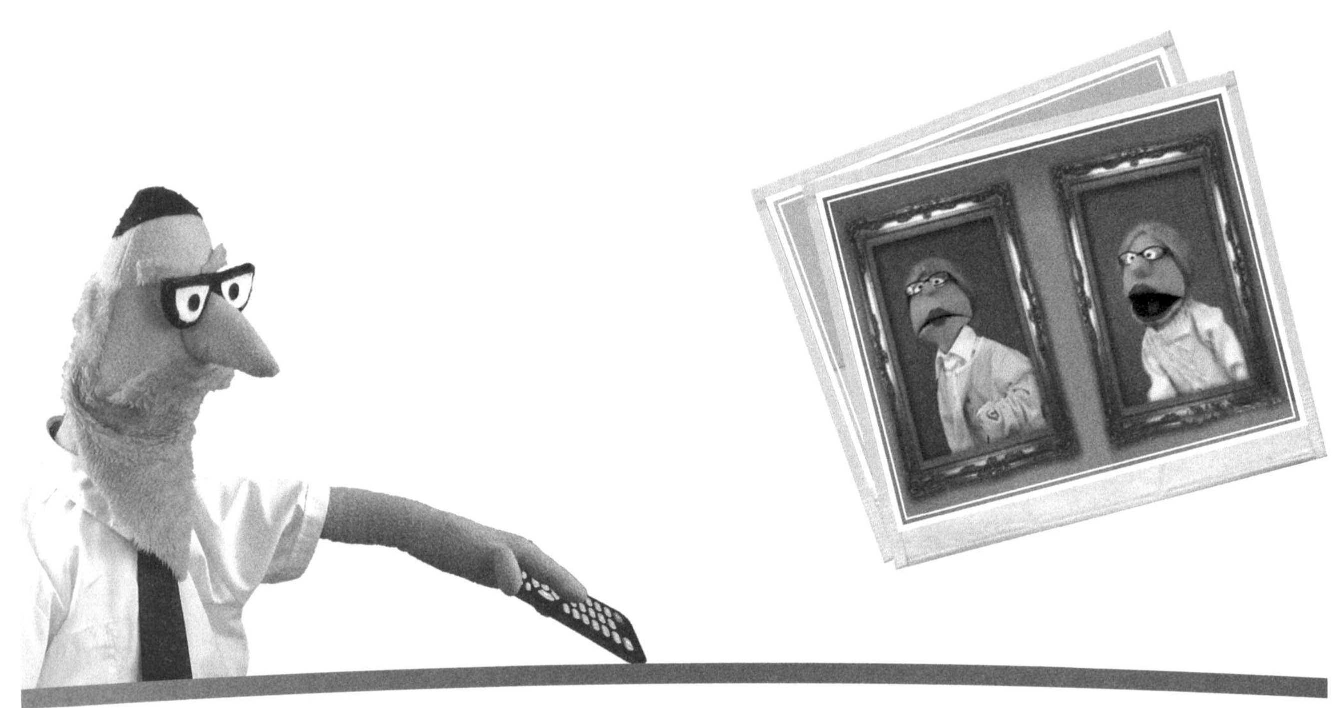

THE CHARITY LADIES

SCENE: Rabbi Itche and Jono are driving

RABBI: (Narrating: After 2 weeks of helping people with their mitzvah pledges, Jono and I started getting pretty good at it.

JONO: So, what's the low-down on the show-down for this ho-down on today's mitzvah card thingy?

RABBI: (Looking at the card) Agnes and Rose Miller pledged to give Tzedakah.

JONO: Agnes and Rose Miller? The Bajillionare old ladies?

RABBI: They're not that old, Jono. I think they must have only been in their fifties when they filled out this card 20 years ago.

JONO: Which would make them approximately 800 years old by now.

RABBI: (Pause) Jono, do you exaggerate numbers to be funny, or do you really just not understand how numbers work?

JONO: I think the first thing you said is kind of a way for me to cover up the second thing you said.

RABBI: Fair enough. I won't mention it again.

JONO: I appreciate that.

(Cut to the van pulling up to a huge mansion. Cut to the miller sisters in their very extravagant parlor the doorbell rings.)

AGNES: Was that the doorbell, Rose?

ROSE: Why, yes, agnes it was the doorbell! (Sing-songy) DOORBELL (The two old women scamper around crazily as they chant, eventually making their way to the door)

AGNES: DOOORBELLL!

ROSE: DOOORBELLL!

(Cut to the sisters welcoming Rabbi and Jono at the door)

RABBI: I'm Rabbi Itche Kadoozy, I called earlier about your mitzvah card.

ROSE: Of course, do come in. Agnes, might you be an angel and bring these young men some tea? (To Jono) You would like a cup of tea, of course?

JONO: Actually, my doctor says…

AGNES: Of course he wants tea, Rose, don't be silly. I'll be right back. (Scampers off singing again) TEA TEA TEA TEA!

(Cut to the miller sisters and Rabbi and Jono sitting in the parlor.)

RABBI: As I told you earlier on the phone, you filled out this mitzvah card 20 years ago, pledging to do the mitzvah of giving charity.

AGNES: Oh yes. The charity. (Picks up her check book from the coffee table.) Just give us a moment to write out a check. (The sisters giggle and whisper to each other as they write the check)

JONO: (Whispers to Rabbi Itche) Get ready to become a bajillionare, Rabbi.

(The sisters hand the check to Rabbi Itche. Cut to Rabbi Itche and Jono driving)

RABBI: (Narration) Much to Jono's disappointment, I did not become a bajillionare.

JONO: 18 DOLLARS?! Those ladies had a crystal toilet bowl and they only gave you 18 dollars?!

RABBI: Calm down, Jono. The mitzvah of Tzedakah doesn't have a minimum. It doesn't matter how much a person gives, just as long as they give something.

JONO: 18 dollars won't even cover the puppy you wanted to buy for me.

RABBI: I never wanted to buy you a puppy, Jono.

JONO: Awww, MAN! Great. Just great.

(Cut to Rabbi Itche and Jono approaching the shul. Marvin is outside)

MARVIN: Hey, Rabbi. Hey wise-guy.

RABBI AND JONO: Hey Marvin.

MARVIN: Rabbi, me and Roy would appreciate if you'd give us a heads up next time you plan a large event.

RABBI: What? What event?

JONO: Please say it's an intervention. I LOVE interventions.

RABBI: What? No. Marvin, what's this all about?

MARVIN: The dinner honoring Rose and Agnes Miller. They're inside now setting things up.

RABBI: Come on, Jono, let's go figure out what's going on here.

(Cut to Rose and Agnes setting up tables in the shul)

AGNES: What an honor this will be for those who get to honor us.

ROSE: Indeed. I only wish I could be so lucky as to honor someone so great as ourselves. OH MY, we've forgotten the Daffodils!

AGNES: Oh but we must have daffodils!

ROSE: We simply MUST!

AGNES: DAFFODILS! (The women run around wildly)

ROSE: DAFFODILS!

AGNES: DAFFODILS!

ROSE: DAFFODILS!

(Cut to Rabbi Itche and Jono in the lobby outside the doors to the large shul. There is a sign on an easel that reads "Welcome to the first annual Rose and Agnes Miller Dinner in Honor of Rose and Agnes Miller." Jono notices something on the wall opposite the doors.)

JONO: Whoa! Rabbi, check that out!

(There are two giant framed portraits of the ladies that take up the entire wall Rabbi and Jono stop and just stare.)

RABBI: Wow. This is very, very strange.

JONO: Rabbi, I think this would be a good time to tell you that I have a very deep and paralyzing fear of old ladies.

RABBI: That's sad, Jono. And disturbing.

JONO: Yeah, that's what my grandmother says.

(They turn around and enter the room)

AGNES: Oh, Rabbi, you've come just in time to practice the speech we've written for you. (Hands Rabbi Itche a stack of papers)

RABBI: You wrote a speech for me?

ROSE: Actually we wrote two!

AGNES: One for before we speak...

ROSE: And one for after!

AGNES: And your little friend will be in charge of carrying us in on thrones!

JONO: Boooooo!

ROSE: Why you bad bad boy! (Jono hangs his head) Go stand in the corner!

RABBI: Jono, you don't have to...

AGNES: Go! Go! Off with you now!

JONO: Sorry, Rabbi, they're about a trazillion times scarier than you. (Runs off screen, and stands in the back of the shul with his face to the wall)

RABBI: Look, Mrs. Miller, I understand that you're proud to have done the mitzvah of Tzedakah, and you have every right to be. It's not always easy to do the right thing, but you were responsible enough to make the right decision anyways, and do what's expected of you. And for that you do deserve credit...

ROSE: Oh no, that won't do!

AGNES: That won't do at all!

ROSE: Not at all!

AGNES: Just stick to what we wrote, young man.

RABBI: (Reads the speech) There are many people in this world who do good things, but they are mere specks of dust beside the giants of generosity, Rose and Agnes Miller.

JONO: (From the corner, still with his face to the wall) Can I go yet?

ROSE: No! Continue, Rabbi.

RABBI: (Sigh. Reads) Today Rose and Agnes Miller went above and beyond the call of duty and did something they didn't have to do. They gave charity to help support this fine institution. (Looks up from the paper) I can't say this.

AGNES: Why of course you can, silly, you just did!

RABBI: No, I mean, it's not true.

ROSE: (To agnes) Tell me I didn't just hear what me thinks me heard!

RABBI: Now hear me out. Tzedakah is not charity. It's translated that way a lot, but a more accurate translation of the word Tzedeka would be Justice. Giving Tzedakah isn't something extra, it's what we're expected to do because it's right and just.

AGNES: You mean to say that we had to give you our money?!

ROSE: Why that's preposterous!

RABBI: No, you could have given it to someone else, and you chose to give it to our synagogue. And for that I'm very grateful. But as far as you're concerned, that money didn't belong to you. It was entrusted to you so that you could give it to someone who needed it.

AGNES: I never looked at it that way.

ROSE: Thank you, young man, for opening our eyes!

RABBI: Thank you for your generous donation. Come on, I'll walk you to your car.

(They exit. Jono is still in the back with his face to the wall)

JONO: Hello? Can I go now? (Slow fade to black as Jono continues to talk) Hellooooooo? Scary old ladies, are you there? (Pause) I'm scared and lonely and cold. And hungry. Hellooooooooooo?

[THE END]

FEELING HAKHEL

SCENE: Rabbi and Jono are sitting behind a desk

RABBI: Shalom Aleichem. I'm Rabbi Itche Kadoozy. There's a lot of interesting things to say about Hakhel, but instead of boring you with a speech, I've asked my friend Jono here to prepare a short video presentation about Hakhel. Jono, tell us a little bit about what we're about to see.

JONO: Well, the first thing I did was go out and buy a brand new camera, which put us a little bit over budget.

RABBI: What? Our budget was $12.

JONO: Yeah. And I wanted our video to be 100 times better than that. Then I sat down to think about the mitzvah of Hakhel and that's when it hit me; I don't know anything about the mitzvah of Hakhel. I've literally never heard of it before.

RABBI: We just had a Hakhel gathering here in the Ira and Edna Bernstein Jewish Center, just a few days ago, there was music and a magician, and I explained the entire concept of Hakhel.

JONO: Rabbi, I zone out when people try to explain things to me. I zoned out when the magician tried explaining to me something about his car breaking down, not having a ride home, I don't know. I zoned out.

MAGICIAN: I've been waiting for a ride to the bus station for five days.

RABBI: What? That's terrible.

MAGICIAN: No. It's magic.

RABBI: Anyways, what did you do about the video?

JONO: Oh. I bought a drone.

RABBI: What?

JONO: And since I still didn't know anything about Hakhel I just recorded a bunch of footage of people being chased by a drone.

RABBI: Well, we're still contractually obligated to fill four minutes, so I guess just show what you've got in the video.

JONO: Hooray. Roll the clip.

(Clip of people running from a drone)

RABBI: I have no idea what that was supposed to mean, Jono, but it made me feel deeply concerned for those people.

JONO: And that, rabbi, is the power of strong visual storytelling.

JONO: And you know what, Jono? That's really the point of Hakhel.

JONO: Oh. See, Rabbi, I knew you could take the random borderline irresponsible stuff I did and turn it into a meaningful lesson.

MAGICIAN: Thank you. You see, even though the mitzvah of Hakhel is to hear the king read from the Torah, the point of this particular

mitzvah isn't learning. It's feeling. According to the Rambam, even people who don't understand a word the king is saying have to be there to concentrate on how the experience makes them feel.

JONO: Oh. Like how you didn't understand my crazy drone video but it made you feel deeply disturbed.

RABBI: Concerned. I said deeply concerned. And yes, but in the case of Hakhel it should make a person feel reverence and awe, rejoicing and trembling, the way the Jewish people felt on Mount Sinai on the day the Torah was given. Imagine that. There was so much to see and feel from the experience of gathering with all the Jewish people to hear the king of Israel read from the Torah that it can make a person feel like they were standing at Har Sinai receiving the Torah themselves, and we can do that too.

JONO: Wait, wait, wait, wait, wait, wait. Hold on. If I don't understand what's going on. How am I supposed to get into it?

MAGICIAN: Through the magic.

JONO: Oh. The magic.

RABBI: Oh. No, no, no, Jono.

JONO: Oh.

RABBI: For me, an example of an experience like that can be watching a video of the rebbe. Sometimes I'll sit in my office and watch a video of a Farbrengen to learn the ideas that the rebbe is teaching, but sometimes, like when we show a video of the rebbe in shul and the acoustics are terrible in the social hall, I can't hear a word, but in situations like that I watch just for what I can gain by seeing the way the rebbe talks to people or the way the rebbe does a mitzvah and paying attention to how that makes me feel, and then using those feelings to be even more excited about doing mitzvot, just like the king reading from the Torah by Hakhel.

JONO: I'm not sure I got all of that, but it made me feel like I should go make another Hakhel video with my $1,200 camera and my $2,000 drone.

RABBI: That's wonderful. Well, that's all the time we have for today. Thank you so much for letting us join together with you for this very special Hakhel gathering.

[THE END]

THE HOLIDAY SERIES

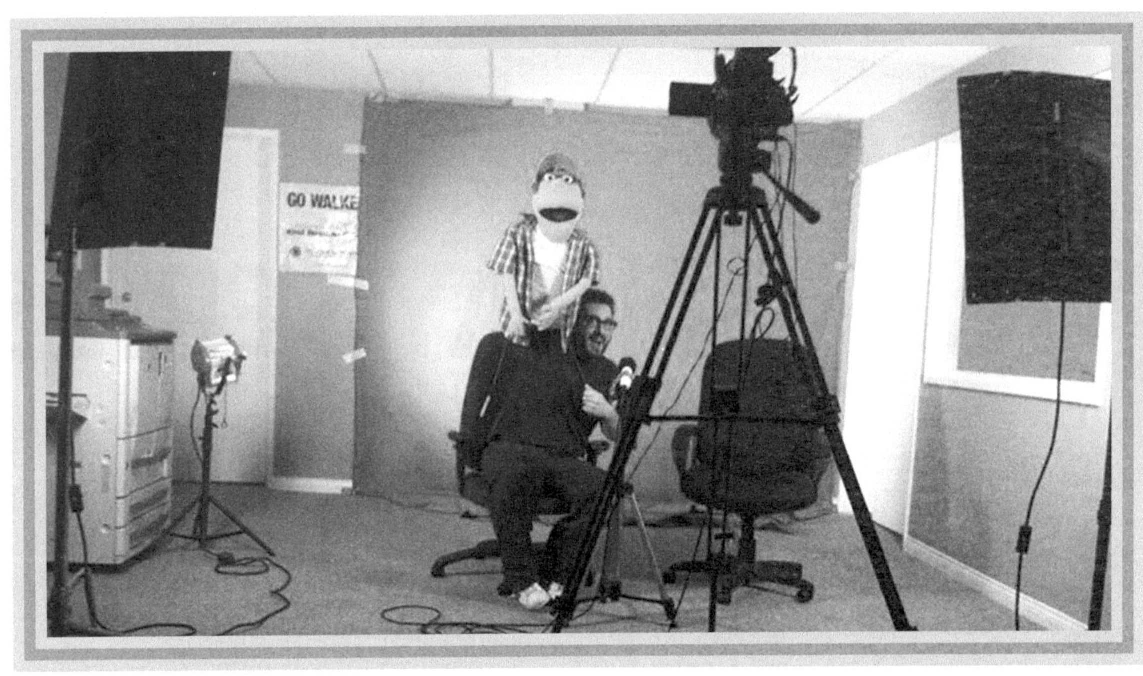

Show co-creator **Jonathan Goorvitch** animating **Jono** for the camera

INTRO & BEHIND-THE-SCENES

by Dovid Taub

In 2006, after a year of **Parsha Reports**, I wanted to try my hand at a long-form story. The last Parsha Report aired right before Simchat Torah, so Chanukah was the next holiday and seemed like a good theme upon which to base a larger, more elaborate iteration of the show. At the time I was particularly enamored with a style of comedic storytelling in which a handful of seemingly trivial occurrences become crucial elements of misunderstanding, ultimately resulting in chaos. Hilarity ensues.

I spent a long time crafting the script with the help of my brother, my sister and Real Jono, each of whom made invaluable contributions. My brother came up with the "plastique dreidels" and the wicker menorah. My sister smoothed out the dialogue and contributed the line "plus, no annoying fly-aways." Real Jono performed his usual job of one-upping all of my jokes, as well as writing most of the dialogue for Jono's personal trainer, who has some of my favorite lines.

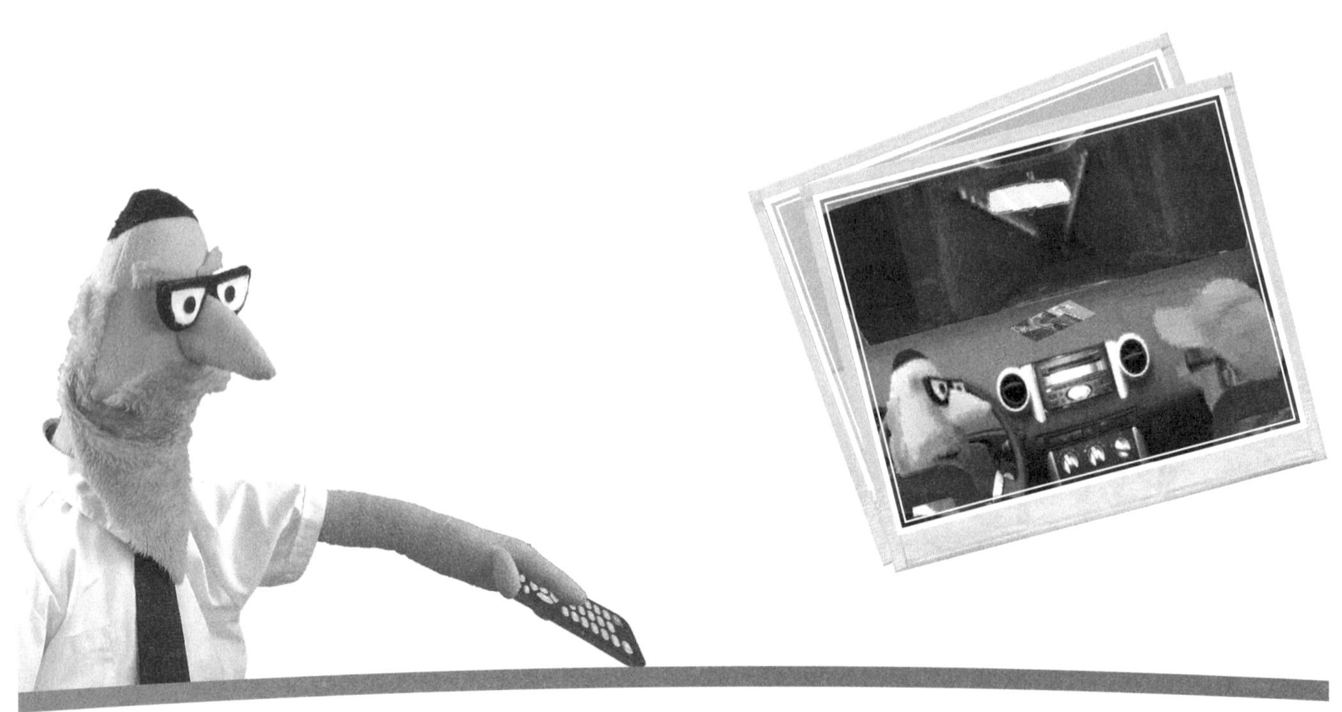

ROAD TRIP: ELUL

SCENE: Rabbi Itche and Jono are in a car

RABBI: Well, the month of Elul is a special time of preparation before all of the special holidays that come in Tishrei. And we seem to be stuck in virtual traffic here in virtual Elul.

(Honking horn)

JONO: Who? What? Who? What? Who? Who? It wasn't me.

RABBI: Relax, Jono. I was just honking the horn.

JONO: Well, why would you go and do something like that and wake me up? The J-Dog needs his beauty sleep.

RABBI: Every day in Elul we blow the shofar. It's almost like a reveille bugle, to wake us up for the special tasks we have ahead of ourselves during the upcoming holidays.

JONO: Whaaa!

RABBI: Are there any special tasks you have to accomplish, Jono?

JONO: Hmm, I already ate my box of Mike and Ikes and drank my Big Gulp, so just wake me up when we get to Rosh Hashanah.

RABBI: Rosh Hashanah means the head of the year. The head of a person makes the decisions that control the rest of the body.

JONO: Right now, my head is telling the rest of my body to dance to the groovy tunes I'm listening to on my iPod.

RABBI: Right. And so too, the decisions we make on Rosh Hashanah to do more mitzvahs sets the tone for and effects the entire year.

JONO: That means I'll be busting moves on the dance floor until 5767, right, Rabbi?

RABBI: Busting moves?

JONO: For some reason, that sounds a lot cooler when you say it.

RABBI: Busting moves?

JONO: Man, why don't you say stuff like that more often? Can I eat yet?

RABBI: No.

JONO: Can I eat yet?

RABBI: No.

JONO: Can I eat yet?

RABBI: No.

JONO: Can I eat yet?

RABBI: No.

JONO: Can I eat yet?

RABBI: No! Jono, we've still got a few more virtual miles left until the end of the virtual Yom Kippur part of our virtual road trip.

JONO: Rabbi, I have to go to the virtual bathroom.

RABBI: Of course, if this were the real Yom Kippur, I wouldn't be driving right now. We'd be in synagogue asking G-d to forgive us for anything wrong we may have done throughout the year, and praying that the next year will be better.

JONO: Rabbi, I was serious before. You might have to virtually pull over to the side of the virtual road. I think I see some virtual bushes.

RABBI: On Sukkot, one of the biggest mitzvahs is to shake a Lulav and Etrog. We take four different species of plants, each with their own qualities, and put them together to do one mitzvah. Similarly, the entire holiday of Sukkot is like that. Jews of all different backgrounds unite to do the mitzvah of celebrating the holiday of Sukkot.

JONO: Coincidentally, I told 50 friends of mine of various different backgrounds that they could crash in your basement.

RABBI: Fifty friends? How do you have 50 friends? I don't even think I know 50 people.

JONO: Personal ads.

RABBI: Look, Jono, your own safety aside, I don't think I can fit 50 people in my basement. Nor do I think it's a very good idea to.

JONO: You're telling me! That junky old couch isn't going to be enough for everyone to sleep on, and you're going to have to get, like, 50 of those junky old couches. We'd better start driving past some virtual garage sales.

[THE END]

HIGH-HOLIDAY BLOOPERS: ROSH HASHANA

SCENE: Rabbi Itche in front of a green-screen

(Take 1)

RABBI: Well, the Days of Awes are upon us once again

DIRECTOR: (OC) Cut. You said "awes"

RABBI: Awes isn't a word. I wouldn't have said that.

(Take 2)

RABBI: The days of awe are almost upon us once again, a time when we think about repentance. Repentance? That's the word right? It's not repentancing?

(Take 3)

RABBI: (Rabbi Itche's tie is flipped over his shoulder) The days of awe are almost upon us once again....

DIRECTOR: Cut! your tie.

RABBI: What? Cut my tie?

DIRECTOR: Your tie is....

RABBI: Why would I cut my tie? If it's too long I could just adjust it, cutting it just seems silly. (Looks down where his tie should be) Oh. I see. Well we didn't have to cut for that, I sometimes go half a day like this.

(Take 4)

RABBI: The days of awe are almost upon us once again, a time when we think about repentancing. Oops. See, now that I said it, I have it stuck in my head.

(A few more outtakes, then)

(Take 255)

DIRECTOR: (Exhausted) Take 255. This is the last time, Rabbi, and then we're shutting down.

RABBI: Ok, I got it. The days of Awe are almost upon us once again, a time when we think about repentance, when we reflect on the mistakes of the year we are about to complete, do what we can to repair those mistakes, and resolve to change for the better in the coming year.

DIRECTOR: Aaaaaaand cut! Fantastic, Rabbi, that's a rap.

RABBI: See, it's never too late to fix your mistakes.

DIRECTOR: Cut! Cut! That wasn't in the script!

[THE END]

HAP-BEE NEW YEAR: ROSH HASHANA

SCENE: Rabbi and Jono are in a Shul

JONO: Well, It's almost Rosh Hashanah again. A time when we commemorate the existence of apples.

RABBI: Actually, Jono, Rosh Hashanah commemorates the creation of the world.

JONO: A world which contains apples. And we thank G-d for giving us honey in which to dip said apples.

RABBI: (Sigh) We thank G-d for another year, and we dip apples in honey to start our new year in a sweet, happy way.

JONO: Happy like a honey bee.

RABBI: Is that an expression?

JONO: Nope. Bzzz.

RABBI: (Sigh) Stay focused, Jono.

JONO: It's also a time when we turn our hearts and minds inwards…

RABBI: Ok, now that's more like it…

JONO: And ask ourselves "what animal parts can we make musical instruments out of?"

RABBI: Oh, and there you've lost it again.

JONO: I was talking about the Shofar Rabbi.

RABBI: I know, but in a very weird and slightly upsetting way. On Rosh Hashanah we use a ram's horn to do the mitzvah of hearing the sound of the Shofar, which helps inspire us to change for the better in the coming year.

JONO: My turn again.

RABBI: Ok, let's try to keep this on topic.

JONO: The name Rosh Hashanah means "Head of the Year."

RABBI: Good.

JONO: Which symbolizes…a head. Of a honey-bee?

RABBI: Good start, Jono. Like the head of a person, or a bee, I guess, which determines the actions of the rest of the body, the decisions and changes we make on Rosh Hashanah are what we take with us through the rest of year.

JONO: And that should keep us all as busy as bees!

RABBI: How does that connect to what I just said?

JONO: I don't know. It just felt like a good way to end. And talk about bees.

RABBI: Fair enough. (To camera) Well, I wish you all a happy and meaningful Rosh Hashanah, and a sweet new year!

JONO: Bzzzz.

[THE END]

CAPTAIN AWESOME: CHANUKAH

SCENE: Rabbi Itche is standing at a menorah

RABBI: Alright Everybody! Ready to light Chanukah candles?

(Jono and Gefilte Fish enter)

JONO: AWYEAH! I'm ready, Rabbi! Ready for the best Chanukah ever! I'm gonna eat jelly donuts 'till I drop, and then get up and eat latkes 'till I drop. And then I'll get up again for an all night dreidel marathon!!!

RABBI: That's the spirit!

MRS K: (Enters) Rabbi, I made your favorite: Zucchini latkes!

RABBI: Oooh, zucchini!

G-FISH: Jonathan, are we gonna play connect four tonight?

JONO: Not tonight, G-Fish. Tonight we play dreidel. And dreidels don't fit in the Connect-4 thing. I've tried (Show picture of dreidels crammed into a Connect-4 board). Rabbi, you ready to light the Channukah menorah?

RABBI: Just about. The chanukah lights are lit to commemorate the victory of the Maccabees over the greek army. When the Greeks wanted to take away our devotion to the holiness of the Torah and mitvos, the small Jewish army of Maccabees stood strong and fought for the freedom to devote ourselves to G-d and to his Torah.

JONO: And that's why we eat donuts.

RABBI: Well...yes. But more directly, that's why we light candles, to show that one little light can fight a lot of darkness.

JONO: And one little donut can hold a lot of jelly.

RABBI: Stay focused, Jono. Each night we light one more candle, because everyday and every moment we have to grow, do more mitzvot, and one little light at a time we are able to eradicate evil and fight darkness.

JONO: Eradicating evil and fighting darkness, eh? This sounds like a job for....(Runs away and zips back wearing super hero attire) Captain Awesome and his sidekick Gefilte Fish...boy!

G-FISH: What?

RABBI: Jono, how did you change so quickly?

JONO: I had it on under my clothes.

RABBI: You always wear a cape and tights under your clothes?

JONO: Yes. Yes I do. It makes me feel more confident. It does wonders during a job interview. No cold stares or intimidating questions can phase me when I know I'm wearing a cape and tights.

RABBI: See, I would feel more ridiculous than confident.

JONO: I guess that's the difference between you and I, rabbi. But no time for chit-chat now! I have to go to the lair of the diabolical Professor Gefilte-Fish!

RABBI: I thought he was your side-kick?

JONO: Yeah, well, there's not many guys willing to play along with this kinda stuff, so I sort of had to double cast.

G-FISH: What? Transition (Dadadadadadadada. Jono and G-Fish are in the "lair". Jono is trapped inside a giant Gefilte Fish jar.

JONO: I'm trapped! In a giant Gefilte Fish jar!

G-FISH: What could be more suitable for a giant Gefilte Fish!

JONO: Yeah, but you look like the kind that's sliced from a Gefilte Fish log, not like a Gefilte Fish ball that comes in a jar...

G-FISH: Enough!! Soon you will sink into the jelly-broth and become completely grossinated! Now I will leave and let you escape. (Exits)

JONO: Must...escape...from giant...novelty jar. (Wiggles. Jar tips over and smashes. Jono escape). Hooray for me! Now it's time to get Dr. Gefilte fish. (Dadadadadada. Jono and G-Fish stand in a room in the "lair")

G-FISH: Oh no, Captain awesome has escaped! Be gentle, I'm boneless.

JONO: Well, now's the perfect time for a cool fight scene, but...there's a lot of kids out there who'd be negatively affected by violence, so...I'm just gonna stand here. (Fight music plays. Jono stands around and coughs and looks at his watch and stuff and bug bursts appear on the screen saying stuff like "COUGH!" "STARE!" "LOOKAROUND!")

G-FISH: This is getting boring.

JONO: You said it G-Fish. I think I know a better, more exiting way to fight darkness and evil...(Dadadadada)

(Back at Rabbi Itche's house. The menorah is lit, and everyone is sitting around eating donuts and playing draidel.)

JONO: Great donuts, Mrs. K!

MRS. K: Thanks Jono, I used extra oil.

RABBI: This is wonderful—everyone here together, enjoying the glow of the Chanukah lights, and having a good time just bein' Jewish.

JONO: You said it rabbi, now let's get ready for some serious dreidel action.

G-FISH: What?

[THE END]

LIGHTS...LATKES...ACTION! CHANUKAH

SCENE: Rabbi Itche is being interviewed

RABBI: What's my favorite part of Chanukah? Well, that's easy. It's the one time of year I get to make my world-famous latkes.

JONO: My most favorite part of Chanukah is most certainly not the Rabbi's latkes.

G-FISH: As a Gefilte Fish, I appreciate Chanukah because it's the only Jewish holiday that doesn't encourage the ruthless consumption of Gefilte Fishes.

JONO: Perhaps, maybe, my favorite part of Chanukah is trying to get the chocolate gelt out of the foil without damaging the foil. So you can put it back together and then give it to your friends.

G-FISH: Yeah, I mean, I have a friend who's a donut and I guess Chanukah's not so great for him. But, you know, them's the pranks.

JONO: And then they open it and they say, hey, there's no chocolate gelt in here! And then you laugh at them. With them. At them. Whatever.

RABBI: The recipe I use for latkes was actually handed down to me from my father, who got it from his father, who in turn got it online after he Googled latkes, I think.

G-FISH: I guess many people don't realize that Gefilte Fishes aren't just ground up, processed fish. We're ground up, processed fish with feelings, okay?

RABBI: I guess, at the end of the day I know my latkes are terrible. But I think the reason I enjoy doing it anyways is because it makes people grateful the rest of the year that I'm actually speaking for several hours instead of giving them my latkes.

JONO: What's your favorite part of Chanukah? I'm not asking, I'm just reading stuff on the screen. Ooh, email this to a friend! Okay, it says it on the screen so you've got to do it, I guess. Oh, visit www.Chanukah.org, okay. Okay, I guess you've got to do that, too. It says it on the screen. Ooh, there's stuff on the side there. A whole bunch of things. I guess you've got to go there, and there, and there. You should probably check that out. Ooh, more stuff!

[THE END]

CHANUKAH MINI-SERIES

SCENE: Rabbi Itche is in his living room. G-Fish, Larry, and others are scurrying around, busily on the phone preparing for Chanukah.

NARRATOR: This year's Chanukah preparations started like any other. Rabbi Itche Kadoozy was planning a public menorah lighting…

RABBI: (On phone) Yes…a 30 foot menorah in the park. I know I need a permit, that's why I'm calling.… Well, I feel that it's not just a Jewish ritual, but a universal symbol of freedom.

NARRATOR: Earlier that day, Rabbi Itche Kadoozy had put up posters all around town stating just that. (Show clips of Rabbi Itche putting up posters that say "The Menorah: Universal Symbol Of Freedom.")

RABBI: (Larry walks by) Larry, can I borrow a pen, thanks.

NARRATOR: G-Fish was ordering 2,000 plastic dreidels for point zero two cents a piece so he could sell them for a dollar each at Rabbi's menorah lighting.

G-FISH: (On phone) Oui, monsieur, how do you say, two thousand plastique dreidels.

LARRY: I thought you were ordering those dreidels from china, why are you speaking in a French accent?

G-FISH: (Holds phone down) They jack up the price if they know you're a rich American. So you just give 'em a French shipping address and intercept the cargo when it comes through JFK.

LARRY: I didn't hear that.

G-FISH: Oh come on, this is completely legal.

LARRY: No, I have a terrible ear infection, I really didn't hear that. HA!

G-FISH: (On phone) PLASTIQUE, PLASTIQUE!

NARRATOR: And Jono was preparing for the 1st annual Chanukah donut eating contest.

(Jono is standing in the living room holding a giant tray of donuts.)

RABBI: (Hangs up phone) Jono, are you still training for that hedonistic donut contest? (Jono does not respond) Oh, come one, Jono. Look, I'm, sorry. I didn't mean that, I know this important to you…

ROY: (Off screen) Think fast!

(A basketball flies on screen and knocks "Jono" over)

RABBI: Oh my….

JONO: (Runs in from off screen) You like my life-size cardboard cut out, rabbi? It's part of an aggressive PR blitz.

RABBI: (Clutching chest) You nearly gave me a heart attack.

JONO: The only way I'm going to beat my competitor is with a large scale over the top publicity campaign.

NARRATOR: Jono's opponent was Ikiru Takamochi, the champion of competitive eating. Ikiru had recently purchased air time on local television stations to promote himself.

(Cut to ikiru's promo. It is a crazy Japanese commercial. It is Japanese with English subtitles including lines like " Ikiru Takamochi is emperor of donut consumption. The mighty intestines of Ikiru Takamochi will squeeze opponents beneath challenge." Cut back to living room)

JONO: But I am confident that I can win this thing. All I need is 300 donuts and my fans.

RABBI: How are you going to eat them all?

JONO: My fans? That's horrific, rabbi. I'm an athlete, not a monster.

RABBI: No, I meant the donuts. And you're not an athlete.

JONO: Oh, I have no idea. I'm thinking some sort of funnel type deal.

RABBI: Oh, wow! I gotta get down to city hall to get that permit for my menorah lighting. Larry, can I keep this pen?

LARRY: You like the red pen, don't you, Rabbi?

RABBI: I just need a pen for…

LARRY: Yes, a red pen is the sign of a powerful man. Consider it my gift to you. Ha!

RABBI: Thanks. And is it also the sign of a powerful man to have an ink stain on his pocket? (Rabbi Itche leaves)

LARRY: (Looks down to see that his chest pocket has a huge red stain on it.) Aw…this is a new shirt. (Sadly, head down in defeat) ha.

(Cut to Roy and Marvin at hardware store with Leslie)

NARRATOR: Meanwhile, Roy and Marvin were at the hardware store to buy materials to build Rabbi's 30 foot menorah.

LESLIE: Well, guys, that's gonna come to about 5,000 dollars. And do you have a truck to get this stuff home?

(Roy and Marvin look at each other. Cut to Rabbi Itche at city hall talking to a clerk.)

NARRATOR: Down at city hall, Rabbi Itche was trying to get his permit from a man he would soon find out was nicknamed "No Permit" Wazinsky.

RABBI: Look, you look like a nice guy…

CLERK: Don't lie to me.

RABBI: I'm not, really. I trust that you'll see that I have all the applications in order so we can get this thing done as quickly as possible.

CLERK: Look, pal, there's a reason they call me "No Permit" Wazinsky.

RABBI: Because your last name is Wazinsky?

CLERK: (Stares him down)

RABBI: It's not Wazinsky?.

(Cut to living room)

NARRATOR: Marvin and Roy returned home without the materials needed to build the menorah.

ROY: How are we going to pay for this. I have 300 dollar budget.

MARVIN: Even if we could pay for it, how would we get it back here?

ROY: And even if we could get it back here, how would we…Ok, no, I guess then we'd be ok.

G-FISH: Pardon me, gentlemen, but I couldn't help but overhear your conversation, and I think I can get you a lightweight 30 foot menorah from china, for 12 dollars, including parts and labor. In return, I ask that you forfeit to me the remaining 288 dollars of your budget.

(Roy and Marvin look at each other. Cut to city hall. Rabbi is exhausted. He approaches Mr. Wazinsky with a stack of papers.)

RABBI: Ok, Mr. Wazinsky, I filled out all 7 eighteen page applications in triplicate. I think I have tennis elbow now, or carpal tunnel, and I don't even know how to play tennis or how to use a mouse, but I think everything should be in order.

WAZINSKY: I'm sorry, sir, but I can't accept any applications after 5:00.

RABBI: But it's 4:58! You can still take it now!

WAZINSKY: Oh, you're right. My mistake, let's just take a look at these…

RABBI: Thank you.

WAZINSKY: Ohhhhh, you stapled these? You're going to have to step out of line and remove the staples. I can't accept stapled applications.

RABBI: But by the time I get in line again and…

WAZINSKY: (Dismissively) See you tomorrow…(Starts to close window)

RABBI: Why do you even have staplers at those tables?

WAZINSKY: (Wazinsky stares at him, then closes the window all the way.)

RABBI: (Kind of to himself) That's it! Rabbi Itche Kadoozy can only be pushed so far.

(Cut to flashback of Jono and Rabbi Itche in the living room. Rabbi is trying to learn.)

JONO: How bout now?

ITHCE: No.

JONO: Now?

RABBI: No.

JONO: Ok…. How bout…. Now? Are you annoyed now?

RABBI: No

JONO: Now?

RABBI: NO!

JONO: Now? How bout now?

RABBI: OK FINE! NOW I'M ANNOYED!

JONO: Ooooh, you owe me a soda, Rabbi.

RABBI: Well, played, Jono, well played.

(Cut back to Rabbi Itche in city hall)

RABBI: This isn't about you and me, Mr. Wazinsky, this is about fighting for something I believe in. If you want a war, you got yourself a war!

(Cut to donut competition hall, the next day)

NARRATOR: The next day, Jono woke up early to go meet with the organizers of the donut eating competition and his competitor, ikiru takamochi, so that they could run through the details of the competition.

JONO: Mr. Takamochi, you may be the hero of Japanese jewry, but I'm the new hero of donuts…eating…eating donuts.

IKIRU: I am not Jewish.

JONO: Yeah, whatever, did you hear my threat though? About becoming the new champion?

ORGANIZER: So, Mr. Weinsteinstein, Mr. Takamochi, let's just run through some of the rules. Obviously, you'll have to eat the actual donuts, in their natural state, without the aid of machinery or hormones. That means no donut shakes, no electronic chewing machines, and absolutely no funnels, people..

JONO: You mean that actually works?

ORGANIZER: The first person to finish all 300 donuts wins. Additional points will be awarded for record breaking time.

JONO: Mr. Judge man, I have never been so psyched about eating so much kosher food before.

ORGANIZER: You mean the donuts? Oh, I can assure you, Mr. Weinsteinstein that the donuts are in no way kosher. (He holds up box of donuts. Close-up on donut box. Box reads "Now With Real Animal Shortening!")

JONO: What do you mean? This is a Jewish event, I just assumed the donuts were gonna be kosher.

ORGANIZER: Well, this isn't necessarily a Jewish event.

IKIRU: I'm not Jewish.

JONO: Quiet, Ikiru. Not necessarily a Jewish event?! It's a donut eating contest on Chanukah! That's about as not necessarily Jewish as an ACLU conference.

IKIRU: I'm not Jewish.

JONO: You don't have to say that, Ikiru. These guys aren't the ancient greeks, you don't have to deny your heritage.

IKIRU: But I'm really not....

JONO: QUIET! Look, mr. judge man, you have no idea how much this contest means to me, and I can't believe I'm saying this, but I don't know if I can take part in a Chanukah celebration that conflicts with the traditions that people like the Maccabees fought for. I gotta think about this.

(Cut to living room)

G-FISH: Guys, the menorah came. 12 bucks, under 20 pounds and best of all, it came with a free carnival prize catalogue. It's in the parking lot, let's go admire it and you can thank me later.

(Cut to parking lot. A giant wicker menorah stands in the parking lot. G-Fish, Roy, and Marvin enter and stare.)

ROY: A wicker menorah?!

MARVIN: Do you realize what kind of fire hazard this is?!

G-FISH: OH, COME OOOOON! If this is some sort of stunt to keep my 288 dollars from me, you guys are sick! I did you a favor!

ROY: Gefilte Fish, this wicker menorah could catch fire. It could be very dangerous.

G-FISH: Look, don't worry about it. Just coat it in scotch guard and hair-spray and it'll be protected from all the elements. And...no annoying flyaways

(Cut to city hall. Mr. Wazinsky opens his window and Rabbi Itche steps up confidently with the stack of papers.)

RABBI: Ok, Mr. Wazinsky, here you go. 378 pages of paper work, written clearly, in print, and ready to go. Find a problem this time, I dare you.

WAZINSKY: (Looks at papers) You filled this out in red pen, you're going to have to do it again in black.

RABBI: THAT'S IT! I'm not going to stand for this any more. What ere you trying to do, keep me here another day?

WAZINSKY: That was definitely part of the plan, yes.

RABBI: Look, I have other things to do, mr. wazinsky. I have a life to live, family to be with, friends to protect from themselves. I mean, seriously, don't you have anything better to do?

NARRATOR: In fact, "No Permit" Wazinsky did not have anything better to do.

WAZINSKY: (Breaks down in tears) No. No. I don't. And now I'm crying in front of all my friends, are you happy now?

CLERK: We're not your friends.

NARRATOR: At that moment, Rabbi Itche Kadoozy realized that the best way to fight his Chanukah war was by spreading light.

RABBI: Hey, look, I'm sorry. Do you...Do you want to come to the menorah lighting?

WAZINSKY: What?

RABBI: And afterwards I'm making a Chanukah party with my friends. You should come.

WAZINSKY: I'm your friend? (Pulls himself together) Well, let's get this baby stamped and approved, friend.

(Cut to living room. Jono is on the phone)

NARRATOR: Meanwhile, Jono also changed his own battle plan.

JONO: (On the phone) Mr. Judge Man...Sorry, Mr. Stevens, how about we move the contest to the Ira and Edna Bernstein Jewish Community center, and we'll provide the kosher donuts.

(Marvin and Roy walk by holding armfuls of cans of hair-spray)

JONO: (To Roy and Marvin) Hmmm, I always pegged you as a gel guy, Roy.

(Fade out. Fade in to public menorah lighting at night.)

NARRATOR: On The First night of Chanukah, everyone gathered for the public menorah lighting.

(Rabbi is getting set up in a cherry picker by Marvin)

RABBI: Marvin, this wicker menorah is definitely original. But are you sure it's safe?

MARVIN: Rabbi, this thing is protected by the staying power of 200 cans of hair-spray.

(Cut to G-Fish standing next to boxes of dreidels, selling them. Roy is watching)

NARRATOR: Gefilte fish was very pleased with the success of his dreidel sales.

G-FISH: Dreidels, get you're tiny plastic dreidels here, only 1 dollar! (To Roy) This is great, I've already sold like 50 dreidels for a dollar each, and thanks to my French shipping address these plastique dreidels cost me next to nothing.

ROY: Plastique? Why would you order exploding dreidels?

NARRATOR: Gefilte fish didn't realize that plastique is not the French word for plastic, but the name of a plastic explosive.

(A dreidel sitting on top of one of the boxes explodes)

G-FISH: (Pause) Exploding dreidels, get your exploding dreidels here, only 10 dollars each!

(Cut to Rabbi being raised in cherry picker to the top of the menorah, holding a lit candle)

NARRATOR: When it came time for the giant menorah to be lit, something terrible happened.

RABBI: Before I light the menorah, I'd like to say a few words.

NARRATOR: Not that.

RABBI: The holiday of Chanukah reminds us all that…. (Candle touches menorah and the entire thing set's on fire) OH MY GOODNESS!

NARRATOR: Yeah, that.

(Cut to crowd screaming.)

GUY: Hey, That guy just set fire to a symbol of freedom! That's a hate crime!

RABBI: I'm a rabbi! Why would I intentionally sabotage a Jewish Ritual?

GUY: It's not just a Jewish ritual, it's a universal symbol of freedom!

RABBI: What?!

(Cut to flashback of Rabbi Itche on the phone in the living room)

RABBI: Well, I feel that it's not just a Jewish ritual, but a universal symbol of freedom.

(Cut back to menorah lighting)

RABBI: Oh, boy.

POLICE MAN: (On bull horn) Rabbi Itche Kadoozy, you are under arrest for hate crimes against the Jewish people and the universe.

—————

JONO: Mr. Judge-man, I have never been so psyched about eating so much kosher food before.

ORGANIZER: You mean the donuts? Oh, I can assure you, Mr. Weinsteinstein that the donuts are in no way kosher. (He holds up box of donuts. Close-up on donut box. Box reads "Now With Real Animal Shortening!")

NARRATOR: After much deliberation, he finally decided that the only solution was to hold the contest in Rabbi Itche Kadoozy's Synagogue and serve kosher donuts.

JONO: (On the phone) Mr. Judge Man…Sorry, Mr. Stevens, how about we move the contest to the Ira and Edna bersnstein Jewish Community center, and we'll provide the kosher donuts.

NARRATOR: G-Fish accidentally ordered dreidels made of plastique—a plastic explosive—while trying to get a better deal on his order by convincing the manufacturers he was from france.

G-FISH: (On phone) *Oui*, monsieur, how do you say, two thousand plastique dreidels.

LARRY: I thought you were ordering those dreidels from china, why are you speaking in a French accent?

G-FISH: (Holds phone down) They jack up the price if they know you're a rich American. So you just give 'em a French shipping address and intercept the cargo when it comes through JFK.

NARRATOR: And Rabbi Itche Kadoozy was arrested for hate crimes after he accidentally lit the menorah on fire at his public menorah lighting

RABBI: The holiday of Chanukah reminds us all that…. (Candle touches menorah and the entire thing set's on fire) OH MY GOODNESS!.

(Cut to crowd screaming.)

GUY: Hey, That guy just set fire to a symbol of freedom! That's a hate crime!

POLICE MAN: (On bull horn) Rabbi Itche Kadoozy, you are under arrest for hate crimes against the Jewish people and the universe.

(Rabbi Itche is on the prison pay-phone. A guard is watching him)

NARRATOR: After several hours in prison, Rabbi Itche Kadoozy was finally able to get through to his lawyer, Larry Goldstein.

(Split screen of Larry and Rabbi Itche on the phone)

LARRY: Hello?

RABBI: Oh, thank goodness you answered, Larry.

LARRY: Rabbi, it's you! Now ALL my clients are currently in jail! HA! Are you OK?

RABBI: I'm fine. Larry, how long is it gonna take to get me out of here? This is obviously all a big misunderstanding.

LARRY: Well, I'd like to say I could get you out of there by tonight, but that would be a lie, so I can't. You see, you've committed a hate crime. You are a hate criminal and unfortunately you have a very strong record of anti-Semitism.

RABBI: What?! I'm a Rabbi!

LARRY: I know you're a Rabbi, rabbi, but there's a lot of strong evidence against you. I mean, you're on record as having stated publicly that quote "Judaism is not a religion."

(Cut to Rabbi Itche at the Bima giving a speech)

RABBI: Judaism is not a religion. It's an inheritance to every Jewish person.

(Back to Rabbi Itche and Larry)

RABBI: I said in was an inheritance!

LARRY: Look, you know that, I know that, the crazy guy in your congregation who misinterpreted what you meant by that sort of knows that… Ha!…but I don't know if the judge and jury is going to buy that from a man who said that Judaism is for criminals.

(Cut back to Rabbi Itche speaking in shul)

RABBI: Judaism isn't just for perfect, holy people. Judaism is for every Jew. Judaism is even for criminals.

(Back to phone call…)

RABBI: I said even! They're getting this all out of context! Judaism is not for criminals!

(Pan over to reveal another inmate wearing a yarmulke standing near Rabbi Itche)

INMATE: Thanks a lot, Rabbi. I thought you believed in us.

RABBI: (Startled, upset.)

(Cut to Jono unloading publicity materials from a van. Jono is carrying a couple of life-sized cardboard cut-outs of himself. One more is left in the back seat)

NARRATOR: Meanwhile, Jono was busy preparing life-sized cardboard cutouts of himself as part of a campaign to promote his participation in the donut eating contest.

JONO: A little help here, people? These things way like.... An ounce.

(Jono crumbling under the weight of the cut-out)

JONO: I'm a competitive eater, not strong-man.

(Cut to shul)

LARRY: (On the phone) Ok, rabbi, I'll give everybody those messages. (Hangs up) Ok, everybody, family meeting.

(Everybody enters)

JONO: (Runs in) OOOH! I get to be the baby!

LARRY: Ok, Rabbi Itche Kadoozy has a message for each of you. First—Roy, Marvin, you two drive the van down to the prison and see if you can get the rabbi out on bail.

ROY: Sure thing. Marvin, you have the keys? Let's go!

MARVIN: You got it, buddy...let's go save the Rabbi...but let's go get sandwiches first.

(Roy and Marvin exit)

LARRY: Jono—the Rabbi says he's very proud of your decision about the donut contest and he wants you to continue your plans to host the event at the shul.

JONO: Roger that. (Jono exits)

LARRY: (To Jono as he exits) It's Larry! We've known each other for three years! Crazy cooky kid. (To G-Fish) Gefilte fish, the Rabbi says he wants you to stay out of trouble.

G-FISH: Does finding a buyer for nineteen hundred exploding dreidels count as not getting in trouble?

LARRY: I'm gonna go out on a limb here, Gefilte Fish, and guess that the answer to that question is—it really depends who you sell them to. HA!

G-FISH: You're gonna have to be a little more specific.

LARRY: No children, no convicted and or war criminals.

G-FISH: Gotcha. And what are you gonna do?

LARRY: I have to stay here and do some legal research to see if I can find a way out of this.

(Cut to Jono on the phone)

NARRATOR: Happy to carry out the Rabbi's orders, Jono got to work right away on arranging the donut eating contest.

JONO: Ok, I'm gonna need 80 dozen donuts...eight-EE dozen.... When I say 80 dozen, I mean 80 dozen...Then you've obviously never met me...oh, you have?...Oh yeah! Sorry about that. I don't know what I was thinking when I did that to your lawn...Anyway, 960 donuts please...And just put that on Rabbi Itche Kadoozy's tab.... Yes, I am the same guy who ordered 100 donuts this morning.... Yes, I do need more.... As a matter of fact, yes, I did finish them all. No, I'm not kidding...No, I will not call an ambulance. I'll have you know that I am a professional competitive eating guy, and my body has been trained to be able to handle that kind of thing. Good day sir. Oh, and please send the bill for your lawn to Rabbi Itche Kadoozy.

LARRY: (Enters, skimming through papers. A horrible grumbling noise is heard) Did you hear something, Jono?

JONO: (Noise is heard again. Jono looks down at his stomach) Hmmm. Yup...That seems to be my tummy. That's funny, cuz I feel fine. Just fine. (Pause) Perfectly fine. (Pause) Absolutely fine. (Long Pause) Completely fi....(Clutches stomach. In severe pain) Ok, there's the horrible, gut-wrenching pain we all knew was coming. Somebody call an ambulance, I think I need to have my stomach pumped! (Collapses)

(Cut to Roy and Marvin driving in the van. Jono's cut-out is in the back seat giving two-thumbs up)

NARRATOR: Meanwhile, Roy and Marvin were well on there way to the prison when they realized they didn't know the way there.

MARVIN: I told you we should've map-quested it.

ROY: You can't map-quest a prison.

MARVIN: Maybe YOU can't map-quest a prison.

ROY: Why must we argue about everything?

MARVIN: Maybe Jono knows where this place is. (Leans back and speaks to "Jono") Hey, Jono, are we going the right way?

NARRATOR: They also didn't know that they were speaking to a cardboard cutout.

ROY: (Looks back at "Jono" giving two thumbs up) Yup. 2 thumbs up. He says we're doing fine.

(Fade out as Roy and Marvin go the wrong way. Fade in to prison. Rabbi is in his cell carving a shoe with a spoon as his cell-mate look on)

NARRATOR: At the prison, Rabbi Itche Kadoozy was busy carving the sole of his shoe with a spoon as part of a plan to regain the acceptance of the inmates he had recently offended.

INMATE 1: (Skeptically) What are you doing, busting out?

INMATE 3: Yeah, you bustin' out?

RABBI: I'm doing something my father did when he was in prison in Siberia.

INMATE 2: Busting out?

INMATE 3: Wait a second, your father was in prison?

RABBI: Yes he was. He was sent to Siberia for teaching Torah to Jewish children.

INMATE 2: What kinda crime is that?

RABBI: It's not a crime. It's a very good thing to do, but in communist Russia it was against the law, and so he was sent to prison. (The inmates gather closer to hear the story) When Chanukah time came, he wanted to light a menorah, and that was, of course, not allowed.

INMATE 1: So what did he do, Rabbi? What he do?

INMATE 2: He busted out!

INMATE 3: HE BUSTED OUT!

RABBI: No! He carved his shoe into a menorah and saved up butter for months to use as oil. And he did that because he believed in it, and no prison was going to stop him.

INMATE 1: (Sniffling a bit) Wow. That's…. amazing. Guys, get your spoons, we're helping the Rabbi dig his menorah!

(Cut to Jono and Larry waiting outside as the ambulance arrives.)

NARRATOR: Back at the Ira and edna Bernstein Jewish community center, the ambulance had arrived to take Jono to the hospital.

(Paramedics get out of ambulance, look back and forth quickly at Jono and Larry, and then go for Larry)

NARRATOR: But when they saw the red stain on Larry's shirt they mistook him as having suffered a major chest wound and took him instead.

JONO: No, wait, I'm in pain!

PARAMEDIC: I know, you are, you're a good friend, but he'll be just fine.

(Ambulance drives off. We see everything spinning around Jono and he passes out. Fade to white. Fade in to dream sequence of scary carousel music and a bunch of talking donuts trying to eat Jono. Fade out. Fade in to prison. Rabbi and the other inmates are excitedly carving his shoe. The guard comes by and unlocks the door.)

GUARD: Ok, everything has been cleared up, Rabbi, you're free to go.

INMATE 2: You've earned your freedom, Rabbi. Good luck, and…thanks.

(The guard is approached by another guard and they whisper things to each other.)

RABBI: I'm gonna miss you guys.

GUARD: Ok, Rabbi, plans have changed, you're being relocated for further questioning.

RABBI: What? What's going on?

GUARD: Officer Wilson here just informed me that the charges against you have changed due to new evidence. It appears that you filled out the request form for the menorah lighting in red pen, suggesting that you are a communist.

RABBI: A communist?!

INMATE 1: A communist?! You lied to us. You said your father was put in prison by the communists.

RABBI: He was!

INMATE 3: That makes it even worse. A son…becoming what his father hates most.

RABBI: He didn't hate…

INMATE 2: Why don't you look you father in the eye and show him that red pen. I bet he'll get a lot of nachat.

RABBI: (To guard) Officer, being a communist, even if I was one, isn't a crime. The cold war has been over for over 15 years.

GUARD: That may be true, but the war on terrorism has only just begun, so we're going to have to release you to the department of homeland security for further questioning. If we don't, the terrorist will win. You're the terrorists. We can't let you win.

RABBI: This is absurd. Can I at least call my lawyer, I'm sure he can sort this all out.

(Cut to hospital room. Larry is in a hospital gown, sitting in a hospital bed. His cell-phone is ringing non-stop as the doctor speaks to him)

NARRATOR: Unfortunately, Larry Goldstein was unable to answer his phone due to hospital policy. (Show sign on wall that says "no cellular phones. No stealing babies.")

DOCTOR: Well, Mr. Goldstein, a quick look at your chest was able to tell us with perfect certainty that you do not have a gaping chest wound, but rather, a red ink stain on your shirt caused by a pen—most likely a red pen.

LARRY: Great, I'm in a big hurry. I have to take a phone call from a client who is in prison.

DOCTOR: Oh, you're a lawyer? In that case I'm gonna run some chest x-rays and do a complete blood workup just to make sure everything is ok. I don't want to risk another malpractice suit.

(Cut to Roy and Marvin in the van)

NARRATOR: Roy and Marvin were hopelessly lost in Brooklyn after taking directions from Jono's life-sized cardboard cut out.

ROY: I thought you lived in NY your entire life!

MARVIN: I lived in queans my entire life, I have no idea how to get around Brooklyn!

ROY: We never should have listened to Jono. (Looks back and sees "Jono" still giving 2 thumbs up.) Will you just cut that out, already! (To Marvin:) He's amused by this!

MARVIN: I think I remember something about taking ocean.

ROY: Ocean Avenue or ocean parkway?

MARVIN: I don't know! Ask Jono.

(Cut to G-Fish sitting in the office of a military officer)

NARRATOR: Gefilte fish had gone to a nearby army base to see if he could sell his exploding dreidels to the military.

G-FISH: Obviously, the most natural choice for a buyer, after children and convicted criminals, of course, would be the army. So what do you say, big guy?

GENERAL ROBERTS: Give me a moment to speak with my associate. (Goes off to the side of the room with his assistant)

GENERAL: (Whispering) Do you have any idea what kind of opportunity this is?

ASSISTANT: No, Sir, I have no idea what you're talking about, Sir.

GENERAL: I've been searching for proof of extra terrestrial life for the past 40 years and now I have my have found it. We're looking at a living, breathing, sliming space alien. I want to keep that creature here for extensive testing.

ASSISTANT: What kind of testing, sir?

GENERAL: Dissection.

ASSISTANT: But sir...

GENERAL: But what?! If he is an alien then he'll probably just regenerate himself from the remaining half.

ASSISTANT: And if he's not?

GENERAL: If he's not, and he is what he says he is. Then court marshal me for cutting open a fish.

ASSISTANT: Is that a joke, sir?

GENERAL: I'm not sure.

G-FISH: (Shouting across room) Look, G.I. Joes, I don't have all day here.. Are you interested in the product or am I gonna have to take my business to the SAUDIIIIIIS?

GENERAL: (Sinisterly) Oh yes, I'm quite interested.

GUARD: It appears that you filled out the request form for the menorah lighting in red pen, suggesting that you are a communist.

RABBI: A communist?

NARRATOR: Larry was unable to answer Rabbi's phone calls due to a no cellular phone policy at the hospital to which he was admitted after a paramedic mistook a red ink stain on his chest for a severe chest wound. (Cut to clips during narration) Jono, for whom the ambulance was originally called, was left unconscious on the street, having collapsed from the 100 donuts he ate while practicing for the donut eating contest he was going to be competing in later that evening.

(Cut to Roy and Marvin in car)

NARRATOR: Roy and Marvin were hopelessly lost in Brooklyn after taking directions from a life-sized cardboard cut-out that they thought was actually Jono.

MARVIN: (Leans back and speaks to "Jono") Hey, Jono, are we going the right way?

NARRATOR: They also didn't know that they were speaking to a cardboard cutout.

ROY: (Looks back at "Jono" giving two thumbs up) Yup. 2 thumbs up. He says we're doing fine.

NARRATOR: And finally, Gefilte fish met with a General in the U.S. army to sell the exploding dreidels he had accidentally ordered.

G-FISH: Obviously, the most natural choice for a buyer, after children and convicted criminals, of course, would be the army. So what do you say, big guy?

NARRATOR: The General was not interested in the dreidels, but he was quite interested in Gefilte fish himself.

GENERAL: I've been searching for proof of extra terrestrial life for the past 40 years and now I have my have found it. I want to keep that creature here for extensive testing.

ASSISTANT: What kind of testing, sir?

GENERAL: Dissection.

(Fade in to Jono wandering around, delirious)

NARRATOR: In his donut induced delirium, Jono decided to enlist in the U.S. army. (Jono's looking at an army recruitment poster.) The army accepted him and sent him to the army base to be fitted for a uniform. (Jono's in a waiting room area at the army base, wearing army fatigues. His head is slumped down, as if he is sleeping) When Jono finally came to his senses, he realized that he had made a big mistake.

JONO: I gotta get out of here! (Jono runs out and runs through a long corridor.)

(Cut to Rabbi Itche in a corridor with an army guy.)

ARMY GUY: Just go down that corridor. It's the 23rd door on the left. (Leaves)

RABBI: The 23rd door out of all the doors, or just the 23rd door out of the doors that are on the left? Hello? (Rabbi Itche wanders down the corridor) This is getting ridiculous. One, two…

NARRATOR: Rabbi Itche Kadoozy was also at the same army base, where he was to be interrogated by the department of homeland security.

(Rabbi is counting doors and Jono runs into him)

JONO: Rabbi, Rabbi, Rabbi!

RABBI: Jono, what are you doing here?

JONO: I accidentally volunteered for the army.

RABBI: That's ridiculous! Of course, I'm here because I accidentally committed a hate crime and some sort of violation of homeland security, so I guess I shouldn't talk.

JONO: Rabbi, we gotta get out of here!

RABBI: Jono, calm down. (They start walking down the corridor) As bizarre as all of this is, there's a logical explanation for everything we've done, and all we have to do is explain ourselves and this whole thing will be over. (As they walk they pass a room with a big sign on it that reads "dissection room." Through a window into the room they see G-Fish strapped to an operating table, hooked up to electrodes.

JONO: What's the logical explanation of that?

RABBI: Dissection Room! That's it! This has gone too far! I don't know what's going on here, but I'm tired of all this. Chanukah is a holiday that celebrates freedom, and it's time for all of us to be free too! Jono, you go get G-Fish, and I'll be waiting outside.

JONO: How are we going to get out of here?

RABBI: I'll take care of that.

(Transition to Rabbi Itche standing outside in the base. A jeep pulls up.)

RABBI: Excuse me, corporal, I'm Rabbi Itche Kadoozy, military chaplain. I'm going to need your jeep, I have to go…perform an emergency bar mitzvah.

SOLDIER: Sir, Yes, Sir!

(Cut to hospital)

NARRATOR: Meanwhile, at the hospital, Larry Goldstein was making an escape of his own.

(Larry is climbing out the window. As soon as he is out of site the doctor enters)

DOCTOR: (Looks around, sees that the hospital bed is empty.) Rats! That's the 5th patient I've lost this week.

(Cut to army base. Rabbi is sitting in the jeep. Jono and G-Fish come running up. G-Fish has electrodes dangling from him)

G-FISH: (To Jono) Man, I new they were gonna want me to pass a security clearance before they bought explosives from me, but what's with the electrodes? And that table saw?

JONO: (To Rabbi Itche) Rabbi, How did you get this jeep?

RABBI: I'll explain later. Get in. If anyone asks, you're 13 years old. (Starts driving) Is anyone following you?

JONO: Yeah the guy who put G-Fish in there saw me as I was leaving, he's probably right behind us.

RABBI: (Looks in rear view mirror. In the mirror we see the general and his assistant in another jeep) He sure is.

(In front of the jeep is a big open gate. Cut to general's jeep)

GENERAL: (Into walkie-talkie) This is general Roberts, there is a communist, a space alien, and a 13 year old new recruit in a stolen jeep approaching the east gate. I order you to close the gate!

(The gate begins to close)

G-FISH: Step on it, Rabbi!

RABBI: I'm going as fast as I can!

(Cut to general)

GENERAL: (Into walkie-talkie) Private, I want that gate closed! NOW!

(Just as the gate is closing Rabbi Itche and Jono get through. The general is stuck behind the gate.)

GENERAL: Rats! (Into walkie-talkie) I want a full search team after these guys!

(Cut to Rabbi Itche's jeep. Everybody is cheering excitedly)

RABBI: We're not done yet, guys. They're probably sending a whole army after us, not to mention that the police are probably gonna come for me too after they find out I escaped. Jono, do you have any idea where Larry is?

JONO: The last I remember, the ambulance was taking him because they thought he had a chest wound.

RABBI: That ridiculous red pen! (Rabbi's phone rings. He answers) Hello?

(Cut to Larry running sown the street in his hospital gown talking on his cell-phone)

LARRY: Rabbi! I'm sorry I didn't answer your calls before, I was in the hospital and they have a no cell-phone policy which made things very difficult for me. And a no baby stealing policy which was less of a difficulty. Ha!

(Cut to Rabbi Itche)

RABBI: Where are you now?

(Cut to Larry)

LARRY: I escaped from the hospital and I'm now on 34th and Elm.

RABBI: 34th and elm, I'll be there in 5 minutes. Wait for me.

LARRY: I'll try, but they might come looking for me soon. Where are you? With Roy and Marvin?

RABBI: Roy and Marvin?

LARRY: Yeah, they went to bail you out.

RABBI: I never heard from them.

(Cut to Roy and Marvin in the van)

NARRATOR: Roy and Marvin were still hopelessly lost

ROY: You know, Marvin, I think the lesson we can learn from this is that you can't always rely on other people for direction. Sometimes that direction has to come from inside yourself.

MARVIN: Hmm. Wow. (Thinks) You know, another lesson we can learn from this is that no matter how bad it get's, always keep a positive attitude—like Jono back there! (Jono is still giving his 2 thumbs up)

(Back to Larry)

LARRY: So where are you? How did you get out of jail?

RABBI: Well, I sort of broke out. I'm in a stolen army jeep with Jono who is going AWOL and G-Fish who was apparently supposed to be the subject of bizarre scientific experiments.

LARRY: I didn't hear that.

RABBI: Come on, Larry, we had no choice!

LARRY: No, I really didn't hear that. You know, with all the tests they ran on me, they still didn't find this terrible ear infection. I think they're looking at a serious malpractice suit. Ha!

(Rabbi pulls up next to Larry)

RABBI: Get in!

LARRY: (Get's in. Looks behind them and sees army vehicles and police cars.) You better step on it, rabbi, there's army vehicles and police cars following you, and the ambulance is not gonna be very far behind.

(Sirens and loud motors are heard. Rabbi is speeding down the road with the army, the police, and the ambulance all on his trail.)

JONO: It's no use, Rabbi, we're out numbered.

RABBI: So were the Maccabees, Jono, that's what Chanukah is all about. A tiny group of Jews standing up against army of the most powerful superpower in the world. And they did it because they believed in fighting for their freedom to be jews. So what do you say, gentlemen? Are you in?!

JONO: I'm in!

LARRY: I'm in!

G-FISH: I'm tingling from these electrodes. Oh, and yes. I'm in.

RABBI: Then let's move. We have a donut eating contest to get to!.

(Car chase sequence. Car chase will be done with toy cars. At some point Jono will say "Whoa, did we just pass a Lego-man?" The chase ends at the Ira and Edna Bernstein Jewish community center. Rabbi's jeep, the army vehicles, the police cars, and the ambulance all converge in the parking lot. Rabbi get's out of the jeep and addresses the crowd.)

RABBI: Everybody, hold it! I want everybody's attention. (Show shots of the crowd getting out of there vehicles and listening.) Now I know that none of this makes sense to any of you. It doesn't make sense that a Rabbi broke out of prison, and it doesn't make sense that my lawyer Larry Goldstein is helping me. And I am most certainly aware that the very existence of Gefilte Fish doesn't make any sense at all. But doing things that don't make sense is what the fight of the Maccabees against the greek army was all about. The Greeks didn't have a problem with the Jews following the logical laws

of the Torah—no stealing, no killing, etc. What they did have a problem with were the laws that didn't make any sense. Laws that Jews follow just because they're jews. Laws like keeping kosher—a mitzvah for which my friend Jono here risked losing the opportunity to participate in an event that meant the world to him, even though it probably didn't even make much sense to him when he did it! But he stuck to his beliefs, as illogical as they may have seemed, and now he has a kosher donut eating contest to participate in, and I'm most certainly not going to let any of you stop him. (To Jono) Go inside, Jono, and get ready. I'll be fine out here. (To crowd) And you know what, people? I want to be there too, and watch him eat those kosher donuts. And I want to celebrate Chanukah with my friends. So if that doesn't make sense to you guys the, well, I guess you can drag me kicking and screaming and lock me up again. Or, you can come inside and have some donuts and celebrate with us.

(Cut to crowd)

POLICE MAN: I could go for some donuts.

GENERAL: Donuts sounds pretty good, actually.

AMBULANCE DRIVER: I worked up quite an appetite during that car chase.

(Transition to shul interior. Everyone is eating donuts)

NARRATOR: And so, the entire crowd gave up their chase and joined Rabbi Itche Kadoozy and his friends for their chanukah celebration.

JONO: Thanks a lot for everything, Rabbi. That was some impressive driving, and the speech was pretty wasome too.

RABBI: Your welcome, Jono. I'm just glad everybody got back here safely, and in time to celebrate Chanukah together.

NARRATOR: Well, not quite everybody.

(Cut to Roy and Marvin in the van)

MARVIN: I'm getting a headache from all this driving. You wanna open the back window?

(Roy opens back window and Jono's cut out gets sucked out)

MARVIN: That's why you never stick your head out of the window of a moving vehicle.

ROY: Why?

MARVIN: Cuz you might get sucked out.

ROY: Huh. I thought it was because if you drive past a telephone pole…

MARVIN: Nope. It's cuz you'll get sucked out.

ROY: Huh. See, that's another lesson we learned.

MARVIN: Yup, I guess it is.

ROY: Do you have any idea where we are?

MARVIN: Absolutely no clue!

[THE END]

THE MIRACLE OF PURIM

SCENE: Rabbi Itche and Jono are sitting in the studio

ANNOUNCER: Live from the Rabbi Itche Kadoozy studios in New York, it's "The Rabbi Itche Kadoozy Show Presents: The Weekly Judaism Related Comedy Show Spectacular!" Starring Rabbi Itche Kadoozy, Jonathan Weinsteinstein, and Gefilte P. Fish.

RABBI: Hello and welcome to the first edition of "The Rabbi Itche Kadoozy Show Presents: The Weekly Judaism Related Comedy Show Spectacular!"

JONO: For all of those of you who are wondering how we came up with the title, a panel of four of our staff got together to come up with a name, and they all won.

RABBI: I voted for Judaism Related.

JONO: And I voted for the exclamation point. It would have been a catchy title, too.

RABBI: Anyways, this Sunday marks the celebration of the rockingest holiday on the Jewish calendar.

JONO: Rockingest?

RABBI: Yes, rockingest. Look, it takes me a long time to figure out that a word is hip and youthful, and by the time I do realize, it usually isn't anymore. So give me a break.

JONO: Now we're even.

RABBI: Even for what?

JONO: Honestly, Rabbi, I don't even keep track anymore. But I'm sure I did something reckless and irresponsible with your property and/or money.

RABBI: I'm sure you have. And now, back to Purim.

JONO: The holiday of Purim celebrates the miraculous victory of the Jews in 356 BCE against Haman, chief advisor to the Persian emperor, who planned to destroy the entire Jewish People.

RABBI: Wow, Jono, that was very impressive.

JONO: Thank you, Rabbi.

RABBI: Thank you? The two people responsible for turning things around were two Jewish leaders by the names of Mordechai and Esther. Mordechai saved the life of the king, and Esther married the king, which made it possible for the two of them to change the king's mind, thus miraculously saving the lives of the Jewish People. And now, for Jono's own commentary on these events, we go to a segment Jono likes to call Analysis Shmanalysis.

JONO: When I first heard about this alleged Purim miracle, I thought to myself, when's snack time? That's because I was nine and in Hebrew school. But when I first heard about it again this year, a different thought crossed my mind. Was this really a miracle, or just a brilliantly executed political strategy? So I embarked upon an undercover journalistic investigation to see just how miraculous it would be to save a political leader's life and/or marry one.

First, I tried sitting in front of the White House for several hours, waiting to overhear an assassination attempt. When that didn't work, I tried taking matters into my own hands, only to find out the hard way that calling up the FBI and warning them of an assassination attempt planned by oneself is not considered saving the President's life, but threatening it. A crime worthy of having dozens of G-men posted outside the television studio where one might work.

Next, I tried plan B, marrying the President. For numerous reasons, this plan was extinguished way before it even started, and of course my earlier warning call regarding the President's life didn't help my courtship at all. In conclusion, while the events leading to the victory of the Jews over the evil Haman might have seemed like a logical, natural plan of action, the fact that it actually worked can only be called a great miracle. I'm Jonathan Weinsteinstein, and that's my Shmanalysis.

RABBI: Well, we're running out of time, but first, what Purim celebration would be complete without a tasty batch of hamantaschen? With us now to explore this tasty triangular treat is our very own Jewish food expert, Gefilte Fish. Gefilte?

G-FISH: Thank you, Rabbi. Before I start, just let me clarify that the title Jewish Food Expert does not mean that I'm an expert on Jewish food, but rather that I'm a Jewish food who is an expert on everything, including Jewish food.

In anticipation of this wonderful holiday, I arranged a poll asking hundreds of people what they think the best filling for hamantaschen is. When asked what their favorite filling is, 24 percent of our participants answered, poppy seeds. Seventeen percent said chocolate chips, and a whopping 59 percent answered, excuse me, sir, we are on the Do Not Call list and if you bother us again, we'll report you.

RABBI: Okay, very interesting, Gefilte Fish. As a Jewish food expert, what is your response?

G-FISH: My response? Report me to whom, buddy? The phone police?

RABBI: No, I mean, what's your response to the poll results?

G-FISH: Oh, yeah. That. Well, whatever your Hamantaschen are filled with, they can help you remember that what seems ordinary can be a chocolatey miracle in disguise.

JONO: Thank you, G Fish. Before we go, let's finish off with a list o' observances.

RABBI: One should hear the Megilla read in the synagogue. There's a special mitzvah on Purim to give charity to at least two needy people, as well as giving a gift of at least two ready-made food items to a friend. Of course, the more people you give to and the more you give, the better. And the fourth and final mitzvah of Purim is the Purim feast. Well, that's all for tonight.

JONO: Thank you for joining us, and please join us again next time for "The Rabbi Itche Kadoozy Show Presents: The Something Something Exclamation Point Show!"

[THE END]

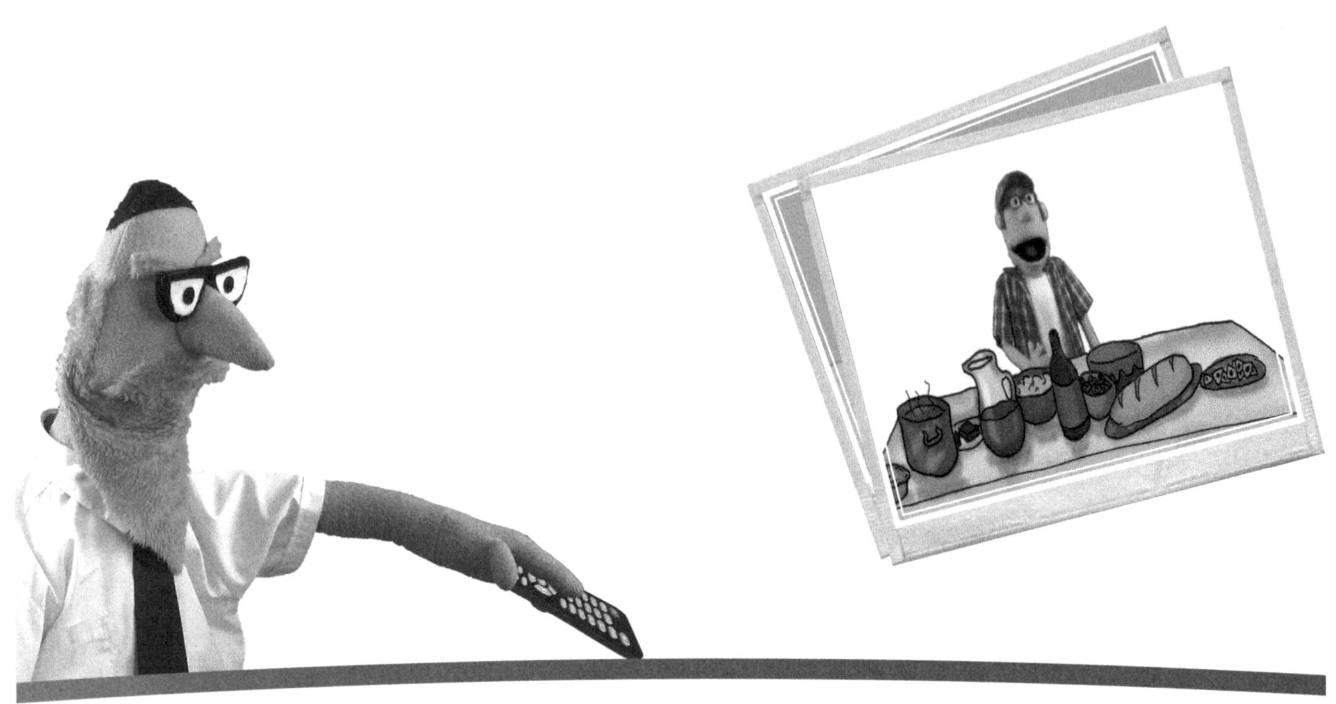

PURIM IS AWESOME!

SCENE: Jono is standing at a rack of Purim costumes

JONO: Well, friends, it's time again for the holiday Purim. What's Purim, you ask? Here's the short version—(Jono begins walking past the clothes rack, and the camera follows him as he walks in front of a drawn backdrop of Persian buildings with domed roofs. G-Fish is there) The story takes place over 2000 years ago in ancient Persia.

G-FISH: Actually, Jono, the domed roofs in your backdrop are painfully anachronistic. Pre-islamic Persian architecture is actually much more…

(Jono walks off past G-Fish, into another blank white background. Haman is there)

JONO: A high ranking advisor to the Emperor and certifiable genocidal sicko named Haman wanted to wipe out the entire Jewish people.

HAMAN: I do indeed.

JONO: But it didn't work.

HAMAN: (Hangs his had and sulks)

JONO: Because G-d made a miracle and the Jews were saved. Hooray!

HAMAN: Boo

JONO: Go away, Haman. (Haman pops out of the scene). That's the short version. Want the long version? Too bad, I don't know the long version. What I do know is that I'm here today—alive and Jewy for all the world to see! And to celebrate that fact, we Jews do 4 things. What's that? You still wanna hear the long version? Well you're in luck, (Jono begins walking again, this time in front of a drawn backdrop of a shul. Rabbi is there reading the Megilla,) because the first mitzvah of Purim is listen to the entire story of Purim read from the Megilla. Twice! Once in the evening at the beginning of Purim, and again the next day. Long version taking it's toll? Don't worry, 'cuz screaming and making obnoxious noises is actually encouraged at certain times when Haman is mentioned.

RABBI: (Get's to a "Haman")

JONO: BLAAAAAAAAGH! (Runs off. Cut to Jono in front of a drawn background of a street.) Feeling generous? Great! No? Too bad! The next mitzvah is giving food or money to poor people. (A beggar enters and puts out his hand) Why? 'Cuz taking care of each other is part of what's kept our people around to this day. (Turns to beggar and gives him money) Here, my friend.

BEGGAR: Thank you, sir. (Walks off)

JONO: And on Purim we give to anyone who asks. No questions asked. (The same beggar comes back in from the other side and puts out his hand) Hey, is that the same guy from before? Who care's? Not me! (Gives him more money then walks off and the camera follows as he walks onto a black white background again). But don't stop the brotherly love there (A festive gift bag falls from the sky and Jono catches it, continues walking and Larry is there) because the next thing we do to celebrate the Miracle of Purim (Hands bag to Larry) is give gifts of food to our friends!

LARRY: (Looking inside the bag) Hey, somebody took a bite ot of my cookie!

JONO: Correction: A fellow Jew took a bite out of your cookie. And a sip from your juice box. (Walks off and camera follows)

LARRY: (As the camera pans past him he is heard saying) Hey, somebody took a sip from my juice box!

(Jono walks in front of a drawn background of a Purim feast)

JONO: And finally, the fourth mitzvah we do to celebrate the miracle of Purim is eat an awesome Purim feast! If you're lucky, you may just get a taste of the awesomest cookies in the world—the Hamantashen! What makes Hamantashen so awesome, you ask? Just a little ancient Jewish secret. Called the TRIANGLE (Draws a triangle in the air with his finger. Once complete, the triangle becomes a giant Hamantash. Jono then reaches his hand out and grabs it, revealing it to be a normal sized Hamantash, just up real close to the camera, then pulls it back towards his face.) Now pardon me as I celebrate the miraculous existence of my people! Happy Purim!

(Walks off. Fade to black)

[THE END]

PESACH MINI-SERIES

SCENE: Rabbi Itche is in his Shul

NARRATOR: For several weeks, Rabbi Itche Kadoozy had been painstakingly planning for Passover so that the Seder could run smoothly without any chaos.

RABBI: (Runs in holding a plunger) This is complete chaos! (Runs off)

NARRATOR: Unfortunately, a leak in the roof had rendered the Ira and Edna Bernstein Jewish center completely unsuitable for hosting a Seder.

(Roy and Marvin walk by carrying boxes of Passover supplies out of the shul)

MARVIN: I told you not to build a meditation duck pond on the roof.

ROY: No, what you told me is that you hate ducks.

MARVIN: And was that untrue?

ROY: No. No it was not.

(Roy and Marvin walk off screen. Cut to Rabbi and Jono in another room)

RABBI: (Scratching his head and body) I can't believe this is happening. I'm so nervous about this that I'm itching all over.

JONO: Oh, yeah, you can thank me for that. I recreated the plague of lice to help me get into the Passover mood. I don't know, Rabbi, I'm just not feeling it this year.

RABBI: I'm sorry you're having a hard time and maybe later I can try to help you work this out. But for now, I'm so distracted I'm not even gonna get upset about you intentionally putting a plague on… (Looks out the front door of the building) WHAT? Did you put diseased livestock on the front lawn?

JONO: I'm going for accuracy, Rabbi. Oh, and if that bothers you, you may want to avoid using the building's water supply for the next few days.

(Roy and Marvin walk by with more boxes)

RABBI: (Sigh) At least now I know why there was a frog in my slipper this morning.

MARVIN: Oh, those were from the meditation pond.

(Cut to G-Fish in another room, "typing" on a Blackberry)

NARRATOR: Gefilte Fish had been busy with his brand new Blackberry, which he used for his constant twitter updates.

(Larry enters)

LARRY: Nice phone, can I see… (Moves his hand towards the phone)

G-FISH: Hey! Whoa! Hands off, buddy! This thing cost me more than you make in a…half an hour.

LARRY: And I'm billing you for this time. HA!

(Jono enters)

JONO: Don't worry about G-Fish, he's just overprotective of his new phone 'cuz it's already missing an "s" key.

G-FISH: Yeah, I guess I must have dropped it a couple of times.

(Flash to G-Fish in the basement on his phone)

G-FISH: Please hold?! I've already been on hold for 10 minutes! Come on! (Throws down phone)

(Flash to G-Fish in the kitchen looking into an open refrigerator)

G-FISH: We're out of orange juice?! COME ON! (Throws down phone)

(Flash to G-Fish in a waiting room somewhere, in front of a sign that says "No throwing cell phones")

G-FISH: No throwing cell phones?! COME ON! (Throws down phone)

(Flash back to G-Fish, Jono and Larry)

G-FISH: Anyways, you wanna follow my tweets? I got 90,000 followers. 20,000 of them are robots with suspended accounts, but that works for me.

LARRY: Sure, I guess. HA!

JONO: And that makes 91,000.

LARRY: You're not so good with numbers, are you, Jono?

JONO: Oh, absolutely terrible. I was kind of into imaginary number for a while, though, until I found out that that's just an exciting name for something really boring.

LARRY: That's actually kind of sad. HA!

G-FISH: More like the square root of negative happy. (G-Fish floats off)

(Cut to Rabbi Itche in another room. G-Fish enters)

G-FISH: Hey, Rabbi, are you still having a Seder? 'Cuz it's been almost 3 minutes since my last tweet, and I gotta find something to announce that takes less than 140 characters.

RABBI: Yes, the Seder is still on. I don't know how, or where, but I haven't given up yet.

G-FISH: Cool cool. (Looks down at his blackberry and starts typing) "Celebrate…the annual…Pesach festival …at the Ira…. and Edna

Bernstein...Jewish...Center." Whew. Thanks, Rabbi, that just bought me another 3 minutes.

(Cut to Roy and Marvin driving in their van)

NARRATOR: After clearing out the shul, Roy and Marvin decided to make up for the leak they had caused by finding another venue for the Seder.

ROY: I'm just saying, most people find ducks relaxing.

MARVIN: Well, I'm not most people, Roy, I thought you of all people could respect that! Now can we please just change the subject?!

(Silence)

ROY: So where are we going, again?

MARVIN: Some clown in Jersey said he had a huge tent to host the Seder in. I think It's worth taking a look at.

(Transition to Roy and Marvin standing with a clown)

ROY: A real clown?

MARVIN: Yeah, it's a circus tent, but I think it could work.

CLOWN: (Squeezes Roy's nose) [honk honk].

ROY: Don't honk my nose.

(Cut to G-Fish typing away on his phone, very pleased with himself)

NARRATOR: During the course of the day, Gefilte Fish's Pesach announcement had received thousands of replies and inquiries. However, due to the missing "S" key on his phone, Gefilte Fish had actually invited thousands of people to celebrate a peach festival.)

G-FISH: (Reading) "will there be produce related activities at the festival?" (Looks up) I think dipping onions in saltwater counts as a produce related activity. (Looks back down at his phone and types). Yes there will be. (Looks up) What a weirdo. (Floats off).

NARRATOR: Meanwhile, as far as Rabbi Itche Kadoozy knew, things were calming down, so he had a moment to help Jono with his lack of excitement.

(Cut to Rabbi Itche and Jono in the shul. Things are a little less chaotic now that everything is moved out)

JONO: I like Passover, Rabbi, I really do. And I really want to get into it, but the only way I know how to pay attention to anything is by getting myself ridiculously over-the-top excited about it. Like those synagogue board meetings.

(Cut to Larry leading a meeting in a room in the shul. There are a bunch of old people and Jono)

LARRY: Next on the agenda is building beautification….

JONO: (Jumps up, holding a tall can, sipping occasionally) Well, I couldn't help but overhear Betty and Al whispering about new plants in the foyer and I was like—BANG! YEAH! PLANTS! Were you guys gonna mention that, it's just a fantastic idea!

AL: I just think it would help make things feel more fresh and…

JONO: That's right, Al! Al's right! You're right, Al! We need plants! And more energy drinks! (Tosses his empty can) And more plants! (Passes out).

(Back to Rabbi Itche and Jono in the shul)

JONO: But for some reason I'm just having trouble pumping myself up about Pesach this year.

RABBI: Have you thought about reading up on the subject?

JONO: I tried, but do you have any idea how much reading goes into reading up on something? Sure it sounds simple "Oh, I'll have to read up on that." But that could mean reading hundreds of letters! And then forming those letters into words in your mind! And then joining those words together into one cohesive concept!

RABBI: So maybe you were on the right track with hands-on experiences. The Pesach Seder is all about reliving the Passover experience through all of our senses, by actually doing things. We drink wine and eat bitter herbs to taste the sweetness of freedom and the bitterness of slavery, we lean to the side to feel the independence of not being a slave to another person. I think you should just keep on trying to

live the Passover experience, and that should do the trick. But try to avoid striking me down with plagues.

JONO: Gotcha. Thanks, Rabbi.

(Cut to Roy and Marvin in the van. Roy is driving)

ROY: I don't feel comfortable about this clown guy, Marvin.

MARVIN: Why, because he squeezed your nose?

ROY: No, because he honked my nose. Noses shouldn't honk, Marvin. It's very upsetting.

MARVIN: Oh, come on. I think it's cute. And besides, we owe to the Rabbi to make this work.

ROY: You're right.

MARVIN: Thank you. Now let me try that...(Reaches for Roy's nose)

ROY: No! (Blocks Marvin's hand) Stop it, Marvin, I can't see what I'm doing!

(Cut to exterior of van swerving dangerously around on the highway. Cut to the front entrance of the shul. Jono is watering the plants in the foyer. A man in a white suit and white straw hat enters).

MR. FINCH: Well, good afternoon, son. Allow me to introduce myself. Harland W. Finch the third. I'm the proud owner of the Finch Family Peach Plantation down the road.

JONO: I'm Jono, the proud owner of some fireworks that I bought on the state border and often think about setting off in your peach plantation.

MR FINCH: Well I do declare, son, I do declare.

(Rabbi walks by and pauses for a moment)

MR. FINCH: I hear you gentleman may be interested in a bushel or two of my delicious peaches.

RABBI: We're not interested in peaches. (Exits)

JONO: I'm interested in peaches. In fact, I'm fascinated by peaches. Particularly gummy peaches.

MR. FINCH: Well, I do declare, son. Perhaps you'd be interested in coming back with me for some hands-on experience with peaches.

JONO: Hmmm.... if taken completely out of context, that's exactly what the rabbi told me to do! I'm in!

(Cut to Rabbi Itche in the shul with G-Fish)

RABBI: Do you have any idea why peach salesmen have been calling and stopping by?

G-FISH: Beats me. Oh, do you mind if I mention the possibility of Pesach marmalade in my next tweet?

RABBI: Yeah, whatever. I have to get back to figuring out how I'm gonna pull off this Seder.

(Cut to Jono working very hard on the peach plantation. he is exhausted and sweaty)

NARRATOR: After taking Mr. Finch up on his offer to gain some hands on experience with peaches, Jono worked all day on the Finch Family peach plantation.

JONO: (To fellow peach picker) Wow. This is hard work. How much do we get paid for this?

PEACH PICKER: I get paid a decent salary, plus fantastic dental coverage. But you're doing this for the "hands on experience" right? You don't get paid anything.

JONO: Aw man! And I totally need to see a dentist.

(Mr. Finch rides in on a golf cart thingy)

MR. FINCH: That's some fine work you're doin' there, folks. Ooh, try not to bruise the peaches, son.

JONO: (Puts down his basket and runs over to Mr. Finch) Hey, Mr. Finch, this has been a very educational experience. For instance, I've learned

that peach fuzz doesn't come off in just one shower. But I think I'm gonna head home now. I have to get ready for Passover.

MR. FINCH: Well, I do declare son, don't you remember? You volunteered for a million hours of work.

JONO: Yeah, about that, I have a very unique learning style. One that doesn't include numbers.

MR. FINCH: Well, let's see if you can understand this, son. You belong to me now, and what I say goes. And I say you best be getting ready for tomorrow, because I'm gonna expect twice as many peaches as you picked today. (Drives off)

JONO: (Shouting to Mr. Finch as he drives off) Well the jokes on you, FInch! I barely picked any peaches today! (Settles down and says to himself) Wait a second...

NARRATOR: And that's when Jono finally realized the full magnitude of the situation he was in.

JONO: (To himself) I'm not getting paid...I can't leave...I'm a slave! Now that's what I call hands-on Passover experience! Now I'm pumped up!

NARRATOR: Well, maybe not the full magnitude.

(Fade in to Rabbi Itche in his office on the phone)

NARRATOR: With Passover only a day away, Rabbi Itche Kadoozy was getting extremely nervous about his Seder. He was also becoming suspicious about the increasing number of calls and visitors asking about peaches.

RABBI: (On the phone) Yes, of course it will be educational, that's the point. What? Well there might be nectarines for desert, but...Yes I do have an ounce of integrity, what is that supposed to.... oh, I have to take another call. (Pushes call waiting) Hello? What? No I am not interested in a peach shaped blimp. (Hangs up and stands up) What is going on here?! (Storms out of his office)

(Cut to G-Fish in the shul with Mrs. Kadoozy)

MRS. KADOOZY: So, what about salmon Gefilte Fish? Is that ok?

G-FISH: What, the pink stuff? Yeah, that's fine.

(Rabbi storms in)

RABBI: Aright, somebody please tell me what's going on here?! Why is everybody calling about peaches?!

G-FISH: Ok, look, I may have had something to do with it. Including -but not limited to—being completely responsible for it.

RABBI: FOR WHAT?!

MRS. K: Rabbi, calm down.

G-FISH: When I tweeted about celebrating Pesach here, I accidentally wrote peach instead of Pesach because the "s" key on this flimsy blackberry fell off.

(Cut to G-Fish outside a window of a house, looking at his phone)

G-FISH: "This Wireless network requires a password?!" COME ON! (Throws down phone)

(Cut back to G-Fish, Rabbi, and Mrs. K in the shul)

G-FISH: So now, basically, the entire internet thinks there's gonna be a peach festival here.

RABBI: WHAT?!

G-FISH: In my defense, what are the odds of a typo like that actually having a compltctly different meaning than the intended one? Although, in retrospect, telling people there'd be Pesach cobbler probably didn't help much.

MRS. K: Gefilte Fish, how could you?! You know it's practically impossible to make a decent Pesach cobbler.

RABBI: This is a disaster. Pesach is the hardest holiday to prepare for under normal circumstances...but with everything going wrong, I have no idea how I can do this.

MRS. K: Now, Rabbi, just calm down, it's not that bad.

(A guy walks into the doorway of the shul)

GUY: Is this where we register for the peach…Oh, wow. This place is wreck. I don't know how you guys are gonna pull of this peach festival by tomorrow. (Exits)

RABBI: That's it. I can't do this. I give up. (Exits)

(Cut to Jono and another guy working on the peach plantation.)

NARRATOR: Down at the Finch Family peach plantation, Jono was doing his best to cope with his new status as a slave.

JONO: (Singing) Go down, Jono, way down to Peach-Pit land, tell old… southern plantation owner that for some reason runs a peach orchard in New York, let my people gooooooo.

(Cut to a wider shot to reveal a crowd of "slaves" applauding. Jono is startled by their presence)

JONO: Ohhh, thank you. Thank you very much. Come back after lunch and you can hear me quietly weeping for several hours.

GARRY: That was beautiful, man. Look, we've been listening to you singing and weeping, and we just wanted to tell you that you've really inspired us.

JONO: Inspired you to do what? Escape?

DOUG: Eh…No, I don't think we could do that. We were just thinking of replacing Mr. Finch's cholesterol medication with placebos.

JONO: Oh wow, that's horrific. How 'bout we call that plan B. Or C. Or Z.

GARRY: Whatever you say, you're the boss.

JONO: I'm the what now?

(Cut to Mrs. K and Rabbi walking through the shul building. Rabbi is moping and wearing his bathrobe.)

MRS. K: Rabbi, I know this must be difficult for you.

RABBI: It's not difficult. It's impossible. I've got a shul full of water, no where to make a Seder, hundreds of people inquiring about peaches…

MRS. K: I know, and you're being so good about the fact that the ducks have nested in the drinking fountain.

(Marvin and Roy are entering the building just in time to overhear this)

RABBI: I actually find the ducks relaxing. (Looks at ducks, takes a deep breath.)

ROY: (To Marvin) See! I told you. (A duck waddles up behind Roy and quacks. Roy is startled) AH!

MARVIN: See, I told you.

MRS. K: You just stay here and relax with the ducks and let your friends take care of all these problems. (Exits into a classroom off the hallway)

(Cut to classroom. Larry, G-Fish, Roy and Marvin are there.)

MRS. K: Ok, everybody, Gather around, this is important. You too, Gefilte Fish.

G-FISH: (Sitting on the opposite side of the room, holding his blackberry which is connected to the wall.) Sorry, no can do, Mrs. K. My blackberry's recharging and I've got another tweet coming up. But don't worry, I'm paying just as little attention over here as I would over there.

MRS. K: [sigh] Everybody, It's up to us to pull everything together so Rabbi can snap out of his rut and we can have the best Pesach Seder ever. Now does anybody know where Jono is?

LARRY: Well, I've got some bad news -Jono left me a voicemail message saying that he's been enslaved on a peach plantation. HA!

MARVIN: (To Roy) Are we laughing about this already? 'Cuz I think it's too soon.

MRS K: Oy vey! Things are worse than I thought. Ok...Larry, you work on finding a legal angle on that. And everyone, we can't let Rabbi find out about this—it may just push him over the edge and then we'll never be able to help him.

MARVIN: Ha! (Everyone gives him an awkward stare) Ok, it is too soon.

MRS. K: (To Roy and Marvin) Roy, how are we doing with finding a place for the Seder?

ROY: We got it taken care of. We rented a circus tent, and all we have to do now is put it together.

MRS. K: Good. G-Fish, you keep an eye on Rabbi to make sure he doesn't find out about Jono or get upset about anything else.

G-FISH: (Without looking up from his blackberry) uh huh.

MRS. K: Ok, Everybody knows what they have to do. Let's get to work.

(Roy, Marvin, Mrs. K and Larry exit. G-Fish remains. From G-Fish's point of view, we can see through the doorway, Rabbi Itche still standing by the drinking fountain)

G-FISH: (Calling out to Rabbi) How you doin' out there, Rabbi?

RABBI: (Without turning to face G-Fish) Still depressed. And a duck ate my tie.

G-FISH: Cool cool. (Looks back down at his blackberry and types some more.)

(Cut to the peach plantation. The slaves are sitting around feeling sorry for themselves)

NARRATOR: Down on the peach plantation, Jono was trying to understand exactly what role was expected of him in his new social circle.

(Jono enters)

JONO: Hey, guys. What's on the slave schedule for today's 5 minute slave break? Slave songs? Slave games? Simon says, perhaps?

GARRY: We're actually waiting for you to call the shots. You're the boss.

JONO: Oh I'm not the boss. If anybody's the boss I'd say it's that guy over there with the whip. Mostly because he makes us call him boss. But also because he has a whip.

DOUG: You got it, chief.

JONO: See, now that's pretty much the same thing as boss. Look, guys, i;m honored that you think so much of me and my crying sessions, but I'm really not leader material. I can;t even take care of a pet.

(Cut to Jono sitting on the couch in itches basement. There is an empty hamster cage next to him. G-Fish floats in)

G-FISH: Jono, where's my hamster? You said you would take care of it!

JONO: I dunno. It probably got eaten by my coyote. By the way, have you seen my coyote?

(Through a window, we see Marvin running frantically. Cut back to the plantation.)

JONO: I'm sorry, guys, but I'm just not your man. (Jono walks off)

(Cut to Roy and Marvin outside the shul, building the tent. There are very large boxes with some weird Ikea name laying around. Marvin is fiddling with tons of polls, Roy is reading from a giant unfolded instruction sheet.)

NARRATOR: Back at the shul, Roy and Marvin were working tirelessly to put together the circus tent.

ROY: How am I supposed to understand instructions without any words? (Show some crazy ambiguous diagram of a little stick figure guy happily doing some vague step) What is this supposed to tell me? And how does that little man use an Allen wrench without fingers?

MARVIN: (Trying to jam a poll into some socket) I don't know, but we've got 4,000 screws, 300 polls, and a whole bunch of crazy looking sockets to put together in only a few hours. (In his efforts to place the poll, it flings out of his hand and flies away) Well, that's one less poll we have to deal with.

ROY: WHY IS THAT LITTLE MAN SO HAPPY?! (To paper) So help me, little man, I will win this.

(Cut to G-Fish still sitting with his blackberry. Rabbi Itche is still in his bathrobe, looking out a nearby window)

RABBI: Gefilte Fish, is that your moped double-parked out there?

G-FISH: Yeah, what about it?

RABBI: Well, it just got ticketed. For the fourth time today. I think the police officer is just giving them as fast as he can write…oh, there's number five.

G-FISH: Aww, man! (Starts to rush out, tugs Blackberry cord and the plug comes out of the outlet. he stops) On second thought, where am I gonna move it to anyways. (Turns back to plug the phone back into the wall)

RABBI: To the shul parking lot. Oh, and there's number six.

G-FISH: I'll have you know that these parking fines help to fund desperately needed government programs.

RABBI: And number seven.

G-FISH: COME ON! WHAT'S WITH THIS GUY?!

(Cut to the peach plantation. Jono is wandering around near the finch mansion by himself)

NARRATOR: Jono had wandered off by himself to think about the responsibility thrust upon him by the other slaves, when he was spotted by Mr. finch's lay-about son Harland Jr.)

HARLAND JR.: Hey, slave! Don't you have a job to do?

JONO: Hey, Harland Jr., don't you have a job? Oh wait, no, I forgot. By the way, I like your neckerchief.

HARLAND JR.: If my daddy sees you out here you'll be sorry. But i'll make you a deal. You do my gardening chores for me and i'll keep quiet.

JONO: Seriously, I wasn't being sarcastic about the neckerchief. I really do love it.

HARLAND JR.: Just get over there and plant those eastern Wahoos. (Exits)

JONO: (To himself) Eastern Wahoo…Where have I heard that before?

(Cut to Jono on the roof of the shul. Roy is showing him the meditation pond Marvin is watering some plants)

ROY: ...And on the other side of the meditation pond, I've planted some shrubbery to obscure the view of the highway. Those bright red plants are Eastern Wahoo, otherwise known as the burning bush plant.

JONO: Cool cool. But the reason I came up here is because the Rabbi said there's a leak in roof.

ROY: Are you kidding me? This pond is absolutely leak proof.

(A little cracking sound is heard. Jono, Roy and Marvin stop and look at each other. Then.... CRASH, Marvin falls down through the roof. Cut to the shul. Marvin is on the floor, water is pouring from the ceiling.)

RABBI: (Runs across the screen waving a mop around) This is COMPLETE CHAOS!!!!

(Cut back to Jono on the peach plantation)

JONO: The Burning Bush plant! It's a sign! I AM supposed to lead the slaves out of peach-pit land! (Runs off)

(Cut back to Rabbi and G-Fish in the downstairs shul. Rabbi is still looking out the window)

RABBI: And there's another one. (Turns around) You're really not gonna leave your blackberry for one minute?

G-FISH: You're really gonna stay in your bathrobe all day?

RABBI: Well played, G-Fish. Well played.

(Mrs. K. runs in)

MRS. K: Rabbi, I have something amazing to show you.

RABBI: If it's a duck trying to cough up a tie, I've already seen it.

MRS. K: Just come outside with me! (She runs out of the room. Rabbi follows.)

(Cut to Roy and Marvin standing proudly in front of the completed circus tent. Mrs. K and Rabbi enter.)

MRS. K: Here it is, Rabbi, this is where you can hold the Pesach Seder.

RABBI: Wow. This…This is amazing!

MARVIN: It can hold 1,000 people, so if any of the peach guys turn out to be Jewish, they can stay for the Seder.

RABBI: Again, all I can say is…wow! It's like you guys fixed everything! Thank you so much.

MRS. K: You're welcome, Rabbi.

RABBI: Well, I guess I gotta get back to work. There's a Seder to prepare for!

(Rabbi starts to rush off toward the shul. A truck and several trailers pull into the parking lot. Rabbi stops.)

ROY: (To Marvin) Ummm, Marvin, what's going on. Did we accidentally order 2 tents?

(A delivery guy walks up to them holding a clipboard)

DELIVERY GUY: Nope. You accidentally ordered a circus. Sign here please.

(Circus performers start emerging from the trailers. Rabbi is standing there speechless. The clown from before walks by and honks Rabbi Itche's nose.)

RABBI: That's it. I quit again.

(Rabbi walks off and into the shul. Mrs. K follows. Cut to G-Fish in the downstairs shul. Rabbi and Mrs. K enter)

RABBI: I can't believe this is still happening. It's just one crazy thing after another!

G-FISH: Wow, he looks even more upset than before. I take it you told him about Jono getting enslaved on the peach plantation?

RABBI: What?!

MRS. K: (Sigh) Oy.

G-FISH: Oops. This is awkward. I'm just gonna go…(Moves a few feet until the cord is pulled as far as it will go) here.

RABBI: Is this true? Is Jono really a slave?

MRS. K: Well…. yes. But you know what, Rabbi, so are you!

RABBI: What?

MRS. K: And you too, Gefilte Fish.

G-FISH: What! That's it. I'm going!...(Moves a few feet again back fore to where he was back over here!)

MRS. K: Yes, Jono accidentally landed up enslaved on the peach plantation down the road. But he's not the only one. You're also trapped. I know you just want to make the perfect Seder, but you're a slave to one way of imagining what that perfect Seder is. If you could just break free from that, maybe you wouldn't be having such a hard time.

G-FISH: Yeah!

MRS. K: And you! You're a slave to that phone! You've been given $4,000 worth of parking tickets, and you still couldn't break free from that phone for even a minute!

RABBI: She's right, G-Fish, we are slaves.

MRS. K: Everyone has these personal slaveries to deal with. But now it's almost Pesach—a time when we celebrate the ability to break free from our own Egypt and do amazing things! And right now, the thing that you two need to do is go down to that peach plantation and rescue your friend!

G-FISH: YEAH! Let's do it! (Looks at phone) In a couple of minutes though, because it's still only at 93%.

RABBI: No! Right now! (To mrs. K) Thank you so much, Faigie.

MRS. K: You're welcome. Now go!

(Cut to an exterior shot of the FInch Mansion)

NARRATOR: At the finch Family Peach Plantation, Jono was finally leading the slaves out of their slavery by marching into Mr. Finch's house and demanding that he let them go.

(Jono bursts through the doors.)

JONO: Come on, boys!

HARLAND JR.: You can't come in here!

JONO: You can't stop us! Go forth, gentlemen! (Dramatically points with his arm, and the slaves enter into the house, past Jono.) But seriously—the neckerchief—AMAZING! (Walks off in the same direction the slaves went)

(Cut to Mr. finch sitting in a fancy parlour. The slaves are there. Jono enters.)

JONO: Harland W. Finch, I demand that you let us leave the peach plantation. Just for the Seder nights, so we can celebrate Passover. (Turns to the slaves and whispers) The jokes on him…I'm not gonna come back for 2 weeks! (Turns back to mr. Finch) So, what do you say?

MR. FINCH: Well, I guess I don't have much of a choice. I like to think of myself as a fair man, and if you young men want to go celebrate your religious holiday, then I don't see how I can say no to that.

SLAVES: Hooray!

(Slaves cheer for a bit. Then Mr. Finch suddenly grabs his chest and gasps. Everyone get's quiet.)

NARRATOR: It was at that moment that Mr. Finch's heart hardened. Mainly due to the fact that his cholesterol medication was replaced with placebos)

MR. FINCH: My Heart!

JONO: (Turns to slaves) Awww, Garry! I told you we weren't going with plan Z!

MR. FINCH: On second thought, I change my mind! Not only will you stay here, but I'll make sure you work harder and more hours than I ever made you work before! I do declare, this is going to be the worst experience of your entire life!

JONO: Uh oh.

(Cut to a man sitting at desk in a government office, using his computer. Behind him is a big governmenty looking logo that

says "New York Department of Agriculture—Peach and Nectarine Division)

NARRATOR: And just when you thought things couldn't get any worse, get a load of this.

MAN: Rabbi Itche Kadoozy is hosting a Grand Peach celebration at the Ira and Edna Bernstein Jewish center! Those guys aren't members of the peach farmers union. Rabbi Itche Kadoozy, I'm gonna shut you down!

NARRATOR: Moments before the sun set and the holiday of Passover began, Rabbi Itche Kadoozy and Gefilte fish prepared to go free Jono from his slavery on the peach plantation.

(G-Fish and Rabbi Itche are standing by the circus tent outside the shul. The sun is almost setting)

G-FISH: I can't believe I gave up my blackberry. This old phone you gave me doesn't even have a color screen. Or a trackball.

RABBI: Don't worry about it. Pesach is starting in a few minutes, so we'll have to leave our phones and stuff here anyways. And for the record, that phone is fantastic. But don't leave it on too long, I lost the charger and they stopped manufacturing it 10 years ago.

(G-Fish puts the phone down on a ledge by the stairs to the shul, and they walk off towards the tent. Larry is standing there.)

LARRY: Rabbi, members of the community are showing up for the Seder. What should I tell them?

RABBI: If we're not back by dark, you'll have to start leading the Seder yourself, Larry. But try to drag it out as long as you can, I don't want to miss much. Do you think you can do that?

LARRY: Are you kidding? When I lead the Seder at home, the first Seder goes directly into the second Seder. With no breaks! HA!

RABBI: Good. Then let's go, G-Fish.

(They exit. Larry enters the tent. Cut to Jono and Garry on the peach plantation. They are sweaty and exhausted.)

NARRATOR: After the failed attempt to free themselves from the peach plantation, Jono and the other slaves were now being forced to work even harder than before.

JONO: This is terrible, Garry. I'm so covered in peach fuzz I feel like a mouse.

GARRY: Pshh. I know what you mean, brother.

JONO: No seriously, I actually feel like a cute furry mouse. (Sticks out his arm) Pet my arm, Garry.

(Cut to Marvin and Roy coming out of the shul and standing at the stairs)

NARRATOR: At the shul, Roy and Marvin had finished setting up the tent for the Seder, and were looking for other ways to help make the celebration a success.

MARVIN: Maybe we should go down to the peach plantation ourselves to give the Rabbi and Gefilte fish some back up.

ROY: That's a good idea. Do you know how to get there?

MARVIN: (Picks up the phone G-Fish left by the stairs) No, but we can use the GPS on G-Fish's fancy phone. (Starts pressing buttons) Ok, this route is as easy as pie. I got it memorized already, let's go. (Puts the phone pack down on the stairs. They walk off)

NARRATOR: Unfortunately, the phone G-Fish left behind was not fancy at all, and the map Marvin found was actually a game of snake. (Show phone screen with a game of snake running. Cut to some peach conference guys and some circus performers standing outside another side of the tent.) Meanwhile, the peach people and circus performers were still confused about the true nature of the event they were attending.

PEACH GUY: (To circus performer) So, what I don't get is why they'd have guys juggling pears at a peach convention. It just seems tasteless.

CIRCUS GUY: We juggle spears not, pears. Thus the name, the amazing spear broth…(Turns around to point to a sandwich board sign standing behind them. The sign has a circusy drawing of guys juggling spears,

and reads "The amazing Pear Brothers.") Aw, Gill! Did you break the "S" key on our computer again?!

(Cut to Rabbi and G-Fish walking along a road. It is getting pretty dark now. There are peach orchards along the sides of the road)

G-FISH: So, Rabbi, what's your plan?

RABBI: I don't know, G-Fish, I haven't really thought it through yet. Do you have any ideas?

G-FISH: Well, normally in a situation like this I'd play a combination of the Thai Gems and a Fiddle Game, and throw in a Pigeon Drop... scratch that—a melon drop for good measure. But we'd need an inside man, a couple of good shills, a violin and a watermelon to pull that off. So I got nothin'.

RABBI: Well, we'll have to think of something soon. Judging by the looks of all these peach trees, I'd say we're getting close.

G-FISH: And judging by the looks of that guy over there, I'd say he's Jono.

(Cut to a shot that reveals Jono in the distance standing amidst some peach trees waving to Rabbi Itche and G-Fish.)

JONO: Hey, guys! Want some peaches?

(Cut to Larry in the tent, at the head of the table. Some of the shul regulars are sitting around the table.)

NARRATOR: Back at the Ira and Edna Bernstein Jewish center, people were getting restless, and Larry was forced to begin the Seder.

LARRY: Before we begin, I'd like to just take a moment to mention my favorite part of the Haggadah, which tells of a Pesach Seder at which Rabbi Eliezer, Rabbi Yehoshua, Rabbi Elazar ben Azaryah,Rabbi Akiva and Rabbi Tarphon were discussing the exodus from Egypt all night long, until morning. I will now perform for you what I imagine that endless Talmudic discussion must have sounded like. [clears throat] Rabbi Akiva! So good to see you. I have a question for you that will take us hours to dissect. (Moves over so as to play another character) Sounds great, Rabbi Tarphon, let's go for it.

(Cut to the peach plantation. Rabbi and G-Fish meet up with Jono and the slaves.)

JONO: Rabbi, Rabbi, Rabbi! Boy am I happy to see you. (Sticks out his arm) Feel my arm.

RABBI: What?

JONO: Never mind. We don't have time for that now. We have to get out of here quick.

G-FISH: Why, because Mr. Finch and his men are coming after us?

JONO: They will be as soon as they realize we're running. But also because I just ate like 12 bushels of peaches and my stomach is feeling craaaaaazy.

RABBI: Well then, we'll have to just run out of here without time to plan—just like our ancestors who had to flee from egypt without even enough time for their bread to rise, depending only on G-d's mighty hand and outstretched arm....

JONO: Seriously, Rabbi, we gotta go.

RABBI: Oh yeah, right. Let's go, everybody!

(They all run off. Cut to Mr. Finch in his parlor sitting in a fancy chair by the window)

MR. FINCH: Finally, some peace and quiet. (Settles into his chair to relax. Rabbi and the rest of the group are seen running past the window. Mr. Finch jumps up.) What in the world?! Harland Jr.! Get the dogs, assemble a search party and incite the local townsfolk into forming an angry mob!

(Cut to Roy and Marvin walking through a scary inner-city street)

NARRATOR: On the opposite side of town Roy and Marvin were starting to wonder if they were going the right way.

ROY: This looks like a pretty bad part of the city, Marvin. Can you please double check the directions?

MARVIN: I tried to check that bus map we passed a few minutes ago, but I was too horrified by the graffitti all over it. Who would write words like that?!

ROY: Somebody who's crying out for help, Marvin. that's who.

MARVIN: That is so true, Roy.

(Cut to Larry in the tent)

NARRATOR: Larry Goldstein was still in the circus tent doing his best to stall the Seder for the Rabbi.

LARRY: If you'll turn to page 86 in your Haggadah, this is the part of the Seder where we finally get to eat the meal! So really, that's only 86 pages away. Not so bad. Now back to page 1. Actually, two pages before page 1.

(Cut to Rabbi, Jono, G-Fish and the slaves running frantically along the road. Dogs can be heard in the background, and behind them in the distance, you can see people running with torches)

G-FISH: So, I appreciate the religious significance of the whole "not having a plan" plan, but seriously—do we really not have a plan?!

JONO: Wait! I have an idea! Everybody follow me! (Turns onto another road and everyone follows)

G-FISH: An idea isn't the same thing as a plan, Jono! Come on, step up!!

(Cut to Mr. Finch riding in his golf cart thingy. Harland Jr. is driving)

MR. FINCH: Well I do declare, we've got 'em now, Harland Jr. That street dead ends at the county Aquarium!

(Cut back to Rabbi and Jono and the rest. They are approaching the entrance to the aquarium. There is a large sign that says "County Aquarium—Featuring the Aqua-walk. Open 9:00 AM to 8:00PM." The Aqua-walk is a long corridor with giant aquarium tanks along each side, and big wooden doors on each end. The group stops at the entrance to the Aqua-walk.)

G-FISH: Oh no! It's a dead end! If only there was an unlikely way out of this that also somehow paralleled the Exodus from egypt in some symbolic way! Oh wait, we're just gonna run through the Aqua-walk.

RABBI: (To G-Fish) Now was the sarcasm really necessary?

JONO: Ok, everybody, this is it! Follow me! (He runs in and everyone follows.)

(Cut to Mr. Finch and Harland Jr.)

MR. FINCH: Drive into the Aqua-walk, Harland Jr. I want to catch those slaves! And also, I heard that a baby whale was just born here and I'd just love to see it. TO THE AQUA-WALK!

(They drive into the Aqua-walk and the mob follows. Cut to the other side of the aqua-walk. Everything is calm. Two guards are standing by the big open doors.)

GUARD 1: (Yawn) Ok, Tom, think it's time to close the doors now?

GUARD 2: (Looks at his watch) Maybe let's wait a bit for any stragglers.

(Silent pause. Then Jono and the gang are heard screaming, running closer, and then running out of the Aqua-walk, past the guards and off screen)

GUARD 1: Well, I guess it's a good thing we waited those 10 extra seconds.

GUARD 2: Yup.

(Each guard takes a door, and they close them shut with a big, deep bang. Cut to inside the Aqua-walk. It is completely dark accept for the light of the torches. The mob is screaming)

MR. FINCH: Now calm down everybody! I do say, just calm down! We'll get out of here soon. In the mean time, let's all try to find the whale baby.

HARLAND JR.: (Looking at a little pamphlet) According to this brochure the whale baby was moved to another aquarium.

MR. FINCH: Well then, son, you better pray this angry Mob don't find that out before we get out of here.

MOB MEMBER: (Off screen) Hey...there's no whale baby here!

(Mr. Finch and Harland Jr. give each other a desperate look. Cut to Rabbi Itche and the rest running along the road. They slow down and catch their breath.)

SLAVES: Yaaaaay!

GARRY: You did it, Jono. Thanks for leading us out of slavery.

JONO: Thanks for showing me I had it in me.

G-FISH: Umm, I hate to break-up this little moment, gentlemen, but I think we better get back to the shul. We've got hundreds of peach fanatics, a circus full of...circus people, and some department of agriculture guys all getting restless, and by now, Larry is probably crossing into new levels of boringness that should never be tampered with by humans.

RABBI: G-Fish is right. We still have a few loose ends left.

(Cut to Larry)

NARRATOR: Back at the Shul, Larry was indeed stretching the limits of boredom.

LARRY: Now if you look in the third set of Haggadot I handed out, you'll notice that there are no slight differences from the first one. That's because it's actually the same edition, we just have a lot of them.

(Cut to outside the tent. A government guy in a suit is standing there.)

NARRATOR: And outside the tent, everybody else was indeed getting restless.

GOV. GUY: That's it. I'm shutting this illegal peach convention down right now. Just as as soon as I'm done watching those clowns practice their delightful circus act.

(Cut to Rabbi and the rest walking up to the driveway of the shul.)

JONO: Wow, Rabbi. This place looks like a circus. And a peach convention. And an FBI raid. I'm sorry you have to deal with this.

RABBI: You know, Jono, I prepared for the perfect Seder for months and when all this started happening, I didn't know how to deal with it. But looking at all these people now, I can't help but feel like this is the perfect Seder.

JONO: Guh?

RABBI: You know, one of my favorite parts of the Seder is the four sons, I feel like this is like that. We have the wise sons, who's questions are about learning and celebrating. (Show Larry and Mrs. K and the community members). And we have some people who are upset about what we're doing, and they're questions will probably be more aggressive. (Show Dep. of Agriculture guys.) Then we have some people who really have no idea what's going on here, but are probably open to hearing what it's all about once they ask their questions. (Show peach people.) And finally, there are those who do not know how to ask. Or rather, refuse to make any sounds at all other than honking noises. (Show clowns). But the point is, everybody is here to ask those questions. And that's what the Seder is all about—asking questions, and trying to understand the answers together.

JONO: That was a great speech, Rabbi. Too bad I'm the only one who heard it.

RABBI: Oh, don't worry, I'll repeat it several times throughout the night. Come on, let's go in.

(They walk into the tent.)

NARRATOR: And so, Rabbi Itche Kadoozy was finally able to lead his perfect Seder, and everybody's crazy problems were all wrapped up nicely. Well, almost everybody.

(Cut to Marvin and Roy walking through the terrible neighborhood. They walk silently for a long time)

ROY: I think something's wrong, Marvin. I feel like we're going around in circles.

MARVIN: Uh oh. According to the map I checked before, if we cross our own path, we'll eat ourselves and explode.

ROY: Hmm. That's good to know. (Pause) Do you think on some level we do this to ourselves on purpose?

MARVIN: Yup. I sure do!

[THE END]

A MATZAH DOCUMENTARY

SCENE: Jono is in his "office"

BAKER: All right. Go ahead.

JONO: All right. So my first question for you is how long does it take to make matzos?

BAKER: Ah, to bake matzah. How long it takes to bake?

JONO: To bake a matzah.

BAKER: It's in the oven about 25 seconds, not more than that. It's done.

JONO: Oh, 25 seconds. That I can pay attention to. My attention span will last 25 seconds for sure.

BAKER: Aha.

JONO: And how long does the whole process take?

BAKER: The whole process is 18 minutes.

JONO: 18. That's one, eight?

BAKER: Yes. One, eight.

JONO: That's way too many minutes for me. Apparently, from the time the flour and water mix until the matzos are completely baked can be no longer than 18 minutes to ensure that the matzah doesn't have time to rise. And my mind was already wondering, why does a matzah have holes in it?

BAKER: Well, actually those holes are to prevent the matzah from rising, so we'll know that chametz, which means dough which has risen to become bread, is no good for Passover.

JONO: All right. So here are the questions. Here's a hunch I had. If you connect all those dots on the matzos, do you get some sort of message, something about the moon landing being a hoax, something about that maybe, maybe government plans to invade somewhere, anything like that?

BAKER: No, sir.

JONO: Uh-huh. So maybe give me a rundown of the whole process.

BAKER: In brief, we take some flour, pour water into the flour, yes, I'm kneading to make that into a nice piece of dough, you know, areas that haven't mixed well. Go take that dough and roll it into a very thin matzah so that it shouldn't rise. Then we take that, we make the holes as you were talking about before and over there, let's put it into the oven for about 20 seconds. Then it gets taken out of the oven and nice fresh matzah.

JONO: How hot is that oven?

BAKER: It's about 900 Celsius, which comes out to about 2,000 Fahrenheit.

JONO: 900, 2,000 degrees?

BAKER: Yes.

JONO: That's a lot of degrees. That's way too many —

BAKER: Yeah. I want to ask you something.

JONO: What?

BAKER: In the house, the oven what you have, how many Fahrenheit is in there?

JONO: How many Fahrenheits are in there?

BAKER: Yeah. It's about 400, right?

JONO: Maybe 1 or 2 Fahrenheits at most, three Fahrenheits.

BAKER: Well, just figure out, this is about 2,000 Fahrenheits.

JONO: Oh. I got to get my Fahrenheits fixed.

BAKER: Sure, you do.

JONO: I was getting confused, but one thing was very clear. I apparently had no idea what a Fahrenheit was. After doing a little bit of research I found that a Fahrenheit was not, in fact, a small sized animal but rather a unit of measurement for measuring heat. So what this guy was trying to tell me is that while a normal temperature for a regular home oven may be 400 degrees, matzah is baked at a whopping 2,000 degrees Fahrenheit. That's a lot of Fahrenheits.

BAKER: Did you get all your questions answered?

JONO: Yes. In other words, no. Not at all. So all I knew was how to bake matzos, but perhaps I should test my attention span one more time with an explanation of why we eat matzah on Passover.

RABBI: Well, well, Passover commemorates the freedom of the Jewish people from slavery.

JONO: Freedom, hey? Well, if my memory of 8th grade history serves me correctly, the Jews declared their freedom from Great Britain in 1776, and I think it had something to do with taxation without representation.

RABBI: No, no. You're mixing things up, Jono. The Jewish people were slaves in Egypt over 2,000 years ago and when G-d Himself finally took us out of Egypt it was so quick, so irregulars and so overwhelming that

we weren't ready spiritually or physically. We didn't even have time to bake regular bread and instead we baked matzos. In a spiritual sense, the flat matzos also represent the humility necessary to begin the journey from slavery in Egypt, to receiving the Torah on Mount Sinai.

JONO: And so, my dear friends, Passover is a time for us to celebrate our freedom, freedom to eat strange foods on various different Holidays, freedom to wear funny skullcaps on our heads and freedom to give each other presents in increments of 18 dollars for some reason, freedom to be who we are as Jews. Freedom. Wow, I'm inspired!

[THE END]

THE PARSHA REPORT

Show creator and writer **Dovid Taub** animating **Rabbi Itche** for the camera

INTRO & BEHIND-THE-SCENES

by Dovid Taub

On Rosh Hashanah of 2005, I was schmoozing with my boss at shul and he theoretically suggested the possibility of doing weekly "**Rabbi Itche Kadoozy**" episodes about the Torah Portion. I had been at **Chabad.org** for about a year and was making videos as consistently as I could. The idea of single-handedly researching the Parsha, writing a script and producing an episode every single week on a consistent schedule seemed daunting and over-ambitious. So I said, "Sure!"

That year was rigorous but thrilling. I spent each Shabbat learning the wrong Parsha, wrote a script at the beginning of the week, shot it by Thursday, and edited it by the time I left on Friday afternoon. One time I cut it so close that the offices were already locked up in preparation for Shabbat by the time I was ready to leave, and I had to go to the roof and climb down the fire-escape to get out. Fun times.

My favorite part of the process was script revisions with Real Jono, who was living in California at the time. Once I had a script I'd send it to him and we'd spend a day or so one-upping each other with jokes; we would often go back and forth a few times on a single joke until it was as funny (Or, more accurately, overly wordy) as possible. Looking back, I kind of feel bad for whoever his employer was at the time.

VAYEIRA

(Looking for G-d in Central Park)

JONO: Good evening and welcome to the Rabbi Itche Kadoozy show weekly news program. Tonight's breaking news takes us to central park where my pet Gefilte Fish has tied himself to a tree. Live on the scene at this very moment is our on-location breaking news and senior waffle eating correspondent…me.

JONO: Jono.

JONO: Jono, tell us what's going on out there…

JONO: Well Jono, It seems that Gefilte Fish has handcuffed himself to a tree, claiming that he is waiting for a revelation from G-d. (Turns to G-Fish). Excuse me, Mr. Gefilte Fish, if I may have a few words with you…

G-FISH: Can't talk now, waiting for G-d. Oh, there he is now!

JONO: Ladies and gentlemen this is an unprecedented moment….

G-FISH: Oh, sorry, false alarm. It was just an ice-cream truck.

JONO: ICE-CREAM TRUCK?!? Oh man, I already took like six ice-cream breaks today. I think the producers are getting concerned. Oh well. Anyway, If I may ask, why are you sitting outside this grossitating tent, chained to a tree with what seems to be an Ethernet cable, waiting for G-d?

G-FISH: Well, sir, if you must know, I'm doing it because of this week's Torah portion.

JONO: Guh?

G-FISH: In this week's Torah portion, G-d reveals himself to Abraham while he is sitting outside his tent.

JONO: And therefore you tied yourself to a tree with a network cable.

G-FISH: Yes.

JONO: Makes sense. (Pause) Ok, I just lied to you. I'm sorry. That doesn't make any sense at all. Let's go live via Satellite to our senior rabbinical correspondent who may be able to shed some light on this situation. Rabbi Itche Kadoozy?

RABBI: Hi, Jono. I think I may be able to shed some light on this situation with a story from one of the great Chassidic masters of our time.

JONO: And I thing I can eat a roast beef sandwich while you do so.

RABBI: There's a story about one of the great Jewish leaders of recent times, Rabbi Sholom Dovber of Lubavitch, when he was a small boy. He asked his grandfather—if G-d revealed himself to Abraham, why won't he reveal himself to me?

G-FISH: Oh boy, this is it! I think I see Him! My G-dly revelation has finally come! Oh…no. That was just a squirrel eating a discarded hotdog.

JONO: Lucky squirrel.

RABBI: From this story we learn that we have entered unprecedented times, when anybody, regardless of what level they may be on, even a child, can have a strong and sincere desire to experience the holy and spiritual parts of life, by learning Torah and doing Mitzvot. Jono, back to you.

JONO: (Finishing sandwich) Oh…yeah. So there you have it folks, something about Torah and mitzvot.

G-FISH: Oh boy!— no, that's not G-D, just a stray helium balloon. Sorry.

JONO: HEY! That's MY Ethernet cord!!!

[THE END]

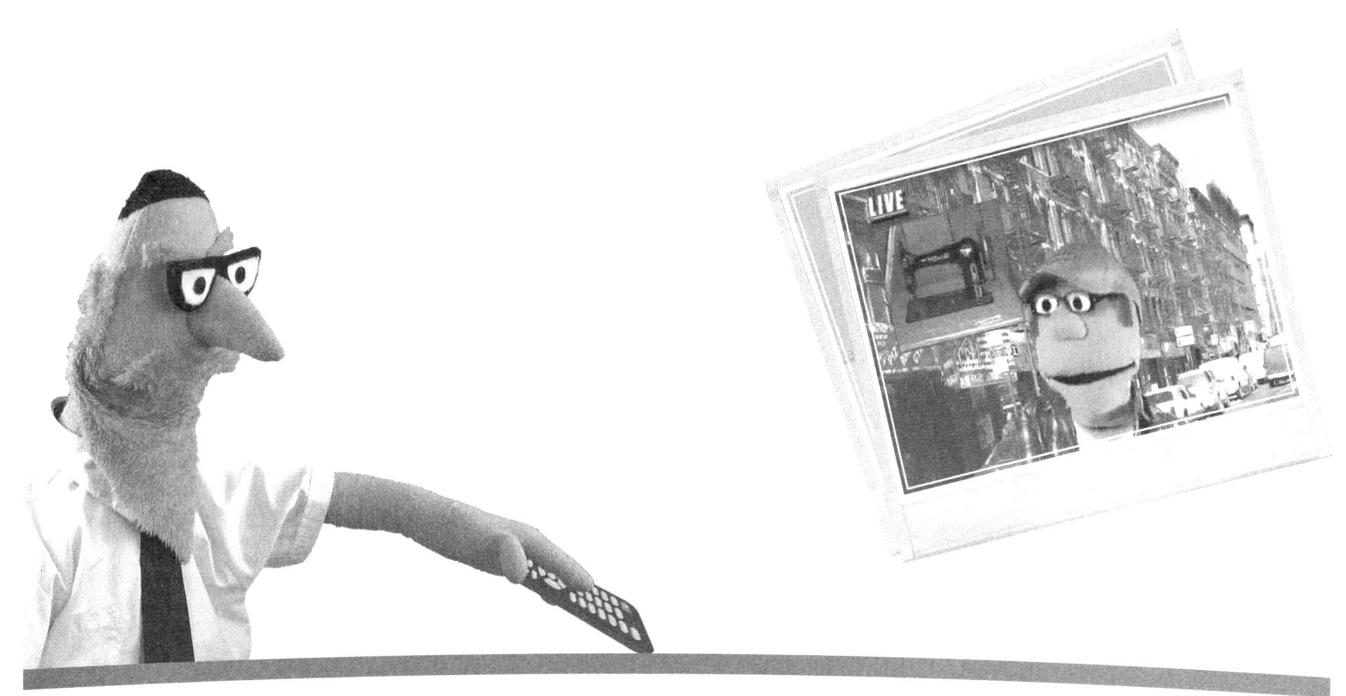

CHAYEI SARAH

(Sarah Redux)

RABBI: Good evening. Some solemn news today: This week in the Torah portion Chayei Sarah, Our matriarch Sarah passed away. We go now to Jono who will give us an on location retrospective on the life of one our most influential ancestors. Jono.

JONO: Thank you, Rabbi. I'm standing here on the lower east side of New York, where our great great, great, great grandparents Abraham and Sarah lived humble and poverty-stricken lives…right down the street from my favorite pizza stand.

RABBI: Lower east side?! Pizza?!

JONO: Yes. They moved here shortly after arriving on ellis island where their names were changed to mr. and mrs. Sydney minkowitz.

RABBI: Jono, I don't think it's possible that Abraham and Sarah lived in New York.

JONO: You know Rabbi, back then it was called Old York.

RABBI: That doesn't make any sense. Jono, where did you get your facts?

JONO: Like any responsible journalist, I'm making them up as I go along. This is a photograph of an early electric sewing machine, used by Sarah day and night to sew matzah ball soup for her family.

RABBI: Sewing soup?!

JONO: Sewing soup? Rabbi, don't be ridiculous. You can't sew soup. She was sewing the matzah balls. In the tenement directly behind me.

RABBI: (Long sigh) Jono, Sarah was born 1,958 years after creation. I think you have your history completely mixed up.

JONO: 1958, eh? The Minkowitz's were born in 1928. I guess I was thinking of the wrong era. Let me revise. Roy, scratch the lower-east-side background. (Background disappears, leaving an empty blue screen.) Ok. Could you bring up a stock image of miami? Fantastic. Great job, Roy…you're a wizard. Never change. (Turns back to camera) I'm standing now, live on location, in Miami, where our ancestors Abraham and Sarah are enjoying being empty-nest snowbirds in the condo behind me. And you'll understand why they chose the place when you see the pool!

RABBI: Jono, you're still way off. Sarah passed away 3,681 years ago.

JONO: What?! Thousands of years ago?!

RABBI: Yeah. 3,681 years ago.

JONO: That's like…A BAJILLION YEARS AGO! By definition, that is NOT news! My career as a journalist has been compromised! Why are we even talking about it?!

RABBI: Jono, the stories of our matriarchs and patriarchs aren't just lessons we can learn from, but rather they're a part of our spiritual genetics. The way Abraham, Isaac, Jacob, Sarah, Rivkah, Rochel, and Leah

acted, their kindness to others and their devotion to G-d and Torah, is an inheritance passed down to us to this day; It's what gives us the strength and ability to have such devotion as well.

JONO: So, in the same way I inherited my black beady eyes from my mom, in a way, I have inherited my Jewish identity from my ancestors?

RABBI: Very good Jono. That's why it's important that we acknowledge and remember their lives the same way we would those of our own family.

JONO: Oh man…I owe Sarah like a bajillion years worth of birthday presents!

RABBI: (Sigh) Well, it looks like we're out of time. Good night, and good luck.

JONO: Roy! Could you please bring up an image of the mall? I have A LOT of shopping to do. (A mall pops up behind Jono) Nice work Roy. Nice work.

[THE END]

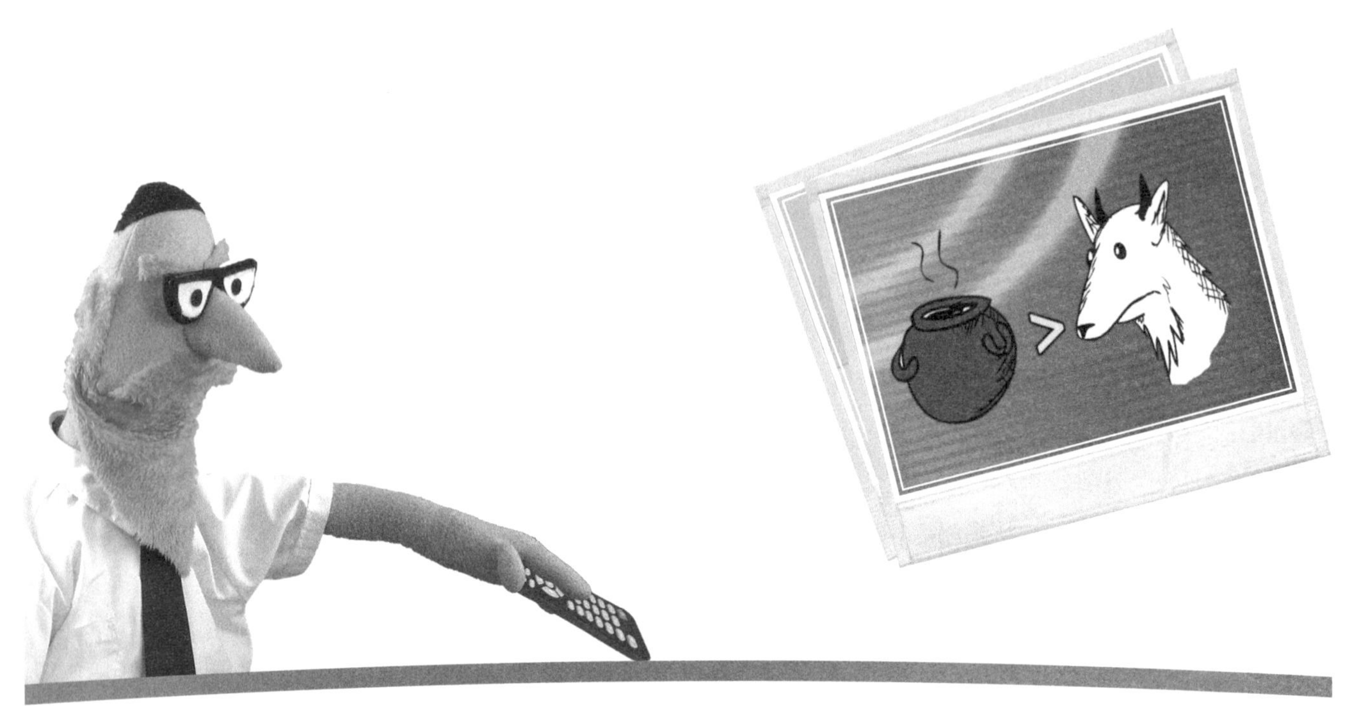

TOLDOT

(Lentil Soup)

RABBI: Good evening, and welcome to the Parsha Report. This week in Parshat Toldos, our holy forefather Yaakov buys the inheritance from his wicked brother Eisav, for a bowl of lentil soup. With us now is our senior cuisine correspondent, Jono, who will share with us a tasty recipe for lentil soup.

JONO: Thank you rabbi, you're a prince. Stay that way. And I mean that. I really do. If you're going to buy your brother's inheritance with lentil soup, it better be DEEE-licious! So allow me to share with you my little recipe that I concocted while watching the Food Network's Lentil Soup Week. It's called 'Jono's Lentilicious Hot Broth' and I will give you my, Jono's, personal guarantee that it's good enough to dupe your brother out of everything he owns. And hey, NO TRADE BACKS! I have shared this recipe with my sources. Yes, the nations top food critics and property appraisers all agree…

(Jono's list is illustrated on the screen:)
Jono's Lentilicious Hot Broth is greater than A GOAT!
Jono's Lentilicious Hot Broth is greater than an Xbox!
Jono's Lentilicious Hot Broth is greater than a robot butler!
Jono's Lentilicious Hot Broth is greater than a monkey who knows karate!
Jono's Lentilicious Hot Broth is greater than or equal to a suit of armor plus an explosion machine plus a tap-dancing worm times a rocket bike minus a flu shot plus a whoopee cushion...which is equal to everything awesome your brother could have possibly acquired in a lifetime!

RABBI: Jono, I am not sure you understand what is meant by inheritance. Do you know what your birthright is?

JONO: Rabbi, please let me finish. Now get ready, people, because I'm about to shock your taste-buds with the Jono's Lentilicious Hot Broth lentil soup recipe even I would sell my "birthright" for...and I have! So here are the simple ingredients...

(The following ingredients pop up on screen:)
1 1/2 tablespoons olive oil—from an olive branch that was carried in a dove's beak over several continents.
1 large onion, chopped with Ghandi's sword
3 garlic cloves, chopped with your sword
2 carrots, chopped with no sword
1/2 cup canned tomato...SQUARE CAN!
1 celery rib, chopped. Don't worry, the celery won't miss a rib, he has seven more!
1 1/4 teaspoons ground cumin, NOT human
1/2 teaspoon salt – from the tears of a clown
1 cup dried red lentils – from your grocer's shelves
4 cups Indonesian mountain spring water
1 1/2 cups three legged chicken broth
2 tablespoons chopped fresh Elvis parsley
2 teaspoons freshly squeezed lemon juice, do not remove lemon from tree

RABBI: Jono, this is absolutely ridiculous!

JONO: By "ridiculous" I am sure you meant to say "delicious". So yes, you are right, it is ABSOLUTELY DELICIOUS!

RABBI: Jono, I'm not even going to get started on how impossible it would be to make your soup. Look, when Eisoy gave his birthright to Yaakov for a bowl of lentil soup, he essentially gave Yaakov his Jewish identity.

JONO: He traded his Jewish identity for lentil soup? Hmmm...he must have used like 3 tablespoons of Elvis parsley.

RABBI: No! Jono, let me tell you something MY sources have told me. It is a fact that anyone's Jewish identity is FAR greater than a goat plus an Xbox plus a robot butler plus a cat who knows karate plus everything "awesome" ANYONE'S brother may have accumulated over a lifetime! (Slurp, slurp, slurp)

RABBI: Jono?

JONO: Sorry Rabbi, just had to finish up a bowl of Jono's Lentilicious Hot Broth. Mmm...that was GOOD! Too bad it's gone, cuz I could sure go for some more!

RABBI: That's exactly my point. Why would anyone ever trade something that they will have their entire lives, something that makes them THEM, for something they can eat and it's gone in thirty seconds?

JONO: Thirty LENTILICIOUS seconds!

RABBI: Jono, Imagine if you agreed to never blow the Shofar again, to never celebrate Chanukah again and to never again get together with your family and friends for a Seder all for the bowl of soup you just finished?

JONO: Whoa! Have you ever seen me blow the Shofar? I'm like Miles Davis on that thing! (Jono turns back to camera) I would like to make a correction to tonight's news cast. The Rabbi Itche Kadoozy Parsha Report is sorry to announce that we have made a grave error. Jono's Lentilicious Hot Broth may be worth trading a horse with lasers for eyes for, but it is not worth trading your birthright for...nothing is. Please send all your angry letters to Rabbi, care of The Rabbi Itche Kadoozy Parsha Report. Rabbi.

RABBI: (Sigh) Well, that's it for this week's Report. Have a pleasant evening!

[THE END]

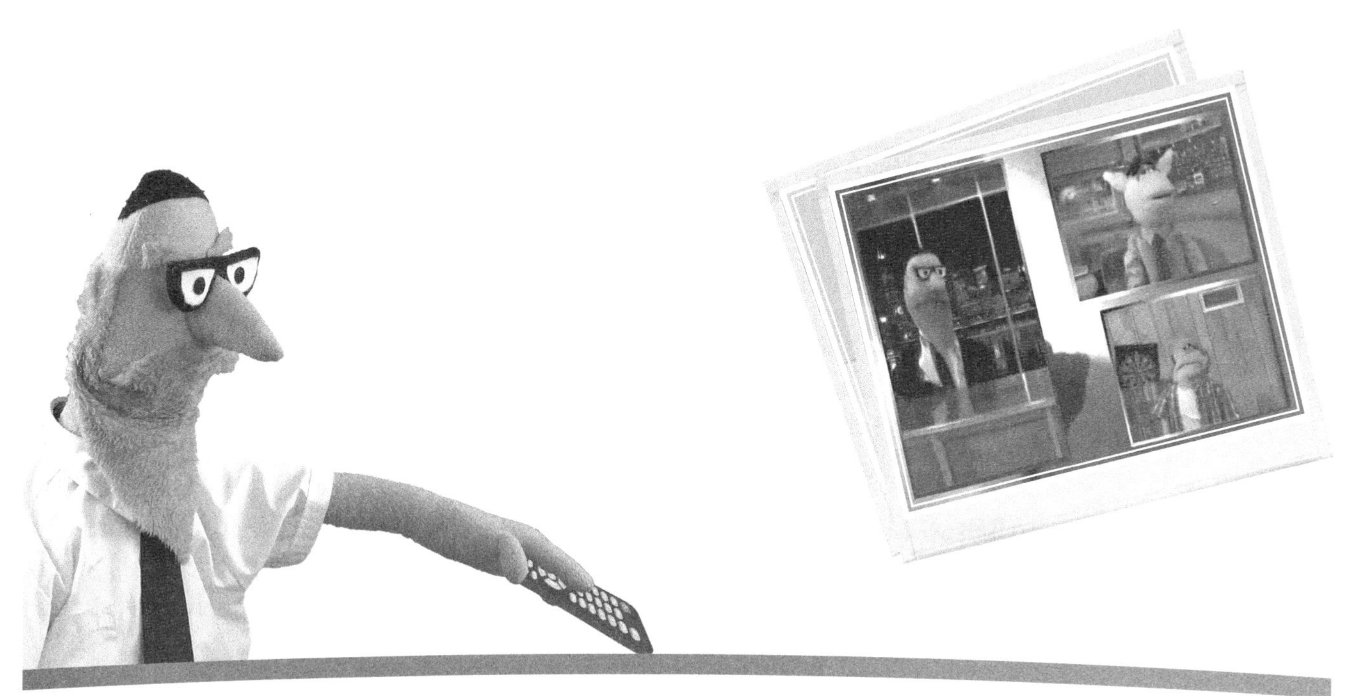

VAYEITZEI

(Staying Awake)

RABBI: Good evening and welcome to the Parsha Report. This week in Parshat Vayeitzei our forefather Jacob travels to Charan where he starts his family and spends twenty years working for his father in-law Lavan. But first, in other news let's go live to Jono who is apparently trying to break a world record. Jono

JONO: (Jono stares blankly. He looks horrible, and disheveled.)

RABBI: Jono!

JONO: (Slowly and deliberately) No, I am not nor have I ever been a member of the Communist party.

RABBI: Jono, snap out of it! (Somebody hands Rabbi Itche a paper) Ok, my stage manager Roy has just handed me a memo, thanks Roy—oh, and if you could get me a tuna sandwich…thanks. …. (Reads note silently) Ok, it seems that Jono is attempting to break the world record for the longest period of time someone has ever stayed awake. At this point in time Jono has been awake for 17 consecutive days. Jono, why are you doing this?

JONO: Well, senator, I think that it's a combination of two very complemental issues, the seventh of which being the shocking statistics invobulating child obesity in this country and the most of which being…Duckies. Rubber Duckies.

RABBI: I see…. (To Roy) What? Ok, Roy has just informed me that we're going to be hooked up via satellite to our senior medical expert, Dr. Gilbert Poznansky, and also that we're apparently out of tuna sandwiches. Dr.?

DR. P: Thank you, rabbi, it's an honor for you to have me here.. It's clear that Jonathan's hallucinatory state is caused by moments of subconsciousness called micro-sleep. Of course, these moments become much more frequent as the patient goes longer and longer without sleep, until he eventually becomes completely unable to function on any sort of higher mental level.

JONO: You're absolutely right, Mrs. President—and that's why I'm cold. So very, very cold. By the way, nice tie, Gil.

DR. P: Please don't call me gil.

RABBI: This is very bizarre.

G-FISH: (Pops up from behind desk) If you think that's bizarre you should come watch me try to break the world record for eating cars…whole! (Goes back down)

JONO: Can I go to sleep yet, I have a stomach and my tooth is screaming.

RABBI: Jono, I'm sorry to say that it's going to be pretty hard to beat the world record for staying awake: Our forefather Jacob didn't sleep for the entire twenty years he was working for his Father In-Law Lavan.

JONO: I could do that (Instantly collapses) Keep talkin' I'm still…(Snores loudly)

RABBI: Jacob spent 14 years learning Torah before he went to begin working, get married, and build a family.. He slept one night before he got there and that stayed awake for the next twenty years. You with me Jono? (Jono continues to snore) Jono?

DR. P: Obviously Jonathan is completely void of intellectual thought at this time, and is of course absolutely incapable of cognitive thought.

RABBI: That's right, Doctor, when we sleep, we lose the advantage we have as intellectual beings. When Yaakov stayed awake for twenty years even though he was involved in farming and other mundane affairs, he kept his mental edge and always remained in charge of his own actions, making sure they were done in accordance with the values of the Torah.

JONO: (Pops up) Guh!

RABBI: It's ok, Jono, go back to sleep.

JONO: Guh.

RABBI: Aright, folks, that's all for this week. Have a pleasant evening.

[THE END]

VAYISHLACH
(The Wrestler)

RABBI: Good evening and welcome to the Parsha Report. This week in Parshat Vayishlach, our forefather Jacob wrestles an angel. With us now is our senior wrestling correspondent—Jono.

JONO: (Jono is wearing a wrestling costume, including a Mexican wrestling mask) Listen up, Angel, I know you're out there and you're watching this, and I've got a message for you, brother—When I get you in that ring I'm gonna take you down, angel. I'm gonna bounce you around off those ropes, brother, and pin you down on the mat, dude! I'm not gonna show you any mercy, angel! I'm gonna walk away with that championship belt, dude, and you're gonna walk away with your metaphorical angel head bowed in shame!

RABBI: Jono...

JONO: Rabbi, with all due respect, I'd appreciate it if when I'm wearing this mask, you'd call me senor piledriver.

RABBI: That's ridiculous, Jono.

RABBI: Ah!

RABBI: (Sigh) That's ridiculous, senor piledriver.

JONO: Thank you.

RABBI: Look, senor, Jacob's struggle with the angel wasn't some sort of phony professional wrestling show.

JONO: Excuse me, Rabbi, are you suggesting that professional wrestling is fake? That's an insult to me, it's an insult to my profession, and it's an insult to my colleagues. I'm gonna get that angel in the ring, and we're gonna really wrestle…in tights…and capes…. And we'll probably have some cool props.

RABBI: Jono, when Jacob fought that angel he really got hurt—he limped away with an injured hip.

JONO: Got hurt? Injured hip? One moment, I have to speak with My manager. (G-Fish enters, they whisper to each other, Jono nods, G-Fish leaves) I would like to kindly ask any and all angels to kindly disregard any dramatic threats I may or may not have made.

RABBI: But even though Jacob was injured, he still arrived back home in Israel safe and sound and stated that he had arrived "whole", and intact.

JONO: Oh, in that case, let's hear some wrestling advice from my great-grandpappy Jacob!

RABBI: Jono, the Jewish People as a nation has also wrestled a difficult opponent. Throughout history many nations have persecuted us and tried to destroy us . We may have been injured, but we've survived it all, and in the end, we to will arrive in Israel "whole", with our Jewish identities intact and our commitment to Torah and Judaism strong!

JONO: And then we'll throw a victory party where we all pour water-coolers full of Gatorade over each other's heads.

RABBI: Um…maybe. Ok folks, that's all the time we have for today, see you next week.

JONO: Same fake news report time, same fake news report place!

[THE END]

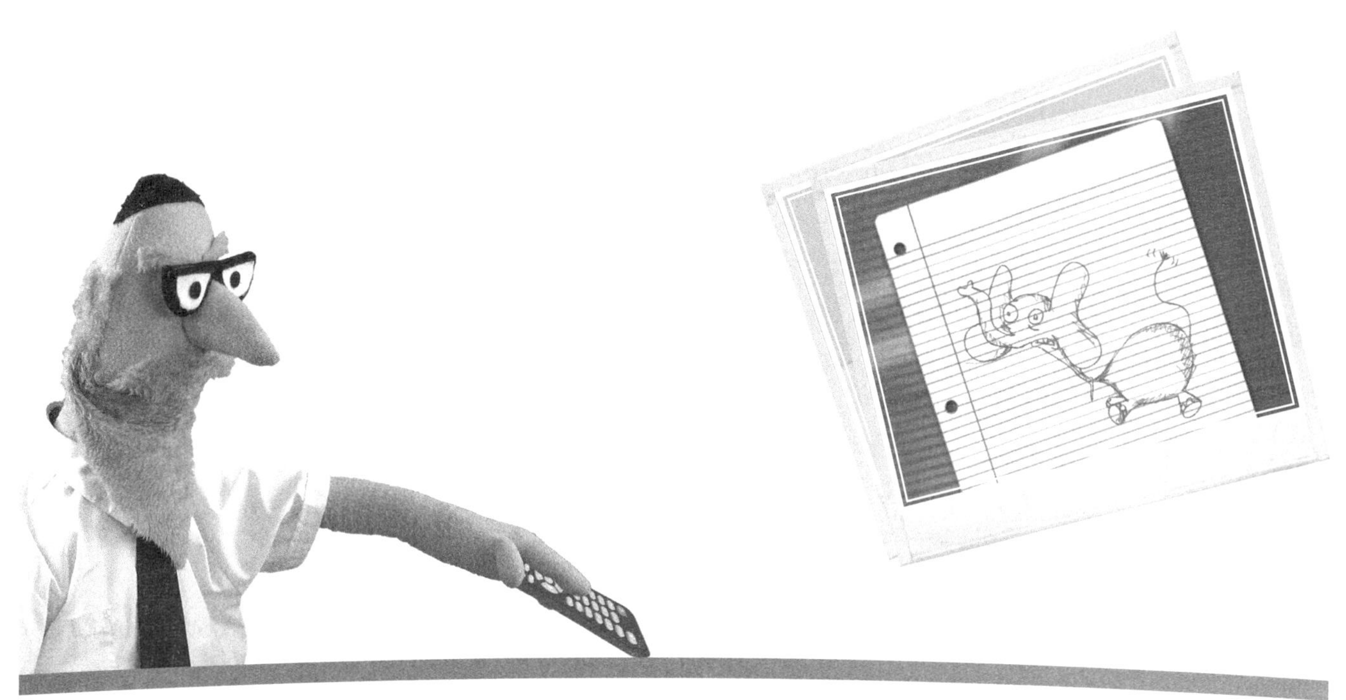

VAYEISHEIV

(Jono's Psychedelic Elephant)

JONO: Good evening, people, and welcome to some show. I've just been informed that this week's Torah portion deals with Joseph's dreams, a topic which interests me greatly for two reasons: The first being my profound love for musical theatre, and second being my fascination with dreams, or rather, my nearly absolute disinterest in reality. Now let's go to the Rabbi for some words of wisdom, which will most likely get me dreaming a little bit. Rabbi?

RABBI: Thank you Jono. One of the things that make dreams so different from real life, is that dreams are inconsistent. Two opposite things can be combined, and what could never be possible in real life becomes possible in a dream. For instance, the Talmud gives the example of an elephant walking through the eye of a needle. That's something you could even begin to imagine seeing in real life!

JONO: I could imagine it.

ITHCE: No…no, Jono, you can't.

JONO: (Drawing a picture) Yes, Rabbi. Yes I can. I could even draw a picture of it. It would look like this. (Shows picture of psychedelic elephant squeezing through needle)

RABBI: Jono, that's not a real elephant. That's some sort of weird psychedelic elephant squeezing down to an impossible size. What the Talmud means is a normal elephant the way it is and a needle the way it is. Two complete opposites, but in a dream they can come together.

JONO: Well, does the Talmud say how big the needle is?

RABBI: No, but…

JONO: And does the Talmud specify the age and medical condition of the elephant?

RABBI: Well, no but…

JONO: Well then, it could be a premature baby elephant walking through a giant novelty needle. (Giant novelty needle ad pops on screen. "Amuse your friends! Dazzle your parents! Be the life of the party! Giant novelty needle is the giant novelty sunglasses of the new millennium!")

RABBI: That's ridiculous, Jono! A premature baby elephant can't even walk at all!

JONO: So, strap him into some roller-blades and push him through. I'm sure that'll count…not to mention, be TOTALLY wasome!

RABBI: The point, Jono, is that dreams are inconsistent—what seems to be one way in our lives can be totally different in our dreams. In a dream, that month old tuna fish sandwich you found behind the fridge and ate before the show could eat you!

JONO: WHOA! Did you just BLOW MY MIND?! I think you did!

RABBI: Yes. Well, sometimes life can be like a dream, full of inconsistencies. One minute we're in a great mood, the next minute we're feelin' down.

JONO: One minute we're drinking coffee, and then BANG, we're sipping tea…through a straw!

RABBI: Kind of. But we can take advantage of these inconsistencies, and the unpredictable dream-like moments, and apply them to real life.

JONO: So in real life I CAN eat my pillow???

RABBI: No. See, sometimes in our lives we might be feeling bad, or might even have done something wrong, but we don't have to stay like that, we can turn right around, encourage ourselves to be happy and do something amazing within moments! From the way our actions and emotions change so quickly in a dream, we can learn to change them for the better when we're awake.

JONO: Wow. That's some pretty crazy stuff! But not as crazy as my Rollerblading elephant. Now if you'll excuse me Rabbi, I have some serious dreaming to do.

(Jono passes out. Transition to dream sequence. Show trippy dream.)

(Jono wakes abruptly from the dream.)

JONO: I knew I shouldn't have eaten tuna sandwich. *Yech!*

(Jono passes out again.)

[THE END]

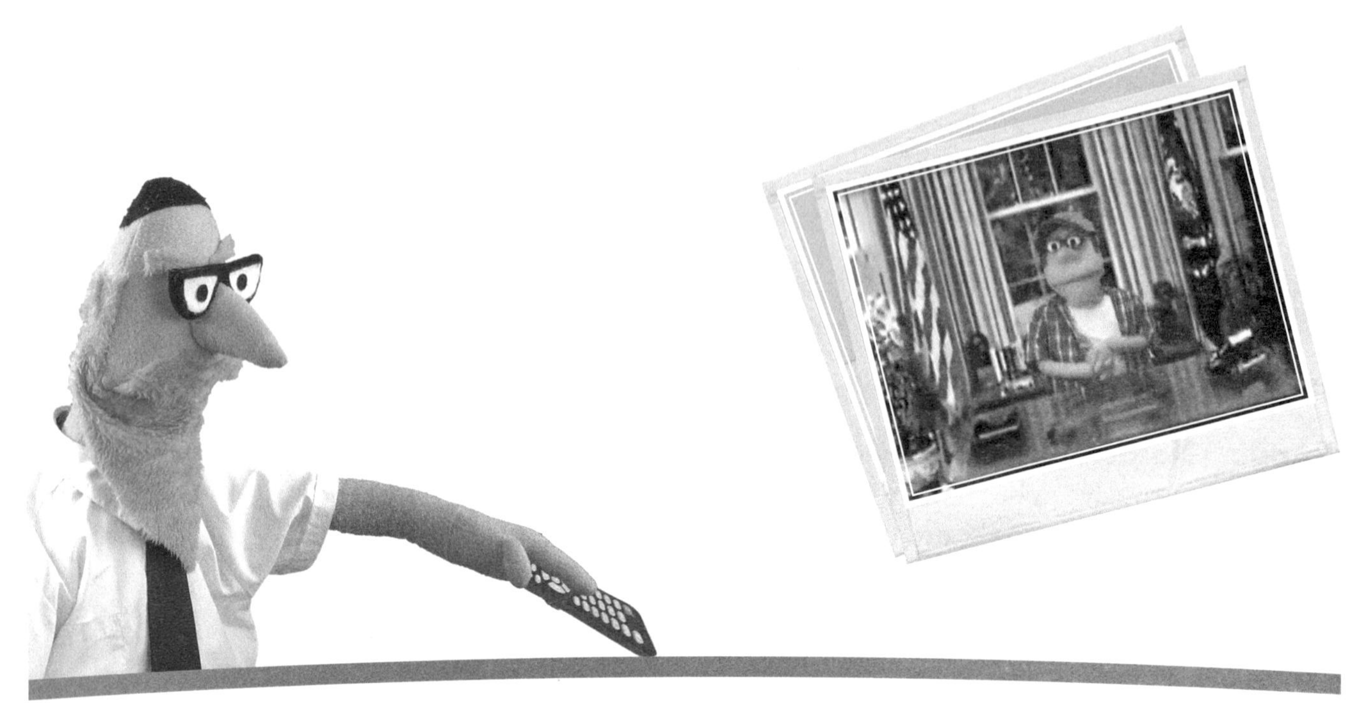

MIKEITZ

(JONO FOR VP)

RABBI: Good evening, and welcome to the Parsha Report. This week in Parshat Mikeitz, Joseph becomes the second in command in Egypt. With us now is our senior political correspondent, Jono.

JONO: Thank you, Rabbi. As you can see, I'm sitting here in front of an image of the oval office, to announce that I am running for Vice President of the United States.

RABBI: Is that so? What party are you running under, Jono?

JONO: Well, to maintain the unbiased nature of this show, I've decided to revive the nearly 200 year-old Federalist party. Either that or the Whig party. Hmmm, wig party—that sounds like fun.

RABBI: Jono, I know I'm probably going to regret asking you this, but, who is your running mate?

JONO: Well, following in the footsteps of such high-profile celebrities turned political figures, I feel that King Kong would be a shoe in for the presidential election.

RABBI: Yep, I regret it.

JONO: I've actually prepared a campaign video for Mr. Kong. Roy, roll the clip.

(Campaign video)

RABBI: Jono, I'm surprised I'm saying this, but underneath all of those stock images of movie monsters, there's actually a very powerful message there.

JONO: I know. I paid a consultant like $50,000 to do that.

RABBI: It seems that in an albeit interesting way, you are following in the path of Joseph. Joseph ascended to power, and became very involved in world affairs. But rather than letting that negatively affect his Jewish Identity, he managed to stay above the obstacles and temptations of the world, stay true to his Jewish beliefs and convictions, and use that to help make the world a better place.

JONO: Just like me and King-Kong are gonna do.

RABBI: Jono, You do know that you're basing your whole plan fantasy.

JONO: Rabbi, most of my life is based on fantasy.

RABBI: Alright, That's all the time we have for now, good night.

ANNOUNCER: Will Jono really run for vice president? Will King Kong win the presidency? Find out in next weeks exciting episode!

[THE END]

VAYIGASH

(A School of Gefilte Fish)

RABBI: Good evening, and welcome to the Parsha Report. This week in Parshat Vayigash, joseph is finally reunited with his brothers, and the whole family moves to Egypt to escape famine. But before Jacob and his family make the move, he sends his son Yehudah ahead to establish a Jewish school for the family to learn Torah. With us now to speak about Jewish Schools, is Gefilte Fish.

G-FISH: Thank you, Rabbi. Jewish schools are actually quite similar in many ways to a school that I went to for a majority of my life…a school of Gefilte fish. For instance, they both contain the word school. (Pause) The similarities end there. Now let's take a look at a school of young Gefilte Fish, swimming in the ocean. (G-Fish continues narrating over footage of a migrating school of Gefilte Fishes.) As you can see, the Gefilte Fish all migrate together in what is called a school. The Gefilte Fish, or Carassius Gefiltus, is easily distinguished

from all other fish because it is the only fish in the entire ocean swimming around with a little slice of boiled carrot on it's head. Thus, for the sake of survival, the Gefilte Fish must swim together in a school to protect their very existence.

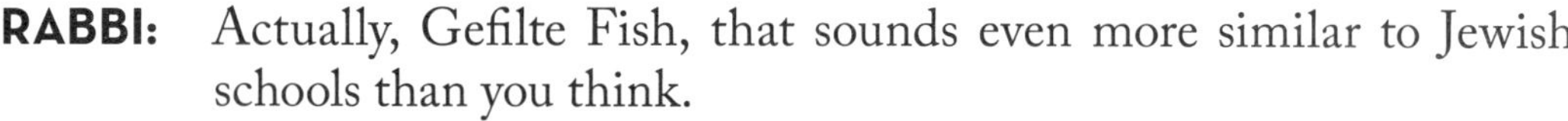

RABBI: Actually, Gefilte Fish, that sounds even more similar to Jewish schools than you think.

G-FISH: You mean that thing on your head is just an appallingly filthy carrot?.

RABBI: No. You see, The Jewish people also need our schools to survive. A Jewish child has a special and unique heritage, and in order for that child to learn about his heritage, to study it's rich past, and to essentially protect it, we too must form schools. Just like your school of fish, our Jewish Schools ensure our survival as a people.

G-FISH: I remember when I was a tiny Gefilte Fish at Gefilte Fish school, when I learned the history of Gefilte Fish, our struggle to survive and our place as The Chosen Fish of the ocean, I became very proud to be a Gefilte Fish…I wore my carrot with pride.

RABBI: And that is exactly what children learn in Jewish schools. Becoming educated in our past allows us to understand our present and look forward to continuing our future—as human beings, as Jews and even as a Gefilte Fish…ies.

G-FISH: Thank you for those insights, Rabbi. While we're still on the subject of school, I would like to share with you some poetry I wrote during a long, emotional semester at Gefilte Fish College…(G-Fish starts making whaley bubbly noises)

RABBI: That's about all the time we have for this week, please join us again next week for the Parsha report.

(A long, slow fade begins…Jono comes running onto the set.)

JONO: Sorry I'm late, I got stuck in traffic and the…oh man! Are you fading out already? Oh man! Is G-Fish reading his poetry again?!?!

[THE END]

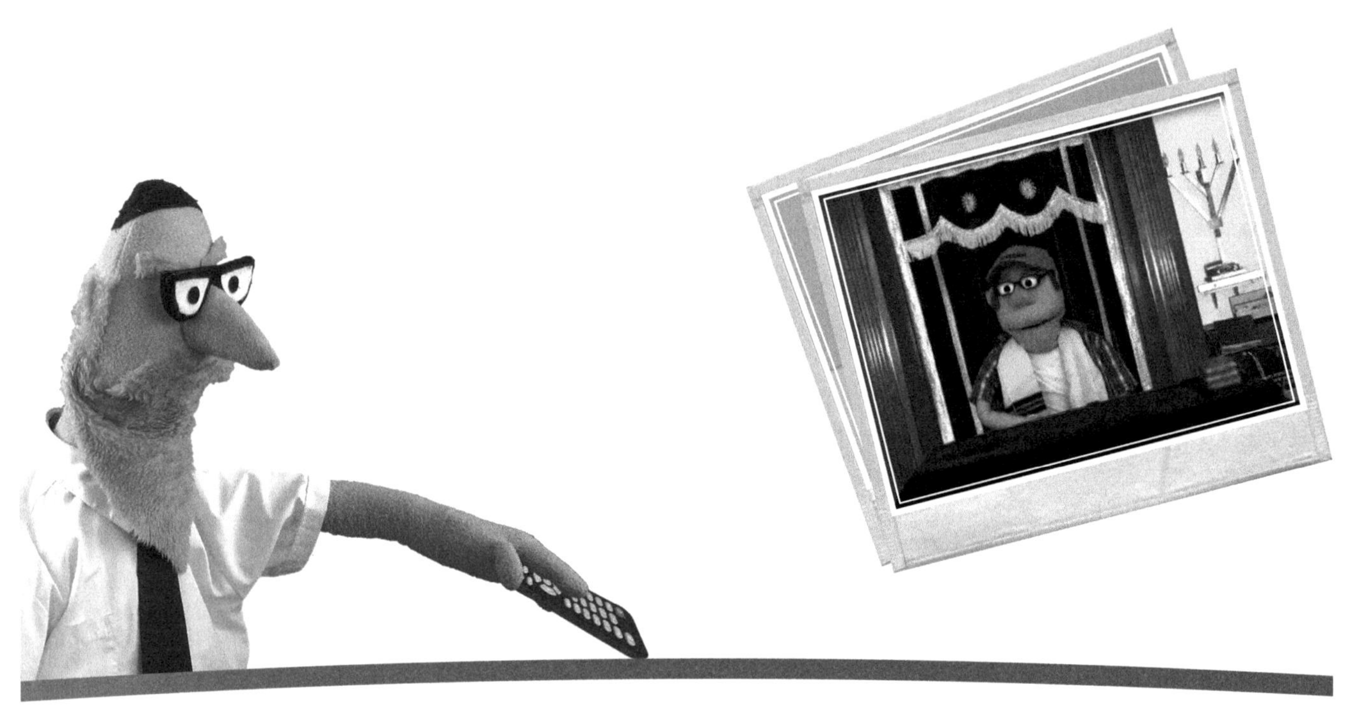

VAYECHI

(Rabbi Jono)

SCENE: Lights come up, Rabbi and Jono are busy arguing.

JONO: I'm telling you, Rabbi, My life is harder than yours. Do you have any idea how stressful it is to play board games with G-Fish?

RABBI: This is a ridiculous argument Jono. With all my responsibilities as a Rabbi, I'd love to be you for a day.

JONO: Okay, then, Rabbi. It's a deal.

RABBI: What's a deal?

JONO: I'll be you and you be me. Just for one day.

(Transition to montage of Rabbi Itche and Jono trading places.)

JONO: (Standing at the front of a shul) Everybody please turn to page elevnty-two in your prayer books. Please rise. (Pause) You may be seated.

RABBI: (In the basement playing connect four with G-Fish)

G-FISH: I win.

RABBI: But you only put one piece in!

G-FISH: You're no fun. I like playing with the real Jono.

RABBI: Why, Jono let's you cheat?

G-FISH: No. He thinks the name of the game is connect one.

JONO: (In shul) Please rise. You may be seated. Please rise. Seated. Rise, Seated, Rise, Seated. Oh! I didn't say Rabbi Says!

RABBI: (Playing operation with G-Fish)

G-FISH: Okay, you go first.

RABBI: Ok, I'll try to get the funny bone…AHHHHH! What was that?

G-FISH: Oh, Jono and I hooked the board up to a car battery. It raises the stakes.

JONO: Please Rise. Please be seated. Be seated again…on the floor. Okay, now please rise. You, in the back, if you could please rise. What? Look, that's not my problem.

RABBI: (Playing scrabble with G-Fish) Ok, superstition. That's 24, and a triple word score…72.

G-FISH: NO FAIR !(Flips over board)

JONO: Please be seate. No, I mean it for real this time. Ahem. In today's Torah portion Abraham makes a flood and has to feed all the animals matzah because there wasn't enough time for them to eat real bread, but then there was a miracle and the matzah lasted for eight days!

(Somebody throws a tomato from the back and yells "BOOOOO") Hey, that tomato was supposed to be for the Kiddush!

(Jono and Rabbi walk back on set and both talk at the same time)

JONO AND RABBI: Jono/Rabbi…I…You were…I'm sorry.

JONO: Rabbi, you were right, I'm really not cut out for your job. And no offense, but G-Fish says you're no great-shakes when it comes to board games.

RABBI: You're absolutely right. You know, everybody, In this weeks Torah Portion, Vayechi, Jacob gives each of his twelve sons special blessing; a blessing that acknowledges the different talents and abilities of each of his sons.

JONO: So, what you're saying is that we each have our own unique purpose in our lives, and we should work to meet our own potential, and not try to be someone else?

RABBI: Exactly. Whether it be speaking in shul, or spending time with a friend, we all have our own responsibilities and talents.

JONO: By the way, Rabbi, your car is in a ditch off the highway. I guess driving your 1978 Lincoln with no turn signals and a hole in the roof is not one of my unique talents.

RABBI: WHAT!

[THE END]

SHEMOT

(Crisis in Egypt)

RABBI: Hello and welcome to the show. This week we're starting a new book of the Torah, Chumash Shemos, and we also have a new intro to the show.

JONO: Give it up for Roy, who put it together. Bang up job, Roy. You are a truly amazing man (Audience Cheers)

RABBI: In world news, this weeks Parsha brings with it another new development: A new pharaoh in Egypt, who enslaved the Jews and made terrible laws against them.

JONO: Roy, Bring up the crisis in Egypt sequence.

RABBI: During the next few weeks we here at the Parsha report will be devotedly delivering up to date news about the slavery in Egypt.

JONO: Now, in order to illustrate the hardships, cruelties and atrocities of slavery, I will be enslaving Gefilte Fish (Show news graphic of enslaved G-Fish)

RABBI: Absolutely not.

JONO: WHATIDOOOO?!?!

RABBI: Look, Jono, you know we've been receiving a lot of angry letters lately (News graphic of angry letters), and I'm sorry, but I can't let you enslave your pet Gefilte Fish. There are laws in place to prevent you from doing such things.

JONO: The MAN is ALWAYS getting this brother down! Now who's gonna build my tomb?!?! (Black silhouette of man building a pyramid with a white question mark flashing on him)

RABBI: Let's just move on, ok Jono?

JONO: (Sigh) Begrudgingly accepted.

RABBI: (Clears his throat) Also this week in Parshat Shmot, Moses is born, and in order to protect him from the Egyptian law against Jewish boys, His mother places baby Moses in a basket in the nile River, thus saving his life. (Graphic of baby Moses in river)

JONO: In order to FURTHER illustrate this, I'm going to put G-Fish…

RABBI: No, Jono.

JONO: Awww MAN!

G-FISH: (Enters) But I wanna be baby Moses!

RABBI: No, Gefilte fish, you can't be baby Moses.

G-FISH: But I wanna be in the basket!

RABBI: No! For your own safety, NO! This is getting out of hand.

MRS. K: Excuse me, just one moment please. Why focus on Moses? You'll have enough Moses later. Why not highlight the role of the Jewish

women who were brave enough to defy the laws of Pharaoh and save the lives of newborn Jewish babies.

RABBI: That's very true, Feigy. That's a very important point in the week's Torah portion.

JONO: And in order to commemorate the brave Jewish Women in Egypt, I'm going to dress G-Fish up as a Jewish Mother

RABBI: NO!

G-FISH: But I wanna dress in…

RABBI: NO! NO! NO! No you certainly do not!

LARRY GOLDSTEIN: Hold it! Order! Order in this court! HA! I'm Larry Goldstein, member of the Ira and Edna Bernstein Jewish community center as well as the lawyer for the Rabbi Itche Kadoozy Show…and as your lawyer, I feel I am obligated to advise you that, in accordance with…animal(?) cruelty laws, enslaving Gefilte Fish would NOT be a good idea.

RABBI: Thank you, Larry.

LARRY: Furthermore, to avoid intentional neglect charges, I would advise you NOT to lock him in a basket and float him down a river…no matter how irresistibly adorable that may look. HA!

RABBI: Hmmm.

LARRY: Lastly, don't dress up Gefilte Fish.

JONO: BUT! G-Fish: I WANNA…! Mrs. K: What about the women?

RABBI: This is out of control. Don't worry Larry…(Everybody is talking over each other). EVERYBODY PLEASE BE QUIET!!! (They stop) Thank you. Look, I just think it's important for all of us to know that this week in history Jews were enslaved in Egypt, Moses was born and Jewish women defied the Pharaoh to save their sons—thus helping to assure the existence of our religion and continuation as a people…something harming Gefilte Fish would not help with AT ALL!

MONSTER: (A furry blue monster walks in, everybody falls silent and looks at him.) Hey, guys, ummm…whoever has an upside-down 1978 Lincoln with a hole in the roof, your lights are on.

JONO: Thanks, Roy. Great haircut, by the way. (Everybody starts up again)

RABBI: Ok, that's all the time we have for now, I gotta go turn my lights off. Be sure to tune in again next week for our ongoing, and hopefully less chaotic coverage on the crisis in Egypt! (Crisis in Egypt logo pops up again) Good night everyone. (Rabbi runs out, obviously frustrated)

(Jono starts singing the outro music as it plays.)

[THE END]

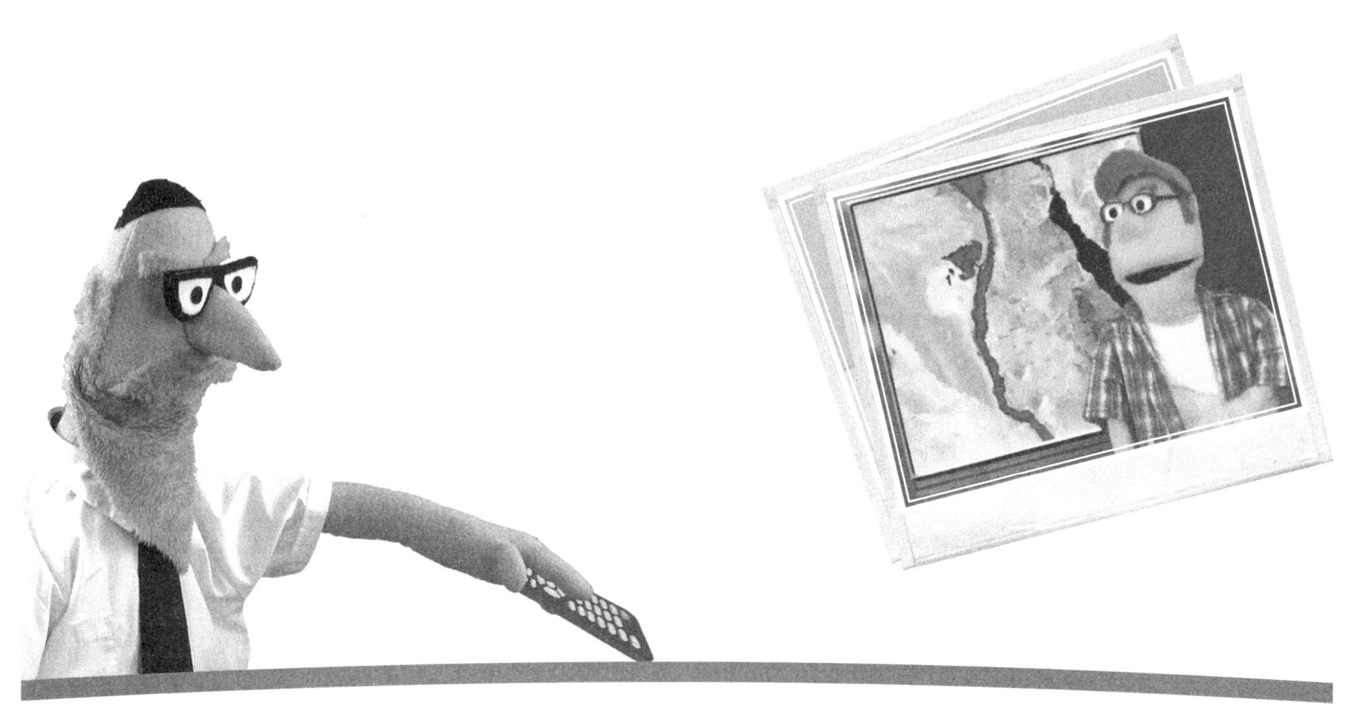

VAEIRA

(Baby Basket Gridlock On the Nile)

RABBI: Welcome back to the Parsha Report. As we promised, we're continuing with our special up-to-the-minute ongoing coverage on the crisis in Egypt. (Crisis in Egypt sequence comes up). This week, in Parshat Va'eira, Moses and his brother Aaron repeatedly urged Pharaoh to free the Jews from slavery and let them leave Egypt. After refusing several times, Egypt suffered from horrible plagues. With us now to report on that is our senior weather and catastrophe correspondent, Jono.

JONO: Thank you, Rabbi. Well, earlier on, things got pretty bloody on the nile river. That's right, Egypt's primary water supply was rendered completely useless and utterly creepy, after it turned into a river of—you guessed it—blood. This also made rush hour baby basket traveling a grid-locked nightmare.

(Image of bumper-to-bumper baby baskets on bloody river. Babies look angry. Much honking is heard)

JONO: The good news for Egyptians is that the blood cleared up, but the bad news is that they were attacked by frogs. (Map of Egypt behind Jono) Egypt experience a swarm-front of frogs coming up out of the nile, over here, and making their way throughout Egypt, into cities, people's homes, and even inside ovens, so if you like froglet chip cookies, I guess that's good news for you. (Froglet chip cookie pops up)

(Screen changes to image of lice)

JONO: Oooh, and look at that nasty little critter. Buy some more shampoo and tuck in your socks, Lice have completely infested Egypt, swarming in quantities matching even the filthiest of third-grade classrooms. Maybe now's a good time for that haircut.

Oh, and watch out for wild animals, because they've invaded Egypt too! (Map shows up again) Looks like there's a wild animal system building up here, and here, making it's way to lower Egypt, which is actually on top over here, and eventually to upper Egypt, which... yup, you guessed it, is down here on the bottom. Complain to the anthropologists for that one.

Move over mad cow disease, and watch out avian flu, because the high temperatures and low pressures have brought A pestilence with them that has moved into Egypt and is killing all domestic animals.

For more in-depth analysis of the next plague to hit Egypt, let's go to Senior Plague Analyst, Gefilte Fish. Gefilte.

G-FISH: Thank you, Jono. The sixth plague which afflicted Egypt was boils. For Egyptians looking for advice on how to treat these boils, I'd give these three pointers:

1. ICE (Visual)

Apply ice to the boils to relieve unsightly swelling and agonizing burning

2. OINTMENT (Visual)

Apply medicated ointment to afflicted areas. Use whatever you have in the medicine chest-creams, lotions, toothpaste, conditioner, cough syrup, whatever.

And, of course…

3. FREE THE JEWS

Let my people go!

Follow those pointers and your boils will be nothing but unsightly scabs in no time. Back to you Jono.

JONO: Thank you, G-Fish. Let's wrap things up for this week with a forecast for the last plague in this weeks Torah portion, which is a devastating fire hail! That fire hail is gonna be hitting Egypt pretty hard, so don't even bother bringing an umbrella, because it'll get simultaneously frozen and melted…Like Mrs. Kadoozy's brisket. (Half frozen half burned/melting brisket) Rabbi?

RABBI: Jono, this forecast sounds horrible. Is there any advice you can give to commuters or visiting tourists?

JONO: Look Rabbi, the Pharaoh brought this upon himself. Moses and Aaron warned him. The answer is quite simple…free the Jewish slaves, see some sunshine. (Graphic?) So if you're thinking about a weekend at the beach, there better be some big changes in Egypt.

RABBI: Let's hope that happens soon.

JONO: Let's hope so Rabbi, cuz I just got me a new badminton set.

RABBI: Thank you Jono. That's all for this week, join us again next week for our ongoing coverage on the "crisis in Egypt."

(Logo pops up)

[THE END]

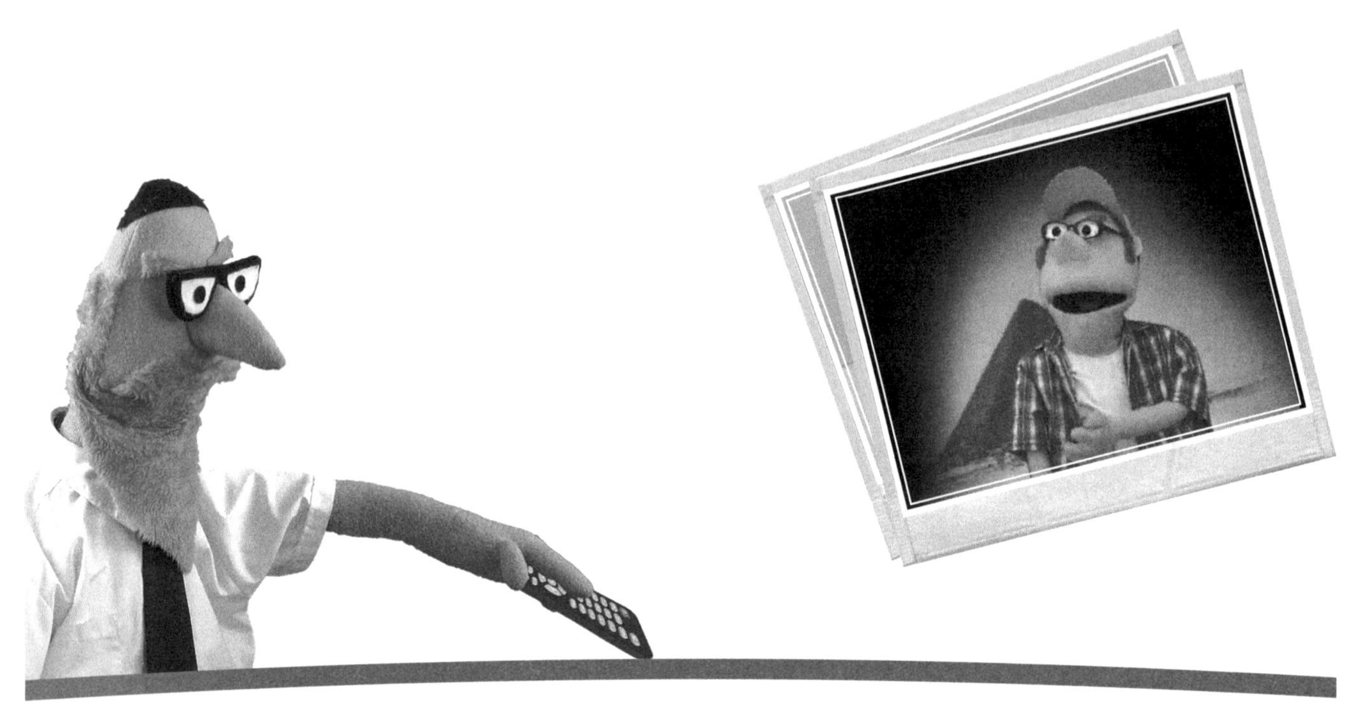

BO

(Blackout in Egypt)

RABBI: Welcome back to the Parsha Report. We continue now with our ongoing coverage of the crisis in Egypt (Crisis in Egypt sequence). One of the final plagues to hit Egypt this week in Parshat Bo is darkness. We go now to an ancient Egyptiab who will give us his impressions as he stands in the midst of this paralyzing darkness.

EGYPTIAN: (Screen is completely dark and all that can be seen are his eyes) Paralyzing is right, Rabbi, I can barely move (Cat screams) Ooh! Sorry. It seems as though the entire land of Egypt is covered in darkness, and nobody can see anything or anybody..(Another pair of eyes shows up and the two sets of eyes collide) Umph

GUY: Hey, watch where you're going buddy!

EGYPTIAN: Sorry! (Moves over, cat screeches) Oooh, sorry about that… again. Anyways, Rabbi, it seems like the darkness is tho thick (Pots and pans crash) oops. SO THICK trying to talk over noises as he smashes into and through things) OUCH! THAT YOU CAN FEEL IT (Crash)…OWW…IN THE AIR! (Big smash, crash, etc.) AHHHHH! (Fall out of picture)

RABBI: Thank you very much for describing what's going on there, or at least trying to. I've just been informed that our senior darkness correspondent, Jono, is on location in Egypt to give us more information on what's going on there.

JONO: Walks onto dark screen. Jono is completely visible, and the background behind him becomes visible, like a glow around him.) I don't know what all this commotion is about, I can see just fine. For example, I just saw that Egyptian guy tumble down into an underground staircase, roll through a sheet of glass, and stumble over that cat again in an inadvertent yet absolutely brilliant moment of three-stoogian physical comedy. Throw in a sledge-hammer gag and this guy is the next Larry Fine.

RABBI: Let me explain what's going on here. During the plague of darkness, while the Egyptians where paralyzed from the complete darkness, the Jewish people had light and were able to see clearly.

JONO: Right now I can clearly see a guy stepping on a rake (Sound is heard of a guy getting smacked in the face by a rake handle).

RABBI: What this teaches us is that just when things seem to be at their darkest, that's when it's most important for us to brighten up the world around us.

JONO: Hey, you! WATCH OUT FOR THAT…. (OWWW)…. pyramid.

RABBI: That's all the time we have for now, but it looks like the Jews are very close to leaving Egypt, so join us again next week as we near the end of the Crisis in Egypt.

[THE END]

YITRO

(Ten for the Price of One)

RABBI: Hello and welcome. This week's Parsha Report promises to be a monumental one, as the Jewish people receive the Torah from G-d on Mount Sinai. Unfortunately, however, the show is being preempted by an infomercial. Look, we gotta pay the bills. (Walks off)

JONO: (In front of gaudy pool) Hello, Friends. Today I wanna tell you about an AMAZING product: The Ten Commandments! By following the Ten Commandments, I was able to afford to stand in front of this image of a gaudy mansion's pool. Now, you may be asking yourself—"Jono, how did the Ten Commandments earn you such a wasome pool?" Well, allow me to divert your question by asking you another one. If the Ten Commandments allowed me to sit in front of this backdrop, what do you think the Ten Commandments can do for you? C'mon, let me show you what I'm talking about.

(Infomercial credits play with cheesy music. "THE TEN COMMANDMENTS" Jono and G-Fish enter a set with a counter and stuff.)

JONO: Now, folks, what I'm about to share with you today is a secret that can CHANGE YOUR LIFE!

G-FISH: Change my life?

JONO: CHANGE YOUR LIFE!

G-FISH: That sounds to good to be true.

JONO: It SOUNDS too good to be true, because it IS too good to be true… but I assure you, it's true. Let's start with the basic package: "I am the L-rd your G-d" and "Thou shalt have no other gods before me." These two doozies will set you up with a monotheistic aproach, and create the foundation for the rest of the belief system of the Torah. That's right, This belief in one true G-d is all yours for only 19.95!

G-FISH: I don't know, Jono. I think I want more.

JONO: More!? Ok, Mr. Fish, you drive a hard bargain. Here's what I'm going to do.

(Graphic of first two Commandments…as Jono "throws the next two in", they seem to fall on top of the others.. creating a pile of Commandments)

I'll give you "I am the L-rd your G-d" "Thow shalt not have any other gods" AND I'll throw in "Thou shalt not take the name of thy G-d in vain" "Remember the Sabbath day, to kccp it holy." And "Thou shalt honor thy father and mother" All for that low low price of 19.95! (BIG $19.95 flashing)

G-FISH: It sounds good, Jono, but so far all you're giving me are commandments about G-d…and my parents. What about how to treat other people?

JONO: G-Fish, I'm glad you asked. If you call today, I'm willing to offer you the deal of a life-time. I'm going to give you the above mentioned commandments AND not 1 (Big 1 graphic), not 2 (Big 2 graphic)

but FOUR MORE COMMANDMENTS! (Big 4 MORE!!!! graphic) That's "Thou shalt not murder" "thou shalt not commit adultery" "Thou shalt not steal" and "Thou shalt not bear false witness". (Graphics for all)

G-FISH: All that, for that low low price of 19.95? You have to be crazy!

JONO: Yes, G-Fish, I am crazy!

G-FISH: And I would be crazy not to order all these Commandments!

JONO: Not so fast, my moist little friend. When you order "I am the L-rd your G-d", "Thou shalt have no other gods before me.", "Thou shalt not take the name of thy G-d in vain", "Remember the Sabbath day, to keep it holy.", "Honor thy father and Mother", "Thou shalt not murder", "thou shalt not commit adultery", "Thou shalt not steal" and "Thou shalt not bear false witness" together, I'm going to give you ONE MORE! (All listed Commandments numbered as Jono read them)

G-FISH: NO WAY!

JONO: Yes. Yes way. I know you must think I'm completely out of my mind and most likely dangerous or at least creepy to be around, but I'm going to throw in "Thou shalt not covet thy neighbors stuff" (Flashing large on the screen) ABSOLUTELY FREE!

G-FISH: So it's still $19.95?

JONO: NO!

G-FISH: No?

JONO: NO! I'm so confident that the Ten Commandments will work for you, that I'm SLASHING the price to $17.48! ($19.95 x-ed out, $17.48 bigger and brighter)

G-FISH: That's not quite slash…

JONO: That's right! All this for $17.48! (Typical infomercial order screen) Call 555-274-357-216-743-841-9320. Now, while you're looking for

your credit card, listen to what people have to say about how the Ten Commandments changed THEIR lives!

IN OFFICE…

LARRY GOLDSTEIN: (Larry Goldstein, Esq., Lawyer, The Law Offices of Goldstein, Goldstein & Gefilte Fish) Following the ten commandments is a sure fire way to keep you out of jail. And if you don't believe me, consider this—I'm a lawyer…. who has visited clients in jail. Clients who did NOT follow ANY of the Ten Commandments."

AT HOME….

MRS. K: (Mrs. Kadoozy, Wife/Mother/Amazing Brisket Maker) I gave the Ten Commandments to my son as a Bar mitzvah present, and it's working out great. When he was 12, oy…you never heard such disrespect…and his room looked like a tornado went through it! But thanks to Thou shalt honor thy father and mother, he's cleaning up that sty right now!

BACKSTAGE…

ROY: (Roy, Stage Manager, The Rabbi Itche Kadoozy Show) Thou shalt not steal is working out pretty good for me. (Roy eyes the last danish on a tray. He reaches for it. Stops.) Roy, that's Rabbi's danish. Walk away…walk away. (Walks away)

(Back to Jono and G-Fish)

JONO: Isn't that amazing!? Call now, and I'll give you a potato dicer for only 12.95!

G-FISH: I WANT THAAAAT!!!!

(Order Screen. Fast announcer voice: "Potato dicer may not actually work, the Ten Commandments are not actually for sale but are available free of charge in your local Torah scroll.")

JONO: (Standing in front of mount Rushmore) The Ten Commandments have been the key to success and happiness for thousands of years. Now, make the Ten Commandments work for YOU!

IN OFFICE…

LARRY: Thank you Ten Commandments!

AT HOME….

MRS. KADOOZY: Thank you!

BACKSTAGE…

ROY: (Still resisting urge to take danish) Walk away…Just walk…away.

(In front of Buckingham palace…)

JONO: The Ten Commandments have changed my life…and I know they will change yours too!

G-FISH: Order NOW!!!

(Cue music and infomercial logo…)

[THE END]

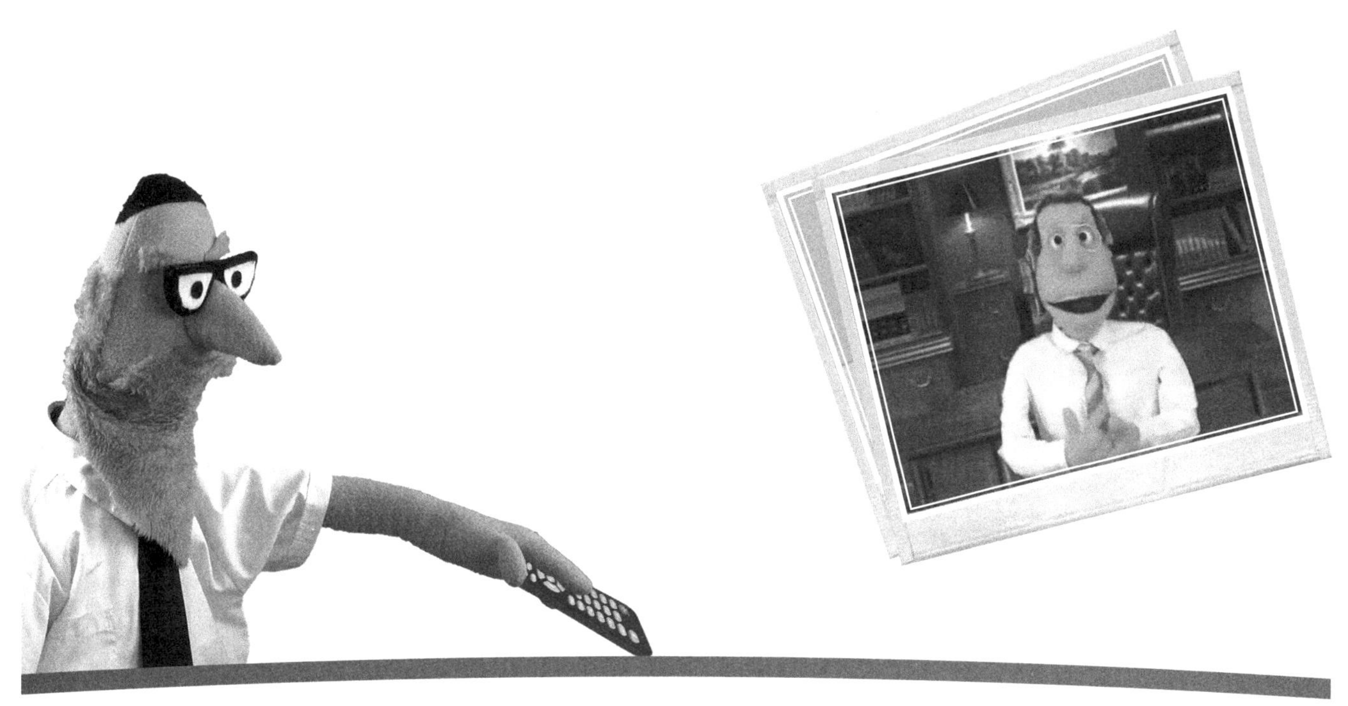

MISHPOTIM

(Goldstein, Goldstein & Fish Legal Services)

RABBI: Welcome to the Parsha Report. This week in Parshat Mishpotim, the Torah tells us many details of civil law, including the responsibilities of someone who has injured someone else, and related topics…Which is a perfect Segway for the following commercial. Will be right back.

(EXT.—Park. Jono violently pops up from the bottom of the screen, whips his head back (CRACK), then puts his hand on his neck.)

JONO: Ouch! I hurt my neck!

(INT.—Doctor's Office. Roy sits in a medical robe. Dr. Gilbert Poznansky points to an X-Ray of Roy's torso with a wrist watch in it.)

DR. P: So, obviously, I wouldn't be able to tell you what time it is right now.

(Roy turns to camera shocked. EXT.—Park. Jono rubs his neck.)

LARRY GOLDSTEIN (VOICE-OVER): Snapped your neck?

(INT.—Doctor's office. Roy is yelling at Dr. Poznansky.)

LARRY GOLDSTEIN (VOICE-OVER): Doctor's wrist watch in your stomach?

(INT. – Law office. Larry Goldstein sits on his desk, animatedly gesturing as he speaks.)

LARRY: Hi, I'm Larry Goldstein. The offices of Goldstein, Goldstein and Gefilte Fish want to help you. (Firm logo pops into the bottom of the screen and stays there the entire commercial)

(INT. – Strange looking office. G-Fish sits at a desk.)

G-FISH: (Gefilte Fish, Esq. – Partner, Goldstein, Goldstein and Gefilte Fish) Larry Goldstein is a thirty two year veteran of the legal system—three of which he spent studying law from where it matters most... BEHIND BARS! (Bars slam down over G-Fish, then disappear) Maybe you don't know your rights, but Larry Goldstein does.

(INT. – Law office. Larry still on his desk.)

LARRY: Injured while attempting to injure yourself? You owe yourself a HUGE cash settlement! (The words CASH SETTLEMENT pop on the screen really large as he says it) Didn't get your homework done on time? Sue the dog for eating it! (A cartoon picture of a dog turning his pockets inside out pops up on the screen) Boss fired you? Fire him back! (The words TAKE THAT, BOSS! pop up). Goldstein, Goldstein and Gefilte Fish want to help you win any Automobile Damage Suits, Personal Injury Actions, Malpractice Suits, Product Liability Suits, Breech of Contract Suits, Negligence Charges, Civil Misconduct Charges, Aggravated Aggravation Charges and both Public and Personal Nuisance Charges.

(INT. – Strange looking office. G-Fish sits at a desk.)

G-FISH: Someone call you a name? Don't ignore them…take them before a jury of their peers!

(INT. – Law office. Larry still on his desk.)

LARRY: Call Me, Larry Goldstein, and the offices of Goldstein, Goldstein and Gefilte Fish for your FREE consultation. Come by the office today and receive this free Gefilte Fish pom-pom ball with googly-eyes. (G-Fish pom-pom pops up – A tiny circle opens up next to the pom-pom—G-Fish is inside…G-Fish: It looks like meeee!)

(EXT.—Park. Jono in neck brace.)

JONO: I had to pay myself $27 in physical and psychological damages! Things are looking up for me…even if I can't! Thanks Larry Goldstein!

(INT.—Doctor's Office)

DR. GILBERT: Thanks to Larry Goldstein, I was able to agree on a settlement… my wristwatch!

INTERCOM: Doctor poznansky, you're late for your 2 oclock

DR. GILBERT: (Looks at wrist) Rats!

(INT. – Law office. Larry still on his desk.)

LARRY: (Wearing a yarmulke) For me, personal injury and civil law is not just a job, it's a mitzvah! Call The Offices of Goldstein, Goldstein and Gefilte Fish today!

(Ambulance sirens scream in the background. Larry perks up and runs off camera. Firm Logo fills screen as Larry's Office goes out of focus. G-Fish appears in a little bubble.)

G-FISH: Well? Call already!

(Back to Show…)

RABBI: Welcome back. That commercial actually makes a really good point. The laws in this weeks Parsha are laws that make perfect sense, ones

that any decent government would enforce. Parshat Mishpatim tells us of laws against murder, theft and any bad things a person could do. But what makes these laws unlike the laws of your city, state and country, is that these are laws from the TORAH itself.

JONO: Hooooold on there, wait-a-minute-stop-the-show-and-explain-something-to-me-Rabbi!

RABBI: (Sigh) Yes Jono?

JONO: Why in the WORLD would we need the same laws enforced by our government AND Torah?

RABBI: I was getting to that, Jono.

JONO: When?

RABBI: RIGHT NOW! You see, the laws set in place by our government are very simple…Don't do this or you go to jail, don't do that or you will pay a fine. The Torah stresses the moral and spiritual implications of committing a crime.

JONO: So the Torah considers my feelings a littler more than the President? Vote Torah in 2008!

RABBI: (Hesitant) Um…well…in a way, yes. I think similar to Larry Goldstein, the Torah considers our crimes and the law on a deeper level than just maintaining law and order. It stresses our responsibility as Jews to not commit such crimes—for ourselves, for the world as a whole, and for G-d.

JONO: And that's why the laws written in Parshat Mishpatim are so important.

RABBI: That's my line!

JONO: For the Parsha Report, I'm Rabbi. Good night.

RABBI: MY LINE!

[THE END]

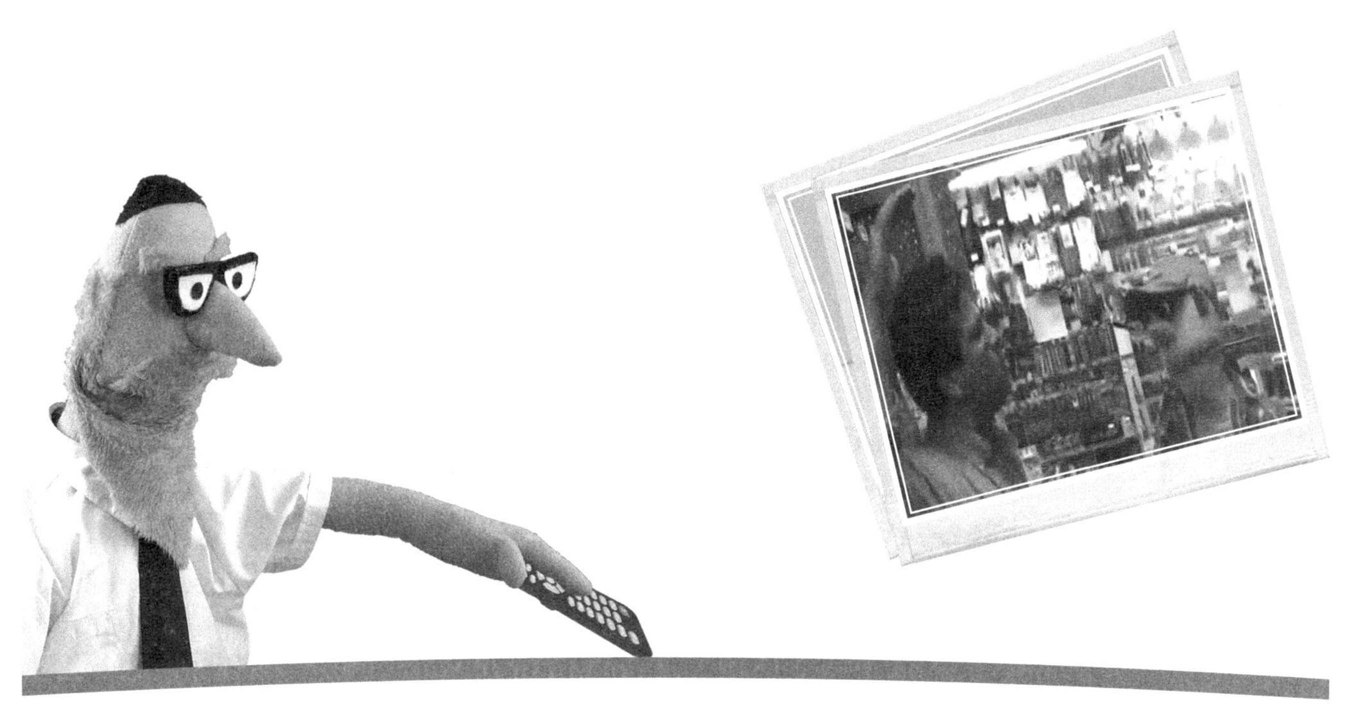

TERUMA

(The Do-It-Yourself Temple)

RABBI: Good evening. This week in Parshat Trumah, G-d gives Moses very specific instructions as to how to build the Mishkan—the portable temple that the jews traveled with in the dessert. This Mishkan was the spiritual home for G-d, so to speak, during the 40 years the Jews spent in the wilderness.

JONO: Rabbi, I recently had the opportunity to go to a hardware store to research how this portable temple would be built. Let's take a look at what I got. I went to New york lumber and Ace hardware in Brooklyn, to see if I could procure some of the materials enumerated in this weeks Torah portion. At first, I figured the easiest way to go would be to see if they had any read-to-go mishkans. (Show clip) So it seemed I would have to gather the parts the hard way. Originally, I had assumed that a home for G-d would have shag carpeted walls, lava lamps, and a hand-shaped chair, but it seems as though the Torah had

a different idea in mind. (Show clip of asking for materials, biblical measurements) The Torah gives very specific instructions for exactly what materials are to be used, but neither me or Leslie had the patience for that. (Show clip of asking for materials and suggesting substitutes). After speaking a bit, Leslie showed me around the store, and brought be out to the lumber yard to show me some two by fours. After a while, Leslie ought on that I had absolute no idea what I was doing. (Show clip of leslie balling out Jono for being inexperienced.) After a while of wandering around the store trying to figure things out, I realized that Mr. leslie was right. I had no idea how to build a temple. So I went to the only guy I know who has experience with this sort of stuff: Rabbi kadoozy!

RABBI: Jono, you can't build the mishkan. It was only used when the Jews were in the desert. But what you can do is make yourself into home for holiness and spirituality-By doing mitzvot and making sure that everything you do is for the right reasons.

JONO: Make myself into a temple, eh?

(Show shot of Jono with a plaque on him that says: donated by Ira and Edna Bernstein

[THE END]

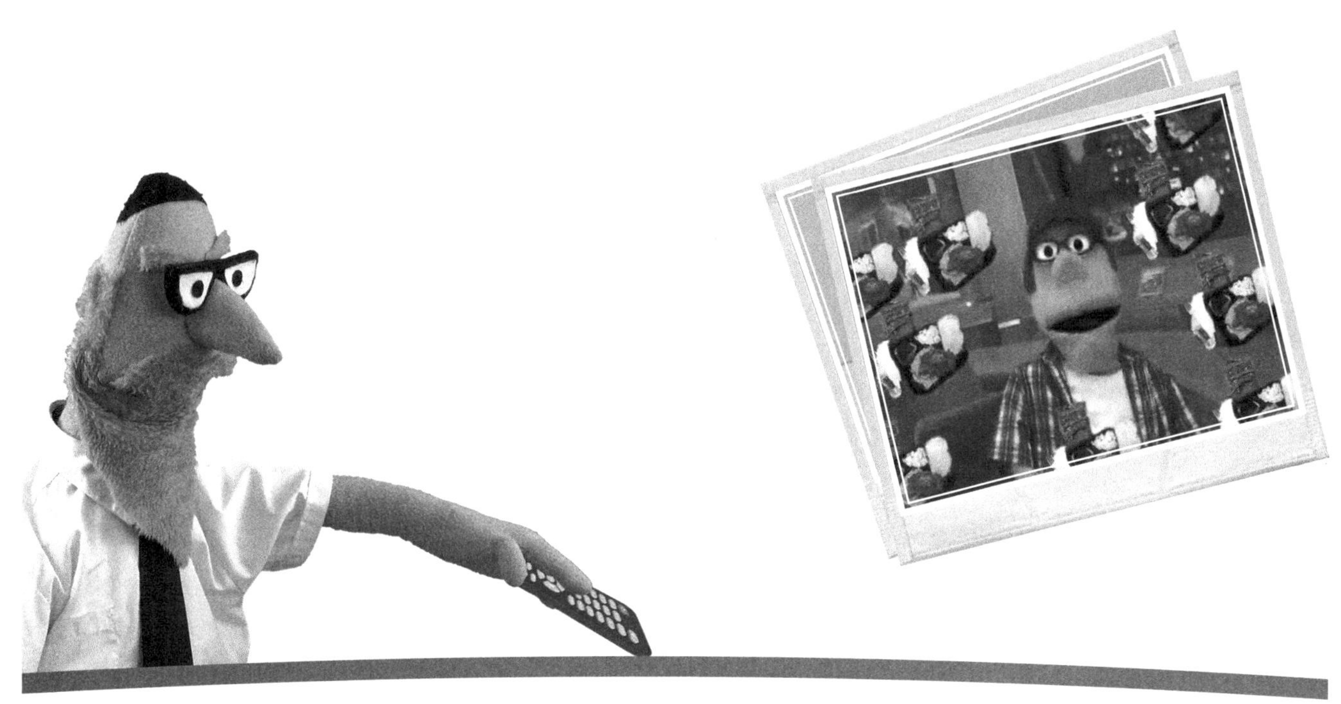

TEZTAVEH

(Press Me!)

JONO: Good evening. I've been informed that this week's Torah portion begins with the commandment to make the oil for the Menorah, pure olive oil, crushed for lighting. At first glance, one may see this instruction as merely pointing out the need to crush the olive to get out the oil, rather than just lighting olives on fire—a mistake I have made all too often (Show graphic of a singed olive sitting in a candle stick). Stiiiiinky!

RABBI: AND dangerous. But on a deeper level, this verse refers to the hardships the Jewish people have faced over the years, how we've been crushed through oppression and discrimination, but these hardships only brought out an even stronger devotion and dedication. Jews were even willing to risk there lives for Judaism if that's what it came to.

JONO: To document these hardships, I recently wrote letters and made telephone calls to various different business establishments, revealing to them my Jewish identity, thus leaving myself open to oppression and discrimination…of biblical proportions. (Graphic of Jewish slave being whipped by Egyptian?)

JONO: My first letter was to a travel agency. (As letters and phone calls are shown/played, corresponding full screen graphics appear). My concern was that by revealing my Jewish identity I might have my passport marked and find it difficult to leave the state. The letter I got back said quote "I would like to thank you for sharing the fact that you are Jewish with me. Although this information is completely unimportant to our business transaction, I can only assume that you were trying to ask for the in-flight Kosher meal. I have gone ahead and made those changes to your itinerary for you at no extra charge." My travel agent continues saying: "In response to your comment: 'Persecute away!' after sharing your religious beliefs with me, I will assure you that I will do no such thing."

(Back to Jono) So far, my search for oppression was coming up dry. But I did order five kosher meals, and all five were, in this reporter's opinion, delicious.

RABBI: Jono, Thank G-d most Jews today live in free countries and are free to practice Judaism in peace, but that doesn't mean that…

JONO: Hang on, I'm not finished. My next stop was a phone call to a country club. This is what I got.

(Play recording of friendly phone call, then back to Jono:)

It seems that no matter where I turned, no matter how hard I tried, I simply wasn't being oppressed. I even mailed a box of bagels and yarmulkes to Russia…NO QUESTIONS ASKED! With freedom and acceptance like this, I feel less like olive oil and more like that stinky olive in a candle stick from before.

RABBI: Jono, the challenge we face now is not so much a fight against oppressive governments, but a struggle within ourselves to not let

the freedom we have cause us to forget our responsibilities as Jews and our unique heritage.

JONO: So…. You're saying that I don't have to get beat up by police officers in order to feel devoted to Judaism?

RABBI: I would certainly hope not.

JONO: So…You're saying that I don't have to sit at a separate lunch counter in order to feel devoted to Judaism?

RABBI: Jono, I think you're getting a little…

JONO: So…You're saying that I don't have to be shipped to the moon via rocket to live on an isolated lunar colony with only other Jews and my trusty Gefilte Fish in order to…

RABBI: NO! No! No, no no no! You see, Jono, you don't need to be personally oppressed to understand the importance of your own Judaism. The hard part now, for all of us, is just pushing ourselves to remember that we ARE Jews…to remember who we are.

JONO: And right now I remember that I'm a guy who has twelve more kosher meals waiting for me at the airport. One, two, skidoooooooooo…. (Jono runs out excited)

RABBI: That's all the time we have for tonight, please join us again next week, for the Parsha Report.

[THE END]

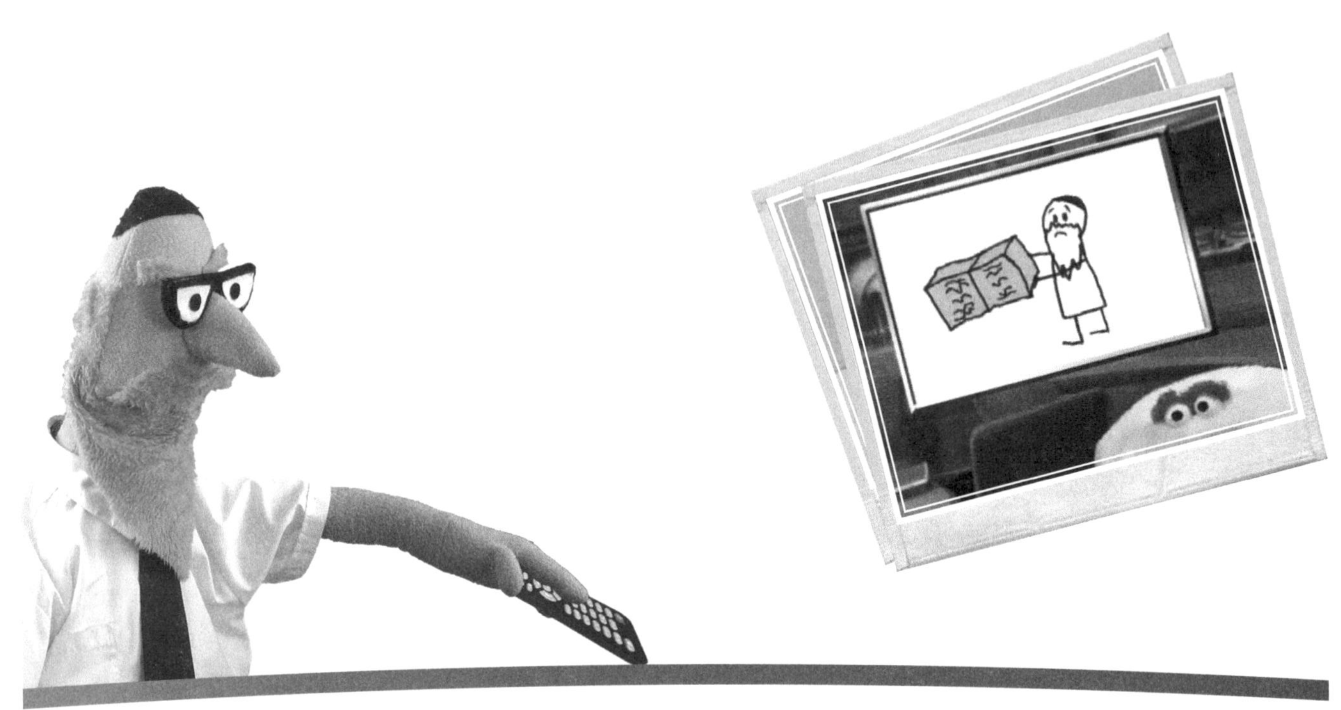

KI TISA

(Image Not Available)

RABBI: This week in Parshat Ki Sisa, the Jews commit the tragic sin of building and worshipping the Golden Calf. With us now to explain this terrible mistake, is our senior theology expert, Gefilte Fish.

G-FISH: Thank you, Rabbi. First let's examine an artist's representation of what the Golden Calf may have looked like…(Stick figure doodle of Golden Calf appears) Roy, who let Jono do the graphics for this show? I specifically requested NO DOODLES! (Sigh) Ok, now let's compare that with a picture of G-d. (Empty gray square shows up with text in the middle reading "Image not available") Oh…great! JUST GREAT!!! How am I supposed to work under conditions like this!!! Not to mention that we're out of Fresca.

RABBI: Gefilte fish, calm down. I think the whole point of your analysis is supposed to be that there can't be any image of G-d.

G-FISH: Well excuse ME, sir, but I think I know what the point of my own analysis is supposed to be! Let's just SEE about that! I'll consult this week's script to…(Script pops up from bottom of screen. G-Fish scans it.) Oh. Hmm. Looks like you're right, Rabbi. I'll buy you lunch after the show. No hard feelings. Ahem. Now let's take a closer look at our (Sigh) diagram. Note that the Golden Calf is made out of…yes, gold. Whereas G-d (Show "image") isn't made out of anything. Another fact worthy to note is that the Golden Calf has eyes—and apparently according to Jono, he had crazy googly eyes – but of course, being an inanimate object, this statue can't see anything anyway. G-d on the other hand, has no eyes, but sees and knows EVERYTHING (Looks up and around). Sort of spooky. I'm scared. Lastly, The Golden Calf was made only out of the gold jewelry that the Jews had available. At the current going rate for gold—roughly $550 per troy ounce—the Golden Calf's value would be estimated at around 200 bucks. Compare that with the figure our experts gave us for the value of G-d—an astounding 4 million dollars.

RABBI: Gefilte fish, you made a lot of excellent points, but I'm going to have to correct you on that last one—You can't put a price on G-d.

G-FISH: WHAT? Ok…let me consult my accountant…

(Jono pops up out of nowhere. He and G-Fish mumble to each other, then…)

JONO: Five million dollars!!!

G-FISH: Five million dollars!!!

RABBI: No! What…what is going on here? Gefilte Fish is Jono's lawyer, Jono is Gefilte Fish's accountant…No offense, but you're both dangerously under-qualified for those positions.

JONO: Pfff. That was completely unprofessional!

(Jono falls back down)

RABBI: Look, Gefilte Fish, the fact is that you, nor anyone, can say that G-d is worth a certain price. You can't put ANY limitations on G-d… not size, color, googly-eyes, or any other physical description. G-d is infinite. You can't say that He looks like any particular person or object, because, essentially, He encompasses every person and object, and beyond.

G-FISH: Yeah, not to mention that I'd be sort of cautious about praying to old crazy eyes here (Show "diagram" again).

RABBI: Well, it look's like that's all the time we have for tonight…

G-FISH: Wait, I didn't get to show the computer simulation of Moses smashing the Tablets (Small stick figure cartoon of Moses dropping the tablet's show's up in the corner) Oh…FANTASTIC!!!! That's it, I'm calling my agent! (Walks off in a huff)

RABBI: Please join us again next week, for the Parsha Report.

[THE END]

VAYAKHEL-PEKUDEI

(The Musical "As a Jew")

RABBI: Good evening and welcome to the Parsha Report. This weeks Parsha tells us how the Mishkan—the portable temple that G-d commanded the Jews to make a couple weeks ago in Parshat Trumah, is actually built..

G-FISH: What?! The portable temple? AGAIN?! Pardon me, but I do hold a degree in ancient history, and I believe that the Temple built in Jerusalem was far more important than the temporary structure the Jews used in the desert. What gives?

RABBI: Well, Gefilte Fish, the special attention that the Torah gives to the mishkan can teach us the importance of carrying our Jewish identity with us wherever we go. Oh, I just heard from Roy that Jono is on location in Antarctica to give us a special on location report.

JONO: Hi Rabbi. I heard what you just said about bringing Judaism with us wherever we go, so I had Roy whip up this backdrop for me. Thanks, Roy. You're simply the best. Anyways, I'm reporting live from Antarctica, where I've chosen to eat a greasy Kugel I picked up this afternoon.

RABBI: That's how you're traveling with your Judaism?

JONO: Yeah, well, I was going to pray here to, but I'm having trouble finding a tenth penguin.

RABBI: Well, Jono, that's definitely one way to do it. But what I meant was more that we can't just confine our Jewish Identity to the Synagogue, but we have to take it with us and incorporate it into our daily lives.

JONO: Incorporate it in our daily lives, eh?

(Music starts up—background changes to what looks like a set on a stage. Jono falls off screen and pops back up in a white shirt and vest. G-Fish joins him on stage, wearing a bow tie. They bob to the music together. (Cheesy musical singing and dancing…)

G-FISH: You need seykhl (smarts) to do your homework

JONO: You need koyekh (strength) to run a mile

G-FISH: It takes geduld (patience) to build a birdhouse

JONO: You'd be meshuga to chase a field mouse

TOGETHER: Just remember every single thing you do, you do it as a Jew.

G-FISH: You can play koyshbol (basketball) wearing a Kippah

JONO: You can eat a kikhl (cookie) in Hebrew school

G-FISH: You can go loifn (running) while thinking about Torah

JONO: You can fress (eat) tacos while you light the Menorah.

(G-Fish runs off screen, Jono ducks and pops back up in his normal clothes and the image of Antarctica comes back behind him. Jono is breathing heavy.)

JONO: So there you have it Rabbi.

RABBI: Jono, I'm actually quite amazed and impressed right now. I'm so used to correcting you, but you have found a beautiful way to express a lesson from Parshat Vayakhel here.

JONO: Thank you! I'll be here all week! You've been great, people! (Blows kisses)

(Jono walks off.)

G-FISH: Jono has left the building.

RABBI: Well, that's all the time we have for now. Please join us again next week, for the Parsha Report.

[THE END]

TAZRIA-METZORA

(Afflictions of Yesteryear)

JONO: Rabbi: Hello, and welcome to the Parsha Report. Tonight we're going to start off the show with a brand new segment called "Afflictions of yesteryear with Jono and Gefilte Fish."

G-FISH: This segment is dedicated to understanding some of history's most fascinating diseases.

JONO: What makes us experts on this subject, you may ask? Easy. My friend Gefilte fish here and I backpacked through Europe last summer in an attempt to find ourselves. Throughout the course of our journey, and thanks to poorly managed youth hostels and several bad choices, the only things we managed to find were a plethora of illnesses, many of which have been extinct for decades, and even centuries. And we contracted all of them.

G-FISH: Let's start our feverish stroll down a plague ridden memory lane with our first stop, Hungary. (Map of Europe is displayed on screen with a red line being drawn as they name

locations. By each location, the name of the place and the disease they contracted there is displayed. Once in a while, touristy pictures of Jono and G-Fish in front of tourist attractions are shown.)

JONO: You know that old saying: never let a monkey feed you grapes? Well, neither do I…and that's how I acquired puking fever at a Hungarian market.

G-FISH: After Jono recovered, we hopped a train to France. Word of advice while in Paris: if performance artist Wheezy Pierre makes you a balloon animal and it pops in your face, hold your breath. Don't breath in the balloon air, that's how I came down with a nasty case of lung fever.

JONO: And last, but most certainly not least—it seems that sharing that banana split with my new friend Nikolai (Picture of Nikolai…gross! [I will take a gross picture of myself to use, if you want]) on the Greek isle of Mikonos turned out to be a mistake I would regret the entire summer. Roy, put trench mouth up there.

G-FISH: After Jono's bout with trench mouth, we decided to cut our losses and go back home. WHERE I GOT CHICKEN POOOOOOOX!!!!

JONO: But don't feel bad for us, the summer wasn't a total bust. Now we are practically immune to every disease known to man. Well, except for the common cold (Sneezes).

G-FISH: Well, it looks like we're nearing the end of the segment, which means it's time for "Ancient Ailment of the Day!" Today's featured affliction is "Tzoraas"— a skin disease mentioned at length in this week's Torah portion. Tzoraas can present itself as terrible, painful white patches on the skin, but it can also appear as green spots on walls of a house, or on clothing. According to our sages, the only known cause for Tzoraas is Lashon Hora—speaking badly about other people. Jewish Tradition also teaches that this disease only occurred during biblical times, and even then only very rarely.

JONO: Whoa whoa whoa, hang on there, G-Fish. Saying bad stuff about people can cause a disease? I'm sorry, but I beg to differ. Sleeping in an out-house in Prague can cause a disease. Borrowing a blanket

from a sick camel in Turkey can cause a disease. But I really don't see how telling people that you shower with swim-trunks on can cause a disease.

G-FISH: Well now you told even more people!!! And EXCUSE ME FOR BEING MODEST!

RABBI: Hang on, just one moment. This is getting out of control.

JONO: Well you try spending a summer with G-Fish!

G-FISH: I carried your passport in my purse THE WHOLE SUMMER! And this is the thanks I get?

RABBI: Look, guys, our Tradition teaches that Tzoraas only occurred very very rarely, effecting only specific people who were particularly spiritually sensitive. But now days you're right, Jono, we wouldn't get a physical disease like that from doing something morally wrong. But we can still learn from the Torah that even though we may not be sensitive to it, the things we say and do have a very real effect on us.

JONO: So you're saying that saying bad things about other people is the spiritual equivalent of drinking a gutter puddle in Bulgaria.

RABBI: Well, I guess so. It's just as bad and the side-effects can be just as unpleasant.

G-FISH: GROOOOSS!!!!

JONO: Sorry I told people about the swim trunks, G-Fish.

G-FISH: You're forgiven...but it's going to take time for me to trust you again.

JONO: (Sadly) Ohhhhh.

RABBI: See, Jono. If you hadn't said something bad about Gefilte Fish in the first place, you wouldn't have had to deal with the consequences.

JONO: Point taken.

RABBI: Well, that's all the time we have for now. May I suggest that you two wait a while before taking another trip together?

JONO: But our safari can't wait!

G-FISH: SAFARI!!!

(Jono and G-Fish run off together.)

RABBI: See you all next week.

[THE END]

ACHAREI-KEDOSHIM

(How to be Holy...Kind Of)

RABBI: Good evening, and welcome to the Parsha report. This week, in Parshat Kedoshim, the Torah commands us to be holy. With us now is our senior holiness correspondent...Gefilte Fish?

G-FISH: (G-Fish has a daisy in his ear(?) , there are flowers all around him, and sitar music playing in the background) Don't look so surprised rabbi, I happen to have a masters degree in holiness. And one in food service management, but that's for another time...when the bank processes my loan request, ignoring my HORRIBLE CREDIT! Anyhoo, hello there friends and welcome to my sanctuary of holiness, tranquility, and love love.

JONO: (Calls from off screen) G-Fish, can I borrow your motorcycle?

G-FISH: I CAN'T SPEAK NOW! I'M IN THE MIDDLE OF A SHOOOOOOOW! (Pause a beat) Oh, and no, you may not! Ahem. Hello again, friends. Let me now teach you an exercise in holiness. First you must get into position.. (Diagram appears on screen ad G-Fish describes the "position") Put point A behind point B, then , tuck point C underneath point A, and pull point D through point Q, as shown in the diagram. (Diagram reveals a horribly twisted and uncomfortable man).

Ahhh, now you may begin to relax and feel the Holiness. Hoooooooliiiiinesssss. Inhale. (Pause) Exhale. Now, Inahle. Hold it. Hold it. Inhale. (Pause) Inhale…. A little more. Good. Now inhale.

JONO: (Again from off-screen) G-Fish, you're mother is on the phone.

G-FISH: Oh MAAAAN!!! IF I'VE TOLD YOU ONCE, I'VE TOLD YOU A BAZILLION TIMES—IF MY MOTHER CALLS DURING A SHOW, TELL HER I'M IN THE HOSPITAL AND I'LL CALL HER WHEN I'M BETTER!! Oh, hello friends. Now where were we?

RABBI: Excuse me, Gefilte Fish, but one of our viewers just called and complained that his brother just passes out because you never told him he could exhale. I think you might have you're priorities a bit skewed.

G-FISH: EXCUSE ME, SIR, BUT I DON'T THINK THIS IS THE TIME OR PLACE TO BE LECTURING ME ABOUT MY PRIORITIES! THΛT'S WHY TIIEY ARE CALLED MY PRIORITIES! THEY'RE MINE! Oh, and everybody can exhale now.. (Pause) Now inhale…

JONO: (Runs into the room) G-Fish, I really don't appreciate the way you've been speaking to me.

G-FISH: (Mimicking Jono) I really don't appreciate the way you've been speaking to me.

JONO: Seriously, it's really bothering me.

G-FISH: Seriously, it's really bothering me.

JONO: Stop repeating everything I say!

G-FISH: Stop repeating everything I say!

JONO: STOP IT!

G-FISH: STOP IT!

JONO: Rabbi! Gefilte fish is bothering me! And he kicked me in the shins yesterday.

G-FISH: I DON'T HAVE LEGS…LET ALONE FEET TO KICK YOU WITH!!!

ITHCE: HOLD IT, GUYS, THIS IS GETTING COMPLETELY OUT OF HAND. Again. I really should ground you two from playing with each other.

G-FISH AND JONO: But Raaaaabbi!!!

RABBI: Gefilte fish, I think you're idea of holiness might be a little bit mixed up. When the Torah tells us to be holy, it continues by giving us several commandments as how to treat other people. Giving Tzedakah, Judging legal disputes honestly, honesty in business, revering your parents, and loving you neighbor are just a few of them. Behaving like a mentsch in everyday life is one of the first and most important steps in behaving in a holy way.

G-FISH: And deep breathing?

RABBI: Well, if the deep breathing helps you behave morally, then yes.

G-FISH: Oh. Well then. I guess I have to go throw away my trick calculator.

JONO: You mean the one that squirts water in my face when I try to use it?

G-FISH: (Takes a deep breath) I feel holier already!

JONO: You should call your mom back while I borrow your motorcycle. And she me might be more than a little upset—I had to add quite a few details to make the whole thing more believable.

G-FISH: (Takes another deep breath) Yes, I will call my mother back and assure her that I am healthy. But please don't touch my motorcycle as you will no doubt hurt yourself. That would be very upsetting for all of us. Kinda.

RABBI: Very good, Gefilte Fish. Now you're starting to sound holy! Kinda. Well, that's all the time we have for now. See you next week, for the Parsha Report.

[THE END]

EMOR

(Party Time)

RABBI: Hello and welcome back once again to another exciting episode of the Parsha Report. This weeks Parsha includes the commandments to observe the Jewish Holidays. With us now to speak about the importance of holidays are our senior Holidays Analysts—Jono and Gefilte Fish.

JONO: Hello, friends. My trusted colleague Gefilte fish and I would like to share with you now our own ideas as how to best observe some of America's special holidays. Perhaps the most exciting holiday on our nation's calendar is Arbor day. Exciting for trees, that is, and positively boring for everyone else. Here's how I suggest the holiday that encourages tree planting and care be celebrated (Graphics accompany suggestion). When the family gathers around the table for the Arbor day feast, begin by staring out the window for several minutes…looking at a tree. Then, after everybody is sufficiently bored out of

there minds, Daddy can unveil the arbor day feast—A bunch of leaves. (Cartoon leaf appears on screen, with the words "Rich in leafy goodness!") Hugging or singing to the tree is also encouraged.

G-FISH: On a more timely note, May 25th marks the observance of National Tap Dance Day. Here's how we recommend you celebrate this important holiday—According to the bajillion year-old custom I just made up, you should cover the dining room table with your finest table-clothery, gather the family, and then jump up on that table and do the shim-sham-shimmy until you drop. Every last one of you. EVEN THE GOLDFISH!!! (Show fish in tap shoes)

JONO: Possibly the most disappointing holidays known to man is march 14th National Pi day. Now, I know most of you out there are imagining the most WASOME holiday in the world—a table filled with apple, cherry, chocolate and maybe even Mike N' Ike's pies, (As Jono says this, the images of the pies appear on a table) but unfortunately a more appropriate celebration for this holiday would include calculators, protractors, and graph paper (These things now appear on the table). And quite possibly no pies at all (Pies disappear). Yes, national Pi day is a holiday celebrated by nerdy high-school geometry teachers who think they're really cool for figuring out that march 14, or 3/14 corresponds to 3. 14, the common three-digit approximation for the mathematical constant—Pi. So until these egg-heads figure out how to build a robot army and make us all their slaves, they can keep their nerdy holidays to themselves, thank you very much.

GEFILTE FISH: Let's move on from that colossal disappointment to one of the GREATEST DAYS EVER—Of course, I'm talking about SANDWICH DAAAAAY!HOORAY FOR SANDWICHES!!! November 3rd marks the birthday of the Earl of Sandwich—the inventor of, yes, the sandwich. The sandwich was quite possibly the greatest innovation in food-stuffs since chickens invented the egg.

JONO: Excuse me, but I do believe that the egg invented the chicken.

GFISH: Whatever. But back to Sandwich Day. Obviously the most appropriate way to celebrate sandwich day is by eating EVERY TYPE OF SANDWICH KNOWN TO MAN!

JONO: I suggest my PATENT PENDING grilled cheese sandwich peanut butter and jelly sandwich sandwich (Image accompanies) Mmmmmmm. Now that's what I call a celebration. Rabbi, back to you.

RABBI: Jono, Gefilte Fish, those are all very nice ways of celebrating. But the holidays described in this week's Torah portion are a different type of Holiday, a Yom Tov, or Jewish Holiday, have very different ways of being celebrated.

JONO: By different I can only assume you mean eating a piece of onion, reading for 5 hours and then eating the flattest, blandest bread in the world.

RABBI: By different I mean that the special meals we eat on Yom Tov aren't just about enjoying the Holiday, but they're about infusing ourselves with an enthusiasm for what the Yom Tov represents, and hopefully giving us the push we need to incorporate that part of Judaism into our daily lives.

G-FISH: So instead of just eating a sandwich or dancing on your table, we should celebrate a Yom Tov by understanding what the holiday means to us as Jews?

RABBI: That's right, Gefilte Fish. We should celebrate our holidays not only physically, but spiritually as well.

JONO: Rabbi, that was probably very beautiful. Unfortunately I was busy worrying about what's gonna happen to me when the high-school geometry teachers make their robot army and their first order of business is to reap vengeance on me for making fun of their Pi day. I'm gonna go hide in the closet. If you need me I'll be under the box of snowsuits.

RABBI: Well, that's all the time we have for tonight. Tune in again next week for another fascinating edition of the Parsha Report.

[THE END]

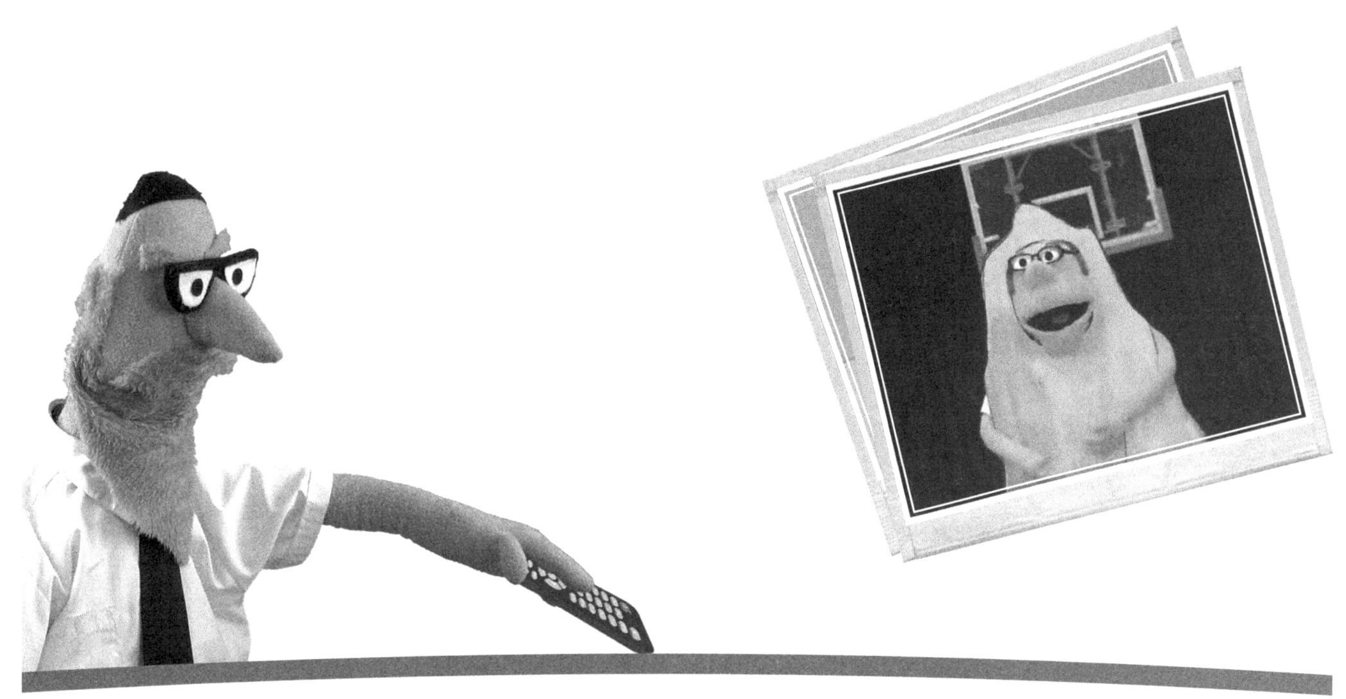

BEHAR

(Jono's Little Mountain Song)

RABBI: Hello, and welcome back to the Parsha Report. This week's Parsha starts by teaching us that the mitzvot and all of their details were given to the Jewish people at Mount Sinai. With us now to illustrate the special-ness of mount Sinai, and why G-d chose it as the place to give us the Torah, is our very own Jono, who will be singing a very cute little song about it.

(Cut to Jono's dressing room door. Roy is standing outside ad Jono's voice is heard from inside)

JONO: I'm not doing it, Roy.

ROY: (Sigh) Look, Jono, let's not make this difficult. I have no interest in making you do something you don't wanna do, but we both have our jobs to do, and right now your Job is to come out here in that mountain costume and sing a song.

JONO: NO NO NO! I'm the star reporter for this show! Get someone less important to do it.

RABBI: Jono, it's not so bad. Have a little bit of humility and come out and do what you have to do.

JONO: Have some humility?! Why in the world would I want to do that?!

RABBI: You'll find out when you sing the song, now get out there and sing, Jono, the show must go on!

(Jono walks out in front of green screen wearing mountain costume)

JONO: Okay let's get this over with. Roy, hook me up with an elementary school gymnasium slash assembly hall. G-Fish, let's hear some a capella backup. Ahem.

(Sings "Little Har Sinai…" song.)

RABBI: Thank you, Jono, that was very…sweet.

JONO: Don't test me, Rabbi.

RABBI: Well, there you have it, Folks. The Torah demands from us to be strong, like a mountain, to make the right decisions, know what's right and wrong, and be proud of being Jewish. But we also have to remember to be a humble mountain, and allow ourselves to do what we have to do, even when we might not want to.

JONO: Right now, this humble little mountain wants to go get a burger. G-Fish, seriously, cut it out. (G-Fish has been continuing his back up the entire time.)

[THE END]

BAMIDBAR

(Sandy Trails)

G-FISH: Hello, and welcome to the Parsha Report. I'm gefilte p, Fish and I'll be filling in tonight for Rabbi and Jono, who are currently hopelessly lost…IN A BARREN DESEEEEEEEEEERT!!!

(Cut to a desert where Rabbi Itche and Jono are riding goats.)

RABBI: Well, it's official. We're hopelessly lost in this barren desert.

JONO: I told you we should have asked for directions.

RABBI: Jono, there's nobody here. This is a barren desert.

JONO: We should have asked that cactus we saw 3 hours ago. He was clearly pointing to the left. (We see a cactus)

RABBI: And we should have followed directions from a cactus?

JONO: Yes.

RABBI: And if a cactus told you to jump off a bridge, you would do it?

JONO: Rabbi, if a cactus told me to jump off a bridge I would sell that cactus to a traveling circus show.

ITHCE: That actually makes a lot of sense.

JONO: Thank you. (Pause) Rabbi, why are we riding these super smelly grossitating goats?

RABBI: Because they were half the price of the super smelly grossitating mules. AND I got a corporate discount. AND...(Pause) I like them. They're cute.

JONO: (Looks down at goat) They are pretty cute. (T0 goat) stop chewing on my shirt Goat, it's the only one I have.

(Silence)

JONO: Rabbi?

RABBI: Yes, Jono?

JONO: I have 2 questions. The first one is—why are we out here in the middle of this barren desert?

RABBI: And the second question?

JONO: What do goats taste like?

RABBI: Seeing as how I'm not the one who thought that the goats look like cotton candy, I'll let you answer the second question yourself.

JONO: Let that be a lesson to all of us! What LOOKS like cotton candy can TASTE like gym socks. Okay, so that answered, what about the first question? Why are we in the middle of this desert?

RABBI: This week's Parsha...

JONO: Here we go...

RABBI: THIS WEEK'S PARSHAH is named "Bamidbar", or In the Wilderness. And it is always read on the Shabbat before the Holiday of Shavuot which commemorates the giving of the Torah.

JONO: Ok.

RABBI: So, there must be some sort of connection between the giving of the Torah and…

JONO: A big, empty, hot, sticky, dry, sandy, sunny and utterly hopeless barren desert?

RABBI: Yes! So what's the connection, Jono?

JONO: Hmmm…Torah and desert, eh? Hmmmm…(Pause) I think I got it, professor! The TORAH was given to us in a DESERT! Boy am I glad I did my detective work on that one. What a great lesson, Rabbi! Ok, now let's go ask that cactus how to get home,.

RABBI: Hold on Jono, the question is, WHY was the Torah given in a desert? The Torah gives us instructions for how to live our lives! So why was it given in a place where nobody lives, and there's nothing going on—no decisions to make, no nothing? (Show Torah alone in a big desert) We're reporters, Jono, we should be able to figure this one out!

JONO: Rabbi, with all due respect, we're puppets who do a satirical news show parody about the Torah portions. If that's what counts as journalism these days then, quite frankly, I'm scared of where our country is headed.

RABBI: Come on, Jono, think!

JONO: Well, where would you want the Torah to be given??? In New York? It would probably smell awful and contain a whole lot of bad words… (We see a picture of Torah in wearing a Yankee's cap)

RABBI: What about Moscow then? My father lived in Moscow for a while, before the war…

JONO: In Moscow there'd probably be less milk and meat, but a whole lot more phone tapping. (Torah in big furry hat)

RABBI: That's it!

JONO: Where?! What?! (Looks around franticly)

RABBI: No, You figured out why the Torah was given in the desert!

JONO: I did?

ITHCE: Yes. The desert, unlike New York or Moscow (Or London for that matter) wouldn't shape the Torah to the style or culture or obstacles of a specific place…. A Torah that's was given in the desert would be truly UNIVERSAL —— something we could apply to EVERY situation without being scared off by the obstacles we all face wherever we live…

JONO: Rabbi, right now I AM being intimidated by this goat. He keeps on givin' me dirty looks. (Close-up of goat's eyes – crazy sound effect)

RABBI: Ok, Jono, now that we have that one figured out, let's start working on how to get home.

JONO: I'm tellin' you, Rabbi, the cactus seemed like our best bet.

RABBI: At this point, Jono, I'm scared enough and sweaty enough to try anything. Let's go. I would much rather apply the lessons of Torah at home than out here in the middle of nowhere with these goats! (Close-up of a Goat's eyes – crazy sound effect)

JONO: Giddy-up, Crazy Eyes!

[THE END]

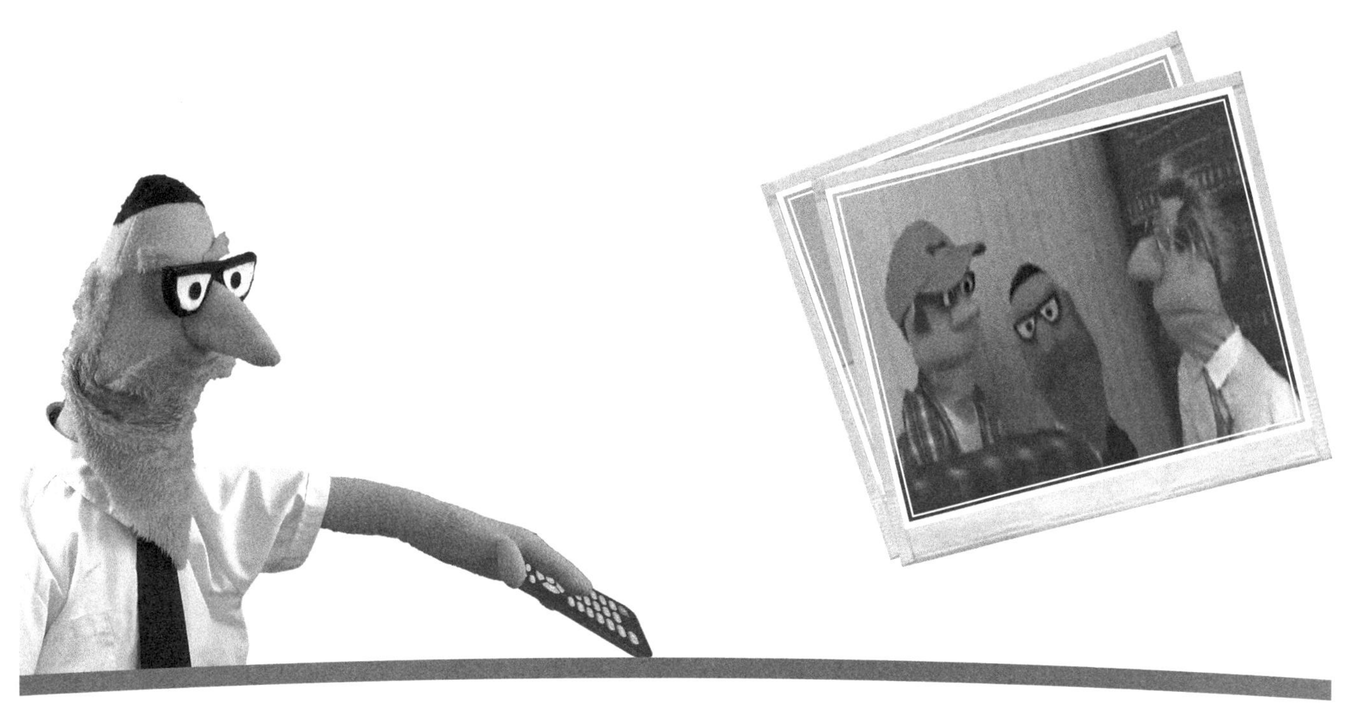

NASO
(The Vow)

LARRY: Ok, Rabbi. Thanks for having me over here for a lunch and learn. Ha!

RABBI: No problem Larry. I'm just sorry that Jono ate your lunch, but we still have time for the learning part.

JONO: (Walks into room) Rabbi, Rabbi, Rabbi! (Crowd cheers for a while) We're out of chocolate cream pies. You better pick up a few next time you go to the store.

LARRY: Ha! Maybe you should take it easy on the pies, Jonathan.

JONO: Neh, the pies don't mind.

RABBI: No, he means, maybe try limiting your over-indulgence.

JONO: Rabbi, if I'd limit my over indulgence, then it wouldn't be over-indulgence, now would it? And then what would be the point.

G-FISH: (Enters room) That's it, who ate my baseball card collection?!

JONO: (Everybody looks at Jono) What's everybody lookin at?! (Laughter)

RABBI: Jono, did you eat Gefilte Fish's baseball cards? And if so, why?

G-FISH: Yeah!

JONO: (Sighs) Yes, Rabbi, I ate G-Fish's baseball cards. And I did it because with a little peanut butter and a marshmallow fluff, they hit a GRAND SLAM HOME-RUN all the way into the upper bleachers of DELICIOUS park!

(Everyone's mouth is agape as the audience laughs)

SCENE TWO

(Rabbi and Larry are learning. Jono is sitting on the couch eating potato chips and holding a newspaper)

RABBI: Ok, Larry, this week's Torah portion is Naso, and one of the things it teaches us is about the Nazir...

JONO: Can anyone think of a 9 letter word that starts with a 7 and ends with a 4?

LARRY: Jono, that's a sudoku, there's no words in it. Ha!

JONO: Hmmm...Sevenvelopefour? Ha. That's a funny word.

RABBI: Jono, please, we're trying to learn.

JONO: Sor-ree! By the way, we're out of soda...and olive oil...and for the record, olive oil is NOT a good alternative to soda. (A beat; laughter) And taste tests have not been favorable for my new drink SODA OIL.

RABBI: Anyways, a Nazir is a person who makes a special vow that prohibits him from drinking wine, becoming spiritually impure, and cutting

his hair, for a certain period of time. This vow is considered by the Torah to be a way of sanctifying oneself. The make yourself holy. Like a spiritual clense.

JONO: Hold-on-wait-a-minute-hold-your-horses-slow-down-explain-something-to-me-just-a-minute, Rabbi! How come you never told me about this Nazir stuff before?

RABBI: Well, it's a very specific mitzvah, for very special people, and nowadays nobody…

JONO: Rabbi, I've been lookin' for an excuse to be sporting a super cool long haircut my entire life. I'd use my hair as a belt.

RABBI: Jono, You overheard something I was teaching somebody else, and it was out of context, and you're getting carried away, here. This is like the time you burnt that bush on my front lawn.

JONO: This is different, Rabbi. Look, you're always telling me to cut down on my over-indulgence, right? Well, this Nazirite vow might be a perfect way to do that. And I'll even throw in a vow of silence if you want too.

RABBI: Okay Jono, start your vow of silence right now.

(Rabbi waits, staring at Jono as we cut back and forth between them. The cuts get quicker and quicker as Jono gets super-antsy. Finally…)

JONO: Baaaaaa! I can't do it. I love talking. But the rest of the stuff I can definitely do.

RABBI: You do realize that this means no more grape juice?

JONO: What about artificial grape flavoring?

RABBI: I don't think that would be a problem…

JONO: Then it's final. I gotta go…NOT get a hair cut. (Exits)

LARRY: How long do you think it will take him to realize that he doesn't have to go anywhere to not get a haircut. Ha!

ICTCHE: I'd say he'll be back in five, four, three, two…

(Jono bursts through the door)

JONO: Ok, I'm back. Anyone miss me?

(Fade to commercial)

SCENE THREE

(Rabbi and Roy are standing around drinking coffee on the set of the Parsha Report)

RABBI: It's only been three days and Jono's hair is already down to his shoulders.

ROY: Yeah, and I haven't seen him drinking wine during coffee breaks for a while. He's really taking this seriously.

RABBI: Well, he says he's only practicing for now, but if I don't talk him out of it soon, this could be more of a mess than the time he tried to recreate the plague of frogs in my living room.

JONO: (Enters. He has long hair down to his shoulders) Rabbi, Rabbi, Rabbi! Oh, hi Roy.

RABBI: (Bird noises are heard) Jono, do hear something? What is that?

JONO: Oh, it's just that pesky hummingbird again. He moved into my hair yesterday afternoon.

RABBI: You have a hummingbird living in your hair?

JONO: Yeah, and he's late with his rent. Do hummingbirds have knees?

RABBI: Jono, this is getting out of hand.

JONO: You're tellin' me? Rabbi, you gotta help me out. My father told me I look like a hippy, and if I don't cut my hair soon, he's gonna stop paying my tuition at the Jay Schandemonier Academy of Moving Pictures. But that's all I can tell you. I really should stop talking now.

RABBI: Why, is this a secret?

JONO: (Hands Rabbi Itche a piece of paper)

RABBI: (Reading) "I'm practicing for that vow of silence again." Jono, this is ridic..

JONO: (Shoves another scrap of paper in itches face)

RABBI: (Reading) "If you go for lunch, please bring me back twelve pastrami sandwiches…what? Oh, ok…and one for the hummingbird too" Jono, this.. (Jono hands Rabbi another scrap of paper) "On rye, with lettuce". (Another paper) "And Tomato."

ROY: Ok, Jono, you're on in 30 seconds. (Jono, Rabbi, and Roy walk off)

(Cut to Roy and Rabbi watching the monitor of the show. Jono is on set.)

JONO: (Holds up sign that reads "And Mustard") Oops. (Flips sign. It now reads "Welcome to the Parsha Report."

RABBI: (Puts his head in his hands) I've gotta take care of this soon.

(Fade out – Fade in…)

SCENE FOUR

(Basement. Jono is eating stuff. A knock on the door.)

JONO: (Hold's up sign that says "Come in")

RABBI: (Enters) Jono Can I have a word with you? (He sits down on the couch with Jono. Warm music is heard as Rabbi and Jono have their heart to heart.) Jono, You don't have to make vows to be a good person.

JONO: I don't? But you're always telling me to limit my overindulgence.

RABBI: The Nazirite in this week's Torah portion is a very special person who takes on a very extreme vow. But regular guys like us can be holy people too. You don't have to take a vow of silence, but maybe you could cut down on those quadruple super-burgers, and keep in mind that the eating and drinking you do is to give you enough energy to do good things, and make the world, and yourself, a better place.

JONO: Huuuuh?

RABBI: You don't need to limit what you do, nor do you need to over-do it. Just do what it takes for you and your body to do good things, to do Mitzvahs, to be a good person.

JONO: So what you're saying is…limiting myself to maybe a triple super-burger instead wouldn't hurt.

RABBI: If that's what it takes.

JONO: I hear you. Thanks Rabbi.

(G-Fish enters holding a newspaper)

G-FISH: You were right, Jono, this crossword puzzle is IMPOSIBLE! There's only one line across, AND NO CLUUUUUUUES!.

RABBI: (Looks at paper) G-Fish, that's a word jumble.

G-FISH: Ohhhh! Then I did it right. The answer is sevenvelopefour.

RABBI: What? Hang on.. I've been meaning to ask you guys…what's SEVENVELOPEFOUR?

JONO: For mailing letters, Rabbi!

(Everybody laughs)

[THE END]

BEHAALOTCHA

(Week in Re-Jew)

JONO: Good evening folks and welcome to the Week in Re-Jew. Let's take a look at what we have for this week on our all new Intelli-compute Parsha-cam. (Jono clicks a remote, and the image behind him changes to static and then to a picture of a menorah.)

First up this week—G-d gives Aaron, the Cohen Gadol, instructions as to how to light the menorah in the mishkan, and then later on in the holy temple. And let me be the first to stress the importance of having instructions on lighting a menorah.

I think everybody around here remembers the incident I had last Chanukah when I tried to light my Chanukah menorah without following the instructions and I ended up lighting the front door on fire, and then the neighbor's cat came over and her tail caught on fire, then the cat got freaked out and ran off to the zoo and lit a monkey on fire. The

monkey went berserk, broke out of his cage, stole an old lady's purse and car keys, and drove to New Jersey. Then, right after he got out of the Holland tunnel, he got pulled over by the cops, and when he handed over the old lady's drivers license, the cop caught fire. (Graphics are seen for each step of this mishap) Needless to say, I got grounded for a week after that one.

NEXT (Clicks remote, static, next picture)

Passover part 2. That's right, the Jews in the desert who were unable to participate in the sacrifice of the paschal lamb, begged Moses for a second chance. Moses relayed their message to G-d, G-d checked his voicemail and dug what Moses was asking. So G-d dropped Moses an e-mail letting him know that the second Passover bill had passed. And that bill became law. (Graphics for all these—answering machine, e-mail, bill/law) Now I know what you're thinking—A second Passover?! Were these guys out of their MINDS! I'd be sitting at that Seder table, listening to my uncle Saul babble on for six hours about Egypt…AGAIN, and the only thing on my mind would be to take MY mighty hand and outstretched arm, grab the doorknob and GET OUT OF THERE. No, but seriously, Passover is great, we could all use 2 of them.

NEXT Manna! Yes, I'm talking about the heavenly food that could taste like anything you wanted and descended every day, for every meal, for every day and every meal that the Jews ate in the desert. Mmmm. See, after a while of eating Manna, the Jews got tired of it and complained "Manna we tired of Manna." (Pause) That was funnier in rehearsal. Actually, it was just as bad in rehearsal, but it's all we had. G-Fish wrote that one.

G-FISH: (Off screen) That's it, I'm calling my…

JONO: NEXT.

Miriam, Moses's sister, says Lashon Hora or bad things about Moses, and gets afflicted with Tzoraas, a biblical skin affliction that served as the punishment for saying bad things about other people. The funny thing is, I said something really bad, and really funny

about Gefilte Fish (Image of G-Fish) and the filthy old blankie (Image of blankie) he insists on sleeping with every night the other day, and I haven't had any problems. Nope, not a single bad thing has happened to me. Well, that's almost all the time we have for tonight, I gotta go to a doctor to check out this horrible rash I got shortly after saying terrible things about Gefilte Fish and his blankie. But first let's go to Rabbi Itche Kadoozy for his 15 second diatribe. Rabbi, you have 15 seconds.

RABBI: (As Rabbi Itche talks, a clock in the lower right-hand corner is counting down from 15.) The second Passover that G-d agreed to in this week's Torah portion teaches us that we always have a second chance to make up for opportunities we missed in the past. But the motivation for that second chance has to come from ourselves, just like the Jews in the desert who asked Moses to plead to G-d on their behalf. This also teaches us that…

JONO: Thank you rabbi, your fifteen seconds are up. And a special thank you to Roy who is in the Parsha report Parsha-copter, manning the Intelle-compute Parsha-cam.

(Cut to Roy in a helicopter)

ROY: I don't know why I have to be in a helicopter just to bring those images up…

JONO: That's all for now. I'm Jonathan Weinsteinstein and this has been the week in Re-Jew.

[THE END]

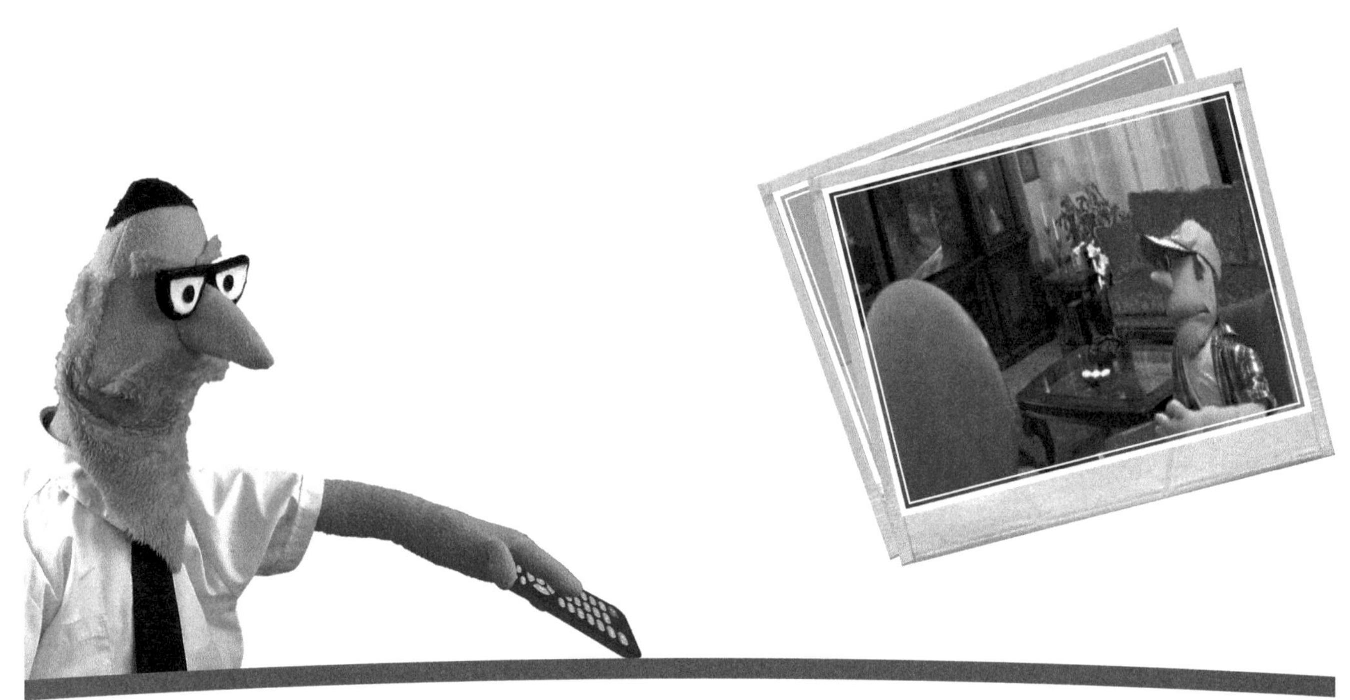

SHELACH

(We've Got a Grape Show!)

JONO: Hello there, people, and welcome to the Week in Re-Jew. Let's take a look at the intellicompute Parsha-cam (Clicks remote, image comes up.) This week, Moses sends out spies to scout out Israel before the Jews move in. But these spies aren't the fearless kind you read about. No, these spies see giant grapes and other giant produce, get scared out of their wits, come back and incite fear in the Jewish people, and end up getting Moses really, really mad. I recently had the opportunity to speak to one of them. And by one of them I mean one of the grapes. Roy?

(Clip starts. Jono is sitting across from a giant grape. Perhaps it is wearing a hat.)

JONO: Giant grape, my first question is, how did you feel when the Jewish spies came in, saw you guys, and said "hey, if the grapes here are this big, then the people must be GINORMOUS?"

Did that make you feel…upset? Proud? Monstrous? What was that like, tell us a little bit about that.

GG: (Nothing)

JONO: Mmm hmm. Fascinating. Now, let me jump to a different topic, and then we'll come back to the spies—what are your personal goals? Do you see yourself as a giant raisin, or perhaps a giant bottle of wine?

GG: (Nothing)

JONO: I see. Ok, back to the spies—Why do you think they were so afraid of you? What is it about a giant grape that would make a Jewish spy say "AAAHHHH! A GIANT GRAPE! OH MAN! IT'S SO HORRIBLE! SO HUGE! I'M SO SCARED THAT I HAVE TO RUN AWAY AND SHARE MY FEAR WITH ANYONE WHO WILL LISTEN! AHHHH!"

GG: (Nothing)

JONO: Ok, one last question—Are you related to Alexander the Grape? (Waits for a laugh)

GG: (Nothing)

JONO: Ahem. Ok. Mr. Grape, or Giant, if I may. Can I call you Giant? It's been a pleasure and we really appreciate you coming out here. (Extend hand to shake, then awkwardly retracts it.)

(Back to Jono on the Week in Re-Jew set)

JONO: Well, that's almost all for now, but first, let's go to Rabbi in the Parsha Report Parsha-Copter, who give us a quick overview…or over-JEW of the Torah portion, as he sees is from a bazillion miles above. Rabbi?

RABBI: Thank you Jono. Well, what I can make out from up here is that after experiencing miracles in Egypt, and receiving the Torah on mount Sinai, the Jews are afraid to settle in Israel and get back into real life. And from a bazillion miles above, it looks like the giant grapes reminded them of the tremendous responsibilities that real

life brings. That's why Moses was so upset, because he knew that the whole point of the Torah is to bring it's lessons into real life, to make it a better, holier place. For the Week in Re-Jew, I'm Rabbi, and I think just lost a shoe.

JONO: Thank you rabbi. Well folks, it's time to sign off for now. I'm Jonathan Weinsteinstein, and this has been the week in Re-Jew.

[THE END]

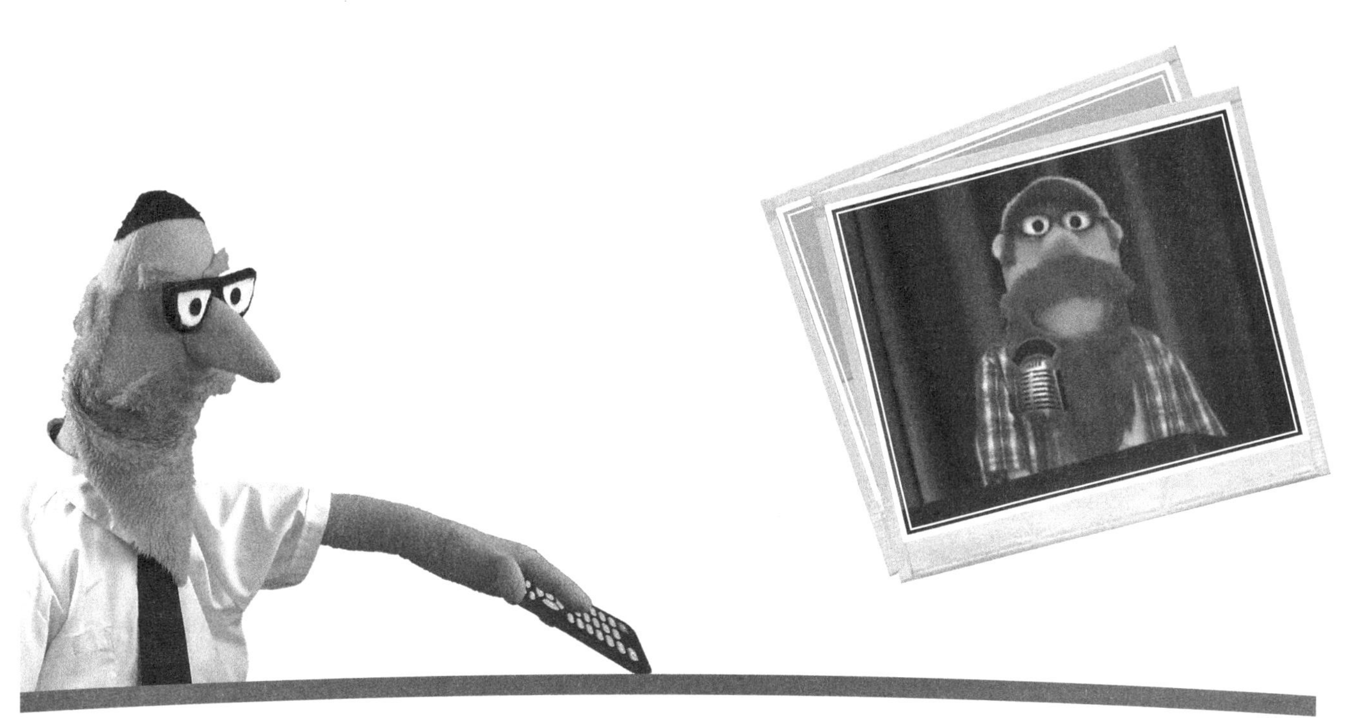

KORACH

(The Great Debate)

JONO: Welcome to the Week in Re-Jew. This week a man named Korach challenges the leadership of Moses and his brother Aaron. In honor of the Torah portion, and in an effort to showcase my talents as a playwright, director and stage manager, I've prepared a one act play depicting a debate between Korach and Moses. The part of Moses will be played by myself, and the part of Korach was written for my good friend and Harvard Drama School graduate, Rolland. Rolland has unfortunately fallen ill, and will be replaced by his untiring understudy—ME. (Clicks remote. Two podiums stand on a very bare stage. Jono runs back and forth between the two to play both parts)

KORACH: Children of Israel, why should this man and his brother be given special status among the Jewish people?

ANNOUNCER: (Offscreen) Moses, you now have 10 seconds for a rebuttal.

(At the bottom of the screen, we read: In tonight's performance, the part of Debate Moderator·will be skillfully played by Jonathan Weinsteinstein.)

MOSES: Was it not I who lead the Jewish people to safety from Egypt? Was it not My brother Aaron and myself who spoke to Pharaoh on behalf of the Children of Israel?

ANNOUNCER: Korach, 10 seconds.

KORACH: Yes, but now we have been given the Torah, and we are all equal in our ability to serve G-d by fulfilling his commandments. Now there is no reason for you to hold a special status.

MOSES: Korach, you are making a grave mistake! What makes my status to special is the fact that I…Hang on a second, a have to make a phone call. (Takes out cell-phone) Hey, G-d? Moses. Yeah. Yeah. Oh she's fine, and the kids too. What? Yes? Thursday sounds great, that would be really nice. Look, there's someone here who wants to speak with you. Ok. Ok. Yeah. Ok. (Holds out phone, then runs back to Korach's podium and draws phone back to his face.)

KORACH: (Static is heard) Hello? Hello? I.. I can't…what? I can't hear you. Are you in a tunnel or something? (Hands back phone)

MOSES: Hey, G-d, it's me again. Yeah. Ok. Bottomless pit? Swallowed by the earth? Ok. Ok. I'll let him know. Ok. Bye bye. Bye bye. Ok. Ha! Priceless. Ok. Bye bye. Talk to you later. Chow.

(Moses looks at Korach, folds his arms and nods knowingly.)

KORACH: Gulp.

(Back to Jono)

JONO: The moral of the story—Moses Rocks and had G-d's phone number on speed dial. BOOYA! And now, let's go to Rabbi Itche Kadoozy for his fifteen seconds of fame. Rabbi, fifteen seconds.

RABBI: Jono, , it seems like you summed it pretty well. There's really not much left for me to say. (Stands around for the rest of his fifteen seconds.)

JONO: Well, folks, that's just about all the time we have for tonight. For the Week in Re-Jew, I'm Jonathan Weinsteinstein.

[THE END]

CHUKAT-BALAK

(Chukat-Balak in Three Minutes)

JONO: Hey and welcome back to, that's right, the Week in Re-Jew. Let's take another exciting look at our illustrious history through a marvel of modern technology: the Intelli-compute Parsha cam. First up is the red-cow. Now, don't ask me what this is about because it makes NO SENSE. The good news, however, is that it's supposed to make no sense. According to what Rabbi Itche Kadoozy told me earlier when I DIDN'T ask him about this, is that this mitzvah is considered to be completely beyond rational explanations.

G-FISH: (Off-screen) I can explain it.

JONO: No you can't, NEXT! The Jews run out of water and start getting SUPER thirsty and WICKED cranky, so G-d tells Moses to get it from a rock. But the rock won't work, so Moses hits the rock. When he does this, WATER STARTS GUSHING AND SPLASHING OUT EVERYWHERE, but G-d isn't happy, so Moses is not allowed to

enter Israel with the Jewish people. NEXT. (Screen doesn't change) NEXT! (Nothing) OH, THIS INFERNAL MACHINE! (Turns to machine) (Hit's remote. Screen changes, lighting and thunder starts.) Oops. Next. Moses's brother Aaron passes away, and the Jewish People mourn. One Aaron's greatest accomplishment was his ability to settle disputes between husbands and wives. I wonder if he's be able to fix up things between G-Fish and Mrs. G-Fish.

G-FISH: (Off screen) THAT'S NONE OF YOUR BUSINESS!

JONO: NEXT. Balam, a Jew-hating Prophet, is hired by Balak, a Jew-Hating King, to curse the Jews. Only thing is, when it comes down to it, G-d won't let him. He tries, but all that comes out is blessings. That's the power of that G.O.D., baby!

G-FISH: (Enters, sinister music plays) Jono, I have a bone to pick with you!

JONO: Ok. Let me have it.

G-FISH: Jono, I think...

JONO: (Clicks remote, playful music plays)

G-FISH: ...that you're doing a great job with the show, and I respect your decisions because you are a genius. And very handsome.

JONO: Thank you, G-Fish.

G-FISH: What?! No?! That's not what I meant!

JONO: Okay, try again.

G-FISH: (Angry, sinister music) JONO (CLICK, playful music) I think you're a wonderful person and I really value our friendship. NO! NO! NO! That's not how it was supposed to come out!!!!! Jono, if you do that one more...(Click! Jono mutes G-Fish...his mouth is moving, he's noticeably teed off, but we hear nothing)

JONO: Man I love this thing! Well, that's all the time we have for tonight. For the Week in Re-Jew, I'm Jonathan Weinsteinstein.

[THE END]

PINCHAS

(Lotto Land)

JONO: Hey, folks, I'm Jono and this is the Week in Re-Jew. First up in this week's Parsha is a guy named Pinchas who stopped the Jewish people from worshipping idols in the desert, thus stopping a plague that was wiping them out, and earning Pinchas the reward of being promoted to the status of a Cohen.

The Kohanim were the descendants of Aaron, and were given the special honor of doing holy stuff in the Temple…I'm going to take the liberty of assuming that that means stuff like reading the brotherhood newsletter, giving Kiddush cups to Bar-mitzvah boys and… making animal sacrifices. Now, if you ask me, there's a much simpler way to achieve the change that Pinchas did—CHANGE YOUR LAST NAME TO COHEN! NEXT!

(Jono puts hand to ear) Excuse me…I've just been informed that changing your name to Cohen wouldn't really work. NO DUH! It's called, like, a joke? Give me a little credit here.

G-FISH: (Enters) Jono, your name change application is in order. Now where's my five bucks and a free Jono hoodie?

JONO: OT-NAY, OW-NAY, EE-FISH…JAY.

NEXT! Before the Jews settled in the land of Israel, the matter of dividing the land had to be dealt with. So, the populations of the tribes were taken into account, but at the end of the day, G-d told Moses that the land was to be divided by lottery. Now, if I would have been consulted about this…WHICH I WASN'T, I would have suggested a scratch-off lottery—much more fun, and you don't have to wait by the radio all day for the results. I took the liberty of creating a mock-up of the scratch-off division of the Land of Israel lottery card. And by I, I mean Roy. Roy, bring up that image I made.

Here is a map of Israel. You scratch off each of the twelve regions, to reveal each REGION NUMBER. Then scratch off the box that says "YOUR NUMBER." If YOUR NUMBER matches any of the REGION NUMBERS, then your tribe wins that region! And unlike the Ohio state lottery, G-d's Israel land lotto doesn't allow the government to tax A bajillion percent of that prize. How's a brotha supposed to make a buck these days? NEXT

Moses appoints Joshua as his Successor. Now…Um…I don't got nothin' for that. G-Fish?

G-Fish (Off screen) Nope.

JONO: NEXT! The Parsha ends with the list of sacrifices to be brought to the Temple on the Jewish Holidays. Last Rosh Hashanah I lost a shoe in synagogue whilst playing tag with a bunch of nine-year olds. Is that enough of a sacrifice? I'VE GIVEN YOU MY SHOE, OH MIGHTY ONE, WHAT MORE DO YOU WANT FROM ME?! Ahem. Okay, while I pull myself together, let's go to the Rabbi for his words of wisdom. 15 seconds worth of wisdom. Rabbi—GO!

RABBI: When the Land of Israel was divided, each tribe received it's portion of the land by use of a lottery—trusting in a force beyond their own understanding. In life, all of us have received a portion by lottery—the people, places and things that we just happen to encounter, and we have to keep in mind that that is OUR portion to take care of in this world. (He was rushing to get all that in.) Phew.

JONO: Thank you, Rabbi. Well, folks …. (Singing:) Now it's time to say good-bye, for me, my G-Fish and The Rabbi.

For the Week in Re-Jew, I'm Jonathan Weinsteinstein.

[THE END]

MATOT-MASSEI

(Anniversary Edition)

JONO: Rabbi, Rabbi, Rabbi! (Crown cheers) Thank you. Thank you. Remember kids, if you stayed up late playing video games and NOT preparing the into to your weekly internet television show, it's always good to open with an old beloved catch phrase.

G-FISH: (Off stage) Ohhhhhhhh.

JONO: Quiet G-Fish! We're on the air! Anyhoo, welcome back to the Week in Re-Jew slash Parsha Report slash the Rabbi Itche kadoozy show! This week is a very special show for us here, because it marks our forty-second season! Yes that's right, 42 wonderful years of the Rabbi Itche Kadoozy Show. But before we show you some exciting and disgustingly old clips from our first season, Let's talk about the Torah portion. This week, in Parshat Massei, the Torah gives us a detailed list of the 42 journeys the Jews made in the desert

throughout the 40 years from the exodus until they entered Israel. Our writers slaved day and night coming up with a fantastic idea for how to present this Torah portion, but unfortunately, they came up with nothing. So, for lack of anything for interesting, let's go to Rabbi Itche Kadoozy who will be reading that list, verse by verse, from the Torah. Rabbi?

RABBI: The children of Israel journeyed from Rameses and camped in Succoth. 6. They journeyed from Succoth and camped in Etham, at the edge of the desert. 7. They journeyed from Etham and camped in Pi Hachirot, which faces Baal Tzefon. 8. They journeyed from Penei Hachirot and crossed in the midst of the sea to the desert. They walked for three days in the desert of Etham and camped in Marah.

JONO: Wow. That…was…not our best work. Now let's take a look at how we tackled this Torah portion 42 years ago, in our first season ever.

(Old timey cartoon Rabbi Itche does the same thing Rabbi Itche was doing)

OLD RABBI: They journeyed from Elim and camped by the Red Sea. 11. They journeyed from the Red Sea and camped in the desert of Sin. 12. They journeyed from the desert of Sin and camped in Dophkah. 13. They journeyed from Dophkah and camped in Alush. 14. They journeyed from Alush and camped in Refidim

(Remote click, but we go to OLD TIMEY CARTOON JONO, who speaks in a high pitched, rocky the flying squirrel voice)

OLD JONO: Thanks, Rabbi, That was great! Now let's go to Roy, in the Parsha Report foot-peddled gyrocopter who will continue reading that list whilst making a non-stop flight form New-York to Paris.

(CLICK, and back to real Jono)

JONO: Roy, in just a few minutes I'm going to ask you to lock that stuff back up in the vault and make sure the climate control is set to encourage speedy decay of that film. But first, let's let old timey

cartoon Rabbi Itche rap things up, with his fifteen seconds of fame. Classic Kadoozy, you're on.

OLD RABBI: The 42 journeys from Egypt can teach us that we, too, must always be traveling from our own Egypt, or freeing ourselves from our own obstacles—constantly breaking out of our own limitations, and pushing to do that one more mitzvah! And now, it's time for our weekly bomb shelter drill! Duck and cover, children.

JONO: What era is that supposed to be anyways? Well, that's almost all the time we have for now, but let's top things off with one more clip from our web debut in 1993. Animated GIF Jono, take us home!

(Animated GIF Jono is displayed. Speech bubble comes up that says "For the Week in Re-Jew, I'm Jonathan Weinsteinstein." As he speaks, low pitched tones are heard (GIF Jono lifts his remote, and we static out.)

[THE END]

DEVARIM

(The 3,000 Year Old Man)

G-FISH: (Playing Chess) Checkmate—I WIN! You know what that means!

JONO: Aww, Dude! Aww, Man! That means I have to do a stand-up comedy routine on amateur night at the giggle room comedy club.

(Transition to Rabbi Itche hanging out on the Parsha Report set. Jono enters.)

JONO: Rabbi, Rabbi, Rabbi!

RABBI: Yes, Jono?

JONO: I have to do a comedy routine tonight at the giggle room, and I was wondering if you could help me write my monologue.

RABBI: You came to me to help you write a comedy monologue?

JONO: Yeah, I was surprised myself when I read that in this week's script, but hey, the show must go on and really, anything could help.

RABBI: Well, Jono, I think you might be interested no know that back when I was a teenager, I was in charge of entertaining the kids at summer camp.

JONO: That's surprising…that you thought I'd be interested to know that.

ITHCE: Me, Mel Brooks, and Carl Reiner were night activity directors in Camp Gan Israel, back when it was in Swan Lake.

JONO: Really?

RABBI: Yeah. We had an act called the 3000 year old man.

JONO: It's the 2000 year old man, Rabbi.

RABBI: No, back when we did it it was the 3,000 year old man. (Looks at watch) Now if you'll excuse me, I have to get started on this weeks show.

JONO: Rabbi, now that I have come to the understanding that you are a comedy legend, despite the fact that you yourself have NEVER laughed, I want to make a deal with you—you come with me to the Giggle room and help me do your 3000 year old man routine, and I'll let you work this week's Torah portion into the routine.

(Transition to Jono and Rabbi Itche on stage at the Giggle Room)

JONO: Ladies and Gentlemen, we have with us a very special guest, a man who arrived a few hours ago at Idlewild Airport. A man from the Middle East, who claims to be 3,000 years old. Sir, it's a pleasure to have you here, how do you feel?

RABBI: Oy vey.

JONO: Oy vey, eh? So you're Jewish?

RABBI: I didn't grow this beard because it's pretty.

JONO: Then let's talk about something that may interest you. Sir, this weeks Torah portion reviews many of the events that occurred while the Jews were wandering in the Desert for 40 years. Do you remember wandering through the desert?

RABBI: Oh, sure. I remember wandering through the desert. I also remember a couple weeks ago, I forgot where I parked at the outlet mall and I wandered around the parking garage for what must have been a half hour. Wandering in the desert for forty years was rough, but wandering around a 7 level parking garage with my arms full of irregularly sized clothing for thoity minutes, now that's moider.

JONO: Fascinating. Now, sir, do you remember when Moses reviewed the entire Torah?

RABBI: Oh, Sure. That was a good speech. A loooong speech, but a very good speech. All the other Rabbis used to be jealous of Moses's speeches. But he had a very good speech writer. His speechwriter could work miracles…and bake the best knishes you ever had.

JONO: Really? Moses did not write his own speeches?

RABBI: No

JONO: Who was Moses's speech writer?

RABBI: G-d.

JONO: Now, as long as we're talking about Moses, I'd like to ask you about what it was like when Moses used to judge all legal disputes himself. Do you remember that?

RABBI: Oh, sure. He used to stand the whole time, and we didn't have supportive shoes back then.

JONO: What kind of legal disputes did people have at that time?

RABBI: Well, usually, there'd be a Tallit, see, sitting in the middle of the road, see, and two guys would come across it, and they'd both grab it at the same time. Both of them wanting the Tallit.

JONO: That's one example…

RABBI: No, that was it. Sometimes there's be other things, one guy would trade a cow for a donkey and they'd argue about it, but most of the time it was two guys grabbing a Tallit and arguing over who should get to keep it. Always a Tallit, I don't know why they couldn't argue over a hat or a nice Italian suit.

JONO: And how would such a case be resolved?

RABBI: Well, sometimes it would go on for months, even years, and it would be a very messy situation, with expert witnesses, jilted lovers and high priced lawyers. But if they were smart about it, they could sometimes solve the whole thing in a second.

JONO: How is that?

RABBI: They would look at the Tallit bag and see who's name is embroidered on it. If it says Murray ben Boinie, then you know who it belongs to, don't you?

JONO: Sir, do you remember the Spies that scouted out the land of Israel?

RABBI: Oh, they were lousy spies. Lousy. Excellent baseball players, by the way, but lousy spies.

JONO: And what made them so terrible?

RABBI: They had a paralyzing fear of grapes. It was very sad, really, they should have seen somebody, talked it out with a psychologist.

JONO: Did you have psychologists back then?

RABBI: We had one psychologist. But we didn't call him a psychologist.

JONO: What did you call him?

RABBI: We called him Murray.

JONO: Couldn't they talk to Murray?

RABBI: Yeah, but he couldn't talk back. He was a mute.

JONO: Could they use sign language?

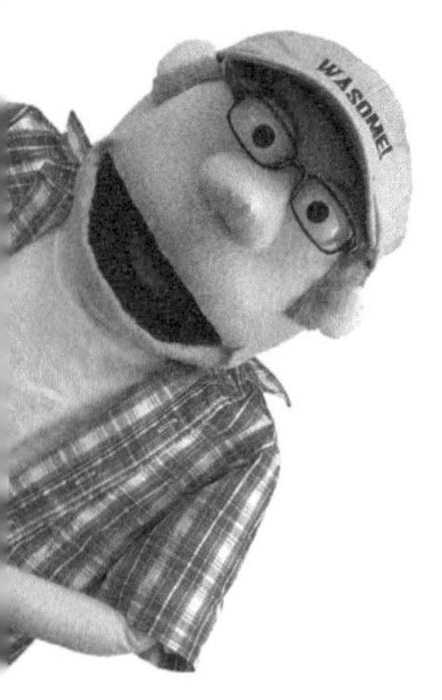

RABBI: It wasn't invented yet. And Murray was blind too.

JONO: Well, sir, we're running out of time, but before we end the program, are there any words of wisdom, gathered throughout your 3,000 years of experience, that you would like to impart on us?

RABBI: Yes. If you're ever standing by Mount Sinai, during the giving of the Ten Commandments, don't blow your nose. It's very distracting.

JONO: Well, sir, thank you very much for joining us, and good night.

(Transition to Jono and Rabbi Itche hanging out back stage. G-Fish Enters)

G-FISH: Nice job, but I believe the conditions of the deal were that you would perform a comedy MONOLOGUE, not a two-person vaudeville act. Go back to the Borscht Belt, promise breaker.

[THE END]

VAETCHANAN

(Technical Support)

RABBI: Hello, and welcome back to the Parsha Report. A very important part of this week's Torah portion is the mitzvah of Tefillin. With us now to talk about tefillin is our very own Larry Goldstein, who just began putting on Tefillin this morning. Larry?

LARRY: Hi, I'm Larry Goldstein, the attorney for the Rabbi Itche Kadoozy Show and it's subsidiaries the Parsha Report at the Week in Re-Jew. And I'm also first time tefillin... putter...onner. This is my grandfather's tefillin, which I've had mounted in a Plexiglas box and hung on my living room wall for years, until I finally decided, hey, I could put these puppies on! Of course, it always helps to have a little bit of a deeper understanding of the mitzvah, so please join me while I place a call to the Tefillin Technical Support line to find out, won't you?

(Larry dials. Ring Ring.)

TS: Hello, You've reached Tefillin Technical Support!

LARRY: Hi, My name is Larr…

TS: If you are calling about purchasing a new pair of tefillin, press 1 now or say "Purchase." If you are calling to have the parchment inside of your tefillin checked to make sure that every word is intact and written correctly, press 2 now or say "I'm calling to have the parchment inside of my tefillin checked to make sure that every word is intact and written correctly." If you are calling to learn more about the significance of the mitzvah of tefillin press 3 now or say "I hate these automated systems!"

LARRY: I HATE THESE AUTOMATED SYSTEMS!

TS: You have chosen to speak to a representative to learn more about the significance of the mitzvah of tefillin. If this is correct say "correct" or mash your palm over all of the buttons on the keypad.

LARRY: (Mashes palm on keypad)

TS: Thanks you. Please hold for the next available representative. (Hold music) your call is very important to us. Please hold while we connect you with the next available…

G-FISH: Good morning sir.

LARRY: Hi, I'd like to…

G-FISH: Please hold a moment sir. (G-Fish hums hold music) Ok, how may I help you this morning, sir.

LARRY: Well, I'd like to learn a little bit about what this mitzvah means and why it's important.

G-FISH: Yes, I can see that you chose that option here on my computer, sir. (Cut to G-Fish's computer and show him playing solitaire.)

LARRY: So, firsts let's start with the basics. Tell me is I have this right: You have parchment with verses of the Torah written on them, including

the Shema and other verses that speak about the importance of remembering the words of the Torah. And you put those parchments in two little leather boxes with leather straps. Do I have that right so far?

G-FISH: Yeah, yeah, you're doing great. (Show G-Fish playing computer games, totally not paying attention.

LARRY: Then, you wrap one of them onto your arm, and place one on your head…

G-FISH: Actually, sir, I don't.

LARRY: What?

G-FISH: I DON'T HAVE ARMS! OR A HEAD!

LARRY: Excuse me, but I don't feel that you're helping me very much.

G-FISH: Sir, I'm going to have to ask you calm down.

LARRY: I am calm…

G-FISH: Sir, you're going to have to stop using that tone of voice with or I'm going to have to release your call.

LARRY: WHAT TONE OF VOICE!?

G-FISH: Sir, this is your last chance. Now do you want me to explain this mitzvah to you or not?

LARRY: I'm sorry. Please do.

G-FISH: YOU wrap one of the boxes on your weaker arm. For most people that's the left arm, which puts the tefillin right next to your heart. Then you place the other box on your head, above your eyes. This symbolizes that both your feelings and your thoughts are wrapped up with Torah and mitzvot.

LARRY: (Larry has been putting on tefillin while G-Fish was talking) That's.. That's beautiful. I…I feel so,,, holy right now.

G-FISH: Ok, all right, save the touchy-feely stuff for someone else. Now if you'll excuse me, I've got a very important game of 3D pinball to finish. (Sounds are heard) OOOOH! Right past my flippers!

(Larry hangs up and G-Fish's screen moves out of the picture.)

LARRY: Well, thank you very much for joining us today. I'm Larry Goldstein, and this has been the Parsha Report.

[THE END]

EIKEV

(We Whined a Lot!)

RABBI: Good evening and welcome back to the Parsha Report. This week, we actually have the amazing opportunity to interview a man who was part of the original generation that left Egypt and wandered through the desert. Roy, why don't you roll that clip for us.

DASAN: Yeah, hi. My name is Dasan. I'm one of the original Jews who traveled through the desert, wandered and followed Moses. I'm not the famous Dasan. It was a very popular name at the time. My best friend in third grade was also named Dasan. We definitely complained a lot in the desert. We made a lot of mistakes. We weren't perfect. We complained a lot.

The Golden Calf, that was not good. The Golden Calf. Now, the thing is at the time, it seemed as though we had two perfectly logical options. Option A, wait a couple more hours for Moses to get back when he said he would or, Option B, tear the jewelry off of

our wives faces, melt it down into a giant Golden Calf and worship it. In retrospect, Option B sounds pretty stupid, but hindsight is always 20/20.

Now, let me just set the record straight about the Golden Calf. We did not intend to replace G-d. No, no, no, no, no, that wasn't the point. The idea was to replace Moses, which wasn't such a great idea either. We never intended on worshiping the Golden Calf. The thing is, though, once you have a giant Golden Calf, you're probably going to end up worshiping that giant Golden Calf.

Now, why did we listen to the spies? They came back. They said Israel was bad; we don't want to go to Israel, even though G-d told us to go to Israel. Why did we listen to them? Answer; because they were spies. I mean, spies are cool. Who would listen to a spy? We shouldn't have, but we did.

One of the things we actually said, and I can't believe we actually said this, was that we wanted to go back to Egypt; we'd be better off there. Yeah, right. Go back there, ring on their doorbells and say hey, guys, remember us? Yeah, yeah, yeah, your firstborn sons died because of us. Remember that? Yeah, the lice, the frogs, remember? Yeah, I'm sure they'd be real happy to see us.

We complained about everything. We complained about the manna; free heavenly food. I mean, I guess it wasn't free enough or heavenly enough. I don't know, but we complained about it.

No matter how many times we messed up in the desert, G-d forgave us. After one of the times, I forget it was, but Moses came down and I was positive that we were going to get, like, 10 seconds to get ready before we imploded and Moses said that we're forgiven. I just sort of nudged the guy next to me and I'm like, did I just hear that right? We made a lot of mistakes. We messed up a lot and the amazing thing is we always ended up getting forgiven, those of us who didn't get smitten, but I'm here to tell the tale.

We whined a lot. Just to give you an idea of Moses was putting up with, let me just show you what it was like. Mm, I don't like the

manna. Mm, I want more water. Blah, I want meat. Blah, blah, blah, I don't like Israel. Mm, Israel is for nerds. I don't want to go to Israel. Blah, blah, blah, I don't like this. Blah, blah, blah. Oh, no, I want to go back to Egypt, oh. That's what it was like.

I'm just trying to think why we did those things. Maybe it was the thrill that you knew you might get smitten. You know, there's that risk. It's like bungee jumping. There's one uprising, which is actually not recorded in the Torah, which I actually started and it was a phenomenal failure. There was a downtime between complaining about water and complaining about food. I said hey, guys, why does Moses always call us the Children of Israel? Let's be called something cool like the wolverines or the eagles. Nobody paid attention to that.

Now, let me set the scene for you. Yom Kippur, Moses comes down with the second set of tablets and this is a fundamental moment, which sets a fundamental precedent in Jewish theology that we can make up for the bad things that we've done and become closer with G-d. But I don't fast well, so I was really out of it and I wasn't really able to appreciate the gravity of the moment.

[THE END]

RE'EH

(Charity Times Eight)

RABBI: Hello and welcome back to the Parsha Report. One very important mitzvah mentioned in this week's Torah portion, is the mitzvah of Tzedakah, or Charity. In order to give proper attention to such a special topic, we've assembled all our friends and cast-members of the Rabbi Itche Kadoozy Show to help us illustrate The Eight Level's of Charity, as outlined by the great medieval Jewish Scholar and Philosopher, Maimonides.

JONO: G-Fish, if you're listening, I told you it wasn't pronounced marmalade. Anyways…let's start with rock bottom.

RABBI: Level 8, The lowest form of Tzedakah, is to give unwillingly.

(Cut to city street. Puppet beggar is asking for money and G-Fish floats by)

BEGGAR: Excuse me, can I trouble you for a dollar…

G-FISH: No.

BEGGAR: please, my car broke down on the expressway, just over there, and my pregnant wife is on her way home from pregnancy classes and I just need 2 dollars to get a train back to…

G-FISH: I said no.

BEGGAR: I just need 2 dollars to get a sandwich…

G-FISH: FINE, HERE, TAKE IT! I can't bare to hear you change your story again.

(Back to Rabbi Itche and Jono)

JONO: Level number 7—giving inadequately, but doing it graciously.

(Cut to Dr. Gilbert Poznansky—the sheep—walking by the beggar.)

DR. P: Here, my good man, take this shiny penny, and with it purchase food for your children and clothes for your pets.

BEGGAR: But a penny won't…

DR. P: No, No, please don't thank me. The thanks I need is in your magical smile. Now go, go deliver the wonderful news to your poverty stricken family!

(Back to Rabbi Itche and Jono)

RABBI: Level 6, is giving money to a person in need, only after they ask for it.

(Cut to Larry Goldstein and beggar. Beggar jingles change as Larry walks by. Larry stops)

LARRY: Do you need something sir?

BEGGAR: (Jingle Jingle)

LARRY: Yes, I see you have a cup. But can I help you in any way, sir?

BEGGAR: (Jingle Jingle)

LARRY: Look, I want to help you, sir, I really do, but I'm not a mind reader. I can't help you unless you tell me what you need. Do you need a new cup? Is that what you're trying to tell me? Or do you need help making that cup NOT jingle. I worked my way through law school as a cup de-jingler, so I know what I'd be doing…but you really need to ask if that's what you want. Or maybe you're making music. I don't know, sir. I'm not a mind reader.

BEGGAR: Buddy, please, can you spare a dime?

LARRY: Oooooooooh, you want money! I'm sorry, I didn't cath that, it makes perfect sense now. Of course, please, take a fifty dollar bill. HA!

BEGGAR: Oh boy!

(Back to Rabbi Itche and Jono)

JONO: Level 5—giving money directly to a poor person, but doing so before he has to ask.

(Cut to Rabbi walking by the beggar)

BEGGAR: (Opens mouth)

RABBI: Ah. (Cuts off beggar)

BEGGAR: Excu…

RABBI: Meh.

BEGGER: Sir, I…

RABBI: Bleh…

BEGGER: I really wish you'd…

RABBI: Neh (Cuts off beggar again) Please, take this. (Places money tenderly in man's hand)

BEGGAR: Then…

RABBI: Eh!

(Back to Rabbi Itche and Jono)

JONO: That was some nice acting, Rabbi.

RABBI: It wasn't acting. We used a real beggar for these things. But, coincidentally enough, as a member of the Screen Actor's Guild, he requested his Union standard minimum payment of $100 a day in nickels and dimes. That was a heavy paycheck. Now on to level 4—Giving money without knowing to whom you are giving.

(Cut to beggar. Jono stumbles by, blindfolded, tossing change behind him.)

JONO: All those in need, take this money. But be careful, I think there's a button in there too. Buttons get stuck in bubble-gum machines. Trust me. (Jono stumble off and we hear crashing off screen)

(Back to Rabbi Itche and Jono)

JONO: By the way, I don't do my own stunts. So, thanks to Roy for that crashing sound.

RABBI: Oh, that was just a sound effect?

JONO: No, he took a spill for me off screen. He's such a good sport. And speaking of Roy, let's let him act out level number 3—Giving money to someone without them knowing that it was you who gave it to them.

(Beggar is standing holding his cup with his arm outstretched and his head facing the opposite direction.)

ROY: (Slowly pops up from the bottom of the screen, behind the beggar, and drops a coin in the cup, unseen by the beggar. When the beggar hears the change drop into the cup he quickly turns to see who gave him the money, but Roy quickly ducks out of view)

(Back to Rabbi and Jono)

RABBI: Very good Roy.

ROY: (Off camera) Don't patronize me.

RABBI: Level Number 2, giving money without knowing who you are giving to, and without the recipient knowing who gave it.

(Cut to Jono licking an envelope. Close up on envelope. Envelope reads as follows, written in crayon: Poor Person, Sheet medal shack #4, Apt. 2J, Shanty Town, NY 00000, Return Address Reads: Anonymous, Nowheresville, NJ. Back to Rabbi and Jono:)

RABBI: That was very sweet, Jono.

JONO: I wrote that myself

RABBI: I could tell..

JONO: And now, level number one, the greatest way of giving to others… Roy, give us a drum-roll (Crashing is heard again)

ROY: (Off screen) OW!

JONO: No, not that one, the drum roll.

ROY: (Off screen) I'm very badly hurt.

JONO: Can someone hit the drum roll button in the control room? (Drum roll plays) Thank you!

RABBI: The greatest level, above which there is no greater, is to support a needy person by giving him a loan or finding him a job, so that he will be able to start supporting himself, and will no longer need to depend on others.

JONO: Oh, by the way, Rabbi, G-Fish complained that his last paycheck from the Parsha Report hasn't cleared yet.

RABBI: Okay, I better go take care of this. In the mean time, all of us should go out and achieve one of these levels of Tzedakah …any one you can. That's all the time we have for tonight, please join us again next week, for the Parsha Report.

[THE END]

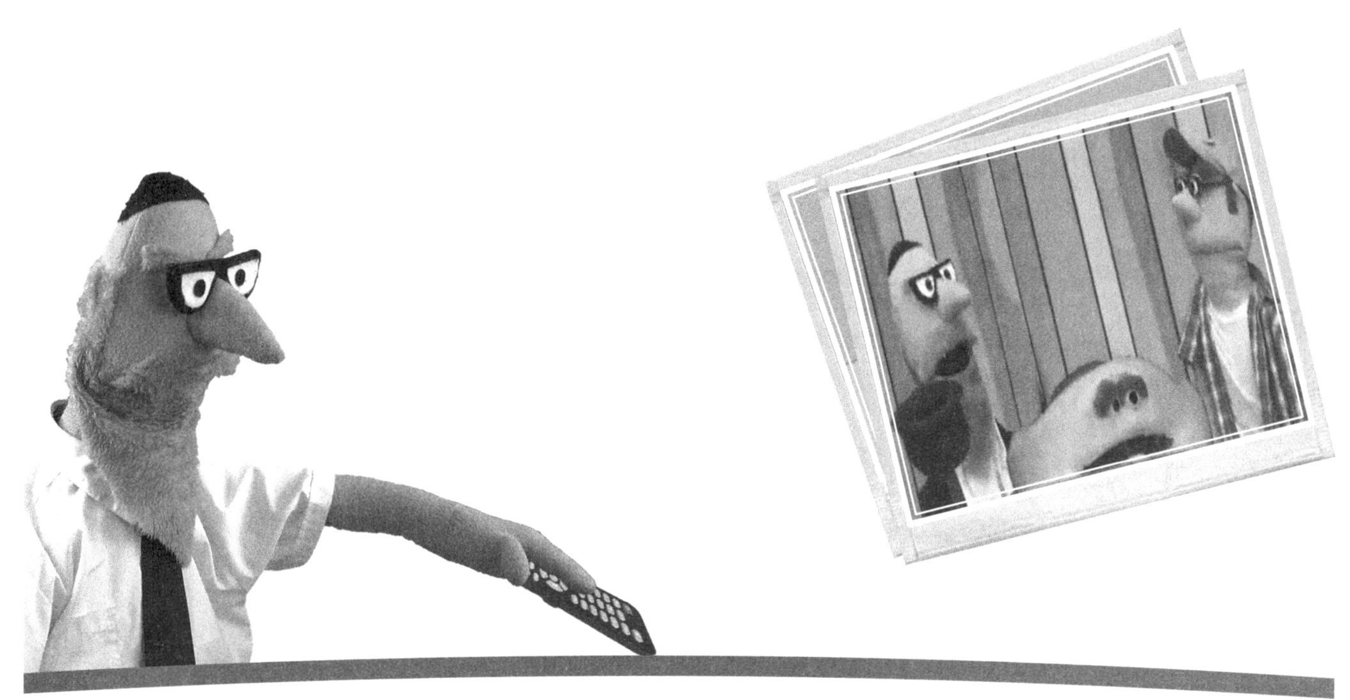

SHOFTIM

(Non-For-Prophet)

G-FISH: (Playing Monopoly) You rolled a seven, that means you owe me 400 dollars. NOW PAY UP!

JONO: Wait just one cotton-pickin' minute, G-Fish. You've told me a lot of rules to these games we play, and well, I started writing them down.

G-FISH: Yeah, and…?

JONO: …And, this isn't one of them. You just made it up.

G-FISH: I didn't make it up, Jono.

JONO: Then where did it come from? You rolled a seven a bajillion times and you never had to pay me 400 dollars. You made it up just now!

G-FISH: Jono, I'm going to tell you something that I haven't told many people before. I have a special gift.

JONO: A remote control airplane?

G-FISH: No, I…

JONO: A robot dog…that flies a remote control airplane?

G-FISH: Jono, stay with me here for just a second.

JONO: I'm here!

G-FISH: Now open your mind…

JONO: Do you have a saw?

G-FISH: NOOOOOOOO!!! I mean figuratively!

JONO: I don't know what that means.

G-FISH: Just listen Jono. The reason I know all of the rules all of the time is because I'm a profit. I have visions of the Al-mighty.

JONO: Wuuuu?

G-FISH: Yup. And just now, before you rolled the dice, G-d appeared to me and told me to change the rules.

JONO: G-d told you to change the rules?

G-FISH: That's what I said, isn't it?

JONO: I don't know about this. I think I need to consult the Rabbi. But are you sure I should use your new and improved method of getting his attention?

G-FISH: It's OK Jono, trust me. I'm a profit.

JONO: Ok. (Takes out a broom and hits the ceiling with it a few times) Rabbi! I FLUSHED A TENNIS BALL DOWN THE TOILET AND THE WHOLE BASEMENT IS FLOODED!

RABBI: (Runs in with a toilet plunger) What is it, Jono? Where's the flood?

JONO: False alarm, Rabbi, I just needed to get your attention.

RABBI: Jono, this is the third time today that you did this to me.

JONO: Hey, I've got your attention, don't I?

RABBI: (Sigh) Anyways, what's the big emergency?

JONO: G-Fish says he's a profit.

RABBI: Ok....

JONO: And G-d told him to change the rules to the bored game we were playing.

RABBI: Mmm hmmm. Change the rules, eh?

JONO: Yeah.

RABBI: Well, Jono, Gefilte Fish is starting to remind me of what the Torah calls in Hebrew—a Novi Sheker.

G-FISH: Yeah, A Novi Sheker. See Jono, even the Rabbi backs me up.

RABBI: Translated into English, that means a false prophet.

G-FISH: Yeah, False...A FALSE PROPHET?!

RABBI: Actually Jono, this week's Torah Portion speaks about a false prophet. And it teaches us that one of the ways to know that a person is a false prophet is if he tells you to do something that the Torah says not to do—if he changes the rules.

JONO: You mean, like if there's something that you know is wrong...

RABBI: Yeah

JONO: Because it's always been wrong, and will always be wrong, and it's even wrong right now...

RABBI: Uh huh...

JONO: ...like telling a sixty-three year-old rabbi that you flushed a tennis ball down the toilet and made him run frantically downstairs to fix

it, when it isn't really true, and you know he has a heart condition, and a "prophet" tells you it's ok?

RABBI: Exactly.

G-FISH: I'm tired of these wild accusations based on circumstantial evidence! As a prophet of the All-Mighty, I will smite you both! CONSIDER YOURSELVES SMOTEEEEEEEEN!!!

RABBI: Gefilte Fish, Prophets have always been an important part of Judaism, but a prophet can never tell you to do something that's against the Torah, something that's wrong.

G-FISH: GULP!

JONO: So…what's the punishment for a false prophet.?

RABBI: Well, we don't have the type of courts these days that can carry out punishments for these kind of things…

JONO: Come on, Rabbi, tell me what it is.

ITHE: No, it really doesn't apply here…

JONO: Come on, Rabbi….

RABBI: No, Jono, please

JONO: Rabbi, just tell me!

RABBI: I…

JONO: PUH-LEEEEEEEEEEZ!!!

RABBI: You…

JONO: LEEEEEEEEEEEEEEEEEEEEEEEEZ!! LEEZ! LEEZ! LEEZ! PLEEEEEEEEZ!!!! EEEEEZ! EEZ! PUH-LEEEEEEEE…..

RABBI: STOP!!! THAT IS SO ANNOYING!! Alright…(Rabbi Itche Jono and G-Fish get into a huddle and Rabbi Itche whispers to them).

G-FISH: DOUBLE-GULP!

JONO: Yikes. Thinks look bad for you G-Fish. Rabbi, let's collect some stones.

G-FISH: Wait a second, wait a second! I'm not a prophet! I'm not even a false prophet! I'm just a...liar.

JONO: What's the punishment for a liar, Rabbi?

RABBI: The punishment for a liar is that nobody can trust you anymore.

(Cut to G-Fish in the bathroom. Water is spraying everywhere)

G-FISH: RABBI! COME QUICK! I FLUSHED A TENNIS BALL DOWN THE TOILET AND IT'S FLOODING EVERYWHERE!

(Cut to Rabbi learning upstairs in his chair)

RABBI: Nope. I won't be fooled this time. (Rabbi buries his nose in his book as Jono swims by.)

JONO: Wheeeeee!

[THE END]

KI TEITZEI

(The Sign)

JONO: Good evening and welcome to the Rabbi Itche Kadoozy show weekly news program. Tonight's breaking news takes us to central park where my pet Gefilte Fish has handcuffed himself to a tree. Live on the scene at this very moment is our on-location breaking news and senior waffle eating correspondent…me.

JONO: Jono.

JONO: Jono, tell us what's going on out there…

JONO: Well Jono, It seems that Gefilte Fish has handcuffed himself to a tree, claiming that he is waiting for a revelation from G-d. (Turns to G-Fish). Excuse me, mr. Gefilte Fish, if I may have a few words with you…

G-FISH: Can't talk now, waiting for G-d. Oh, there he is now!

JONO: Ladies and gentlemen this is an unprecedented moment....

G-FISH: Oh, sorry, false alarm. It was just an ice-cream truck.

JONO: ICE-CREAM TRUCK?!? Oh man, I already took like six ice-cream breaks today. I think the producers are getting concerned. Oh well. Anyway, If I may ask, why are you sitting outside this grossitating tent, chained to a tree with what seems to be an Ethernet cable, waiting for G-d?

G-FISH: Well, sir, if you must know, I'm doing it because of this week's Torah portion.

JONO: Guh?

G-FISH: In this week's Torah portion, G-d reveals himself to Abraham while he is sitting outside his tent.

JONO: And therefore you tied yourself to a tree with a network cable.

G-FISH: Yes.

JONO: Makes sense. (Pause) Ok, I just lied to you. I'm sorry. That doesn't make any sense at all. Let's go live via sattlelite to our senior rabbinical correspondent who may be able to shed some light on this situation. Rabbi Itche Kadoozy?

RABBI: Hi, Jono. I think I may be able to shed some light on this situation with a story from one of the great Chassidic masters of our time.

JONO: And I thing I can eat a roast beef sandwich while you do so.

RABBI: There's a story about one of the great Jewish leaders of recent times, Rabbi Sholom Dovber of Lubavitch, when he was a small boy. He asked his grandfather—if G-d revealed himself to Abraham, why won't he reveal himself to me?

G-FISH: Oh boy, this is it! I think I see Him! My G-dly revelation has finally come! Oh...no. That was just a squirrel eating a discarded hotdog.

JONO: Lucky squirrel.

RABBI: From this story we learn that we have entered unprecedented times, when anybody, regardless of what level they may be on, even a child, can have a strong and sincere desire to experience the holy and spiritual parts of life, by learning Torah and doing Mitzvot. Jono, back to you.

JONO: (Finishing sandwich) Oh…yeah. So there you have it folks, something about Torah and mitzvot.

G-FISH: Oh boy!— no, that's not G-D, just a stray helium balloon. Sorry.

JONO: HEY! That's MY Ethernet cord!!!

[THE END]

NITZAVIM-VAYAYLECH

(The Sit-In)

RABBI: Hello, and welcome to the Parsha Report. You'll have to excuse the mess, we only have 2 more shows left after this and Roy started cleaning up early.

(Roy walks in carrying a heavy box)

ROY: It's called "striking". I'm striking the set.

RABBI: Roy, please, we're in the middle of a show here. I'd expect a little bit more professionalism from you.

ROY: I'm sorry, Rabbi, but today is the only day I could get my friend Marvin to come help me move these boxes.

MARVIN: (Comes in carrying a big heavy box) Watch out, watch out. Comin' through, hot soup, move it or loose it. (Stops at Rabbi Itche and removes his hat respectfully) Very nice to meet you, Rabbi. Any friend of Roy is friend of mine. Anytime you need help movin' or disposin' of anything, give me a call.

RABBI: Well.. that's very nice, Marvin.

MARVIN: No problem, only 5 bucks a box. (Continues moving) Ok, hot soup comin through, move it people, move it! (Roy and Marvin exit)

RABBI: Anywho, this week's Torah portion is actually a combination of two Torah portions, and the name of this double Parsha is the first word of each of the two portions—Netzavim-Veyeilech.

(Marvin and Roy come back in carrying a big 2x4. they talk as they walk and push Rabbi Itche off screen)

MARVIN: So he says to me, he says, Marvin, I don't want you drving that forklift on the highway no more. So I says to him, I says, Pete, I'll stop driving the forklift on the highway if you stop using the jack hammer as a can opener.

(Marvin and Roy pass and Rabbi Itche cautiously re-enters the frame)

RABBI: (Clears his throat) The word Netzavim, means standing, and the word Vayeilech means "he went" or "he walked." Each of these words are just the first of 2 different stories in the Torah, but combined as one name of this week's double Torah portion, they can also teach us a lesson.

MARVIN: (OS) Ok, wiseguy, what's the big idea? I gotta move that box!

JONO: (Off screen) No way! You wanna move this box, you gotta move me with it!

MARVIN: (OS) You got it, wise guy!

(Marvin enters carrying a big box with Jono popping up out of it!)

RABBI: This is ridiculous! I'm in the middle of a show here, what do you guys think you're doing?!

MARVIN: I was just tryin' to clear this studio out for you's guys, and wise guy here decided to play games!

JONO: It's not a game, Marvin, it's a sit-in. The form of non-violent civil disobedience that practically ended racial segregation in this country! Ever heard of it?! Oh, and I like being in a box.

RABBI: What exactly are you protesting, Jono? Do you have something against cardboard boxes?

JONO: Why of course not, Rabbi! Don't be silly, cardboard boxes are a man's best friend. Oh no wait, that's a dog. Or maybe a dog in a cardboard box, or a cardboard box dog…The point is, I'm protesting the end of the Parsha Report. This show is my life! Or at least it's the only thing I got going for my resume these days besides nose inspector. I'm dangerously under qualified for every other job on the face of the earth. This is all I got. And I'm not going to let it be taken away from me by this…this…monster!

RABBI: Now calm down, Jono, let's not start with name calling.

MARVIN: Well, I am technically a monster…

JONO: Look, Rabbi, I've worked too hard to make this show the marginal success that it is, and I'm not gonna give that up. I'm staying right here on the Parsha Report set ready to disrupt your attempt at making a serious show with my youthful antics week after week for as long as I can!

MARVIN: I'm just doin' my job, wise guy. Roy told me I gotta get the studio cleared up to make room for a new set, and that's what I'm tryin' to do, ok, wiseguy?

JONO: You can see, Rabbi, how I'm really stuck between a box and a hard place here.

RABBI: So let me run this by you guys to see if I understand all this—Jono is sitting still in that box, refusing to budge, in order to avoid losing

everything he's achieved with this show, and Marvin is trying help us move out our old stuff so we can do new things. Is that right?

JONO AND MARVIN: Right

RABBI: Listen guys, this is exactly what the name of this week's Torah portion is teaching us…

JONO: Oh boy, here's the part where the rabbi kills two boxes with one stone by conveniently resolving my personal dilemmas with a lesson from this week's Torah portion.

RABBI: Nitzovim Vayeilech—Standing and Going. Judaism demands both from us. Jono's right, we have to stand firm in our traditions and our Jewish identity and not lose one tiny bit of the beautiful heritage we have. But Marvin is also right—we also have to grow as Jews, to always try to do good things we weren't able to do before. Now do you guys understand what you should do?

JONO: Nope.

RABBI: This is infuriating. One of these days I really wish you would listen to what I have to say to you Jono.

JONO: From your mouth to boxes ears.

RABBI: I…Give up.

MARVIN: You know, that was a very nice speech, Rabbi, but you didn't clear up how to actually resolve my little situation with wiseguy here.

RABBI: No need to thank me, Marvin, I'm just doing my job.

MARVIN: Uhhhh…

JONO: Don't worry Marvin, he's always a little bit cryptic.

MARVIN: Hey, wise guy, I got an idea.

JONO: And I'm pretending to listen.

MARVIN: How's about you let me strike this Parsha Report set, and when Roy and I build a new one…

JONO: No.

MARVIN: Let me finish, wise guy.

JONO: Fine.

MARVIN: We clean up the set and when we build a new one, I'll give you a box to sit in off-stage of it.

JONO: Hmmm.

RABBI: Jono! That's a perfect compromise! We get to change and grow as a show, and you get to.... Sit in a box!

JONO: Hmmm...throw in one of my super wasome peanut butter and jelly sandwich grilled cheese sandwich sandwiches...patent pending!... and you got yourself a deal.

MARVIN: Done. I have no idea what that is, but if you come with me to the kitchen, I'll whip one up for you's right now.

JONO: Good. I'm so hungry I could eat a box!

RABBI: That's ridiculous.

JONO: There's more than one way to skin a box? A box saved is a box earned? When in Rome do as the boxes? One in the hand is worth two in the box? You win some you lose some...boxes? When life gives you boxes make lemonade? I keep my friends close and my cardboard boxes even closer? Life is like a box of boxes?

[THE END]

HAAZINU

(A Chat with Planet Earth)

RABBI: Hello, and welcome once again to the Parsha Report. This week, in Parshat Haazinu, Moses appoints the heavens and the earth as eternal witnesses to observe whether or not the Jewish People will continue to fulfill G-d's commandments for all time. With us now to comment on this is the Earth. Earth?

EARTH: Oh, hello. I'm the Earth. Yes, the whole wide world. Now, you might ask yourself if Earth has hands. Well, of course I have hands. How am I supposed to drink tea without hands? Now, of course everything I do has an effect on you, because I'm the whole world. But watch this —— (Makes funny sound). All right, that just collapsed about 500 skyscrapers. But did you know that everything you do has an effect on me? It's true. It affects me at my core, at the center of the earth, which is the center of me. Because I'm the Earth. Oh, one moment please...Brazil is itching me.

Every mitzvah you do has an effect on me. I feel it. For instance, right now, someone right here is respecting their mother and father. Oh, oh, and right now somebody down here is giving tzedakah. Oh yes, yes, and over here somebody just didn't steal, which is good. I mean, he didn't steal. He wanted to, but he didn't. Oh, this, this is just an itch I have in Canada right now. Oh yes, oh. Oh, that—ah.

Now, I'll illustrate with a story. The other day I was at lunch with the moon, and there was a moon here, that conceited, hotheaded braggart he is. And I'm going to tell him so. For instance, a few centuries back I remember the moon and I were having a heated discussion. And the moon told me Earth, you are boring. And I told him, Moon, you are a conceited, hotheaded braggart. And the moon said to me, touché.

Anyways, back to the story. The moon and I were having lunch. Well, it started out as lunch, but then I turned around to get a coffee and then it became dinner, due to my position in relation to the sun. But then I turned back and it became lunch again. And the moon started bragging, the hotheaded, conceited braggart that he is, and he started saying, oh, I'm so happy, my life is so great. There are no people living on me, no people polluting me, no people littering on me, no people making wars on me. Woo-woo-woo.

I said to him, Moon, there may be people living on me, making wars on me, polluting me, littering me, but those same people can make the decision to do something good. I have people living on me that can celebrate Shabbat, people living on me that can celebrate Rosh Hashanah, which mind you is a celebration of my creation. I have people living on me that will take their hard-carncd moncy and givc it away to somconc lcss fortunatc than thcm, rcgardlcss of how poorly dressed or foul-smelling that recipient may be. And then the moon gave some lame excuse why he had to leave; he had to go ready for an eclipse or something. And I said, oh hogwash. And he said, what? And I said, hogwash, it's an expression. I'm not quite sure what it means myself.

[THE END]

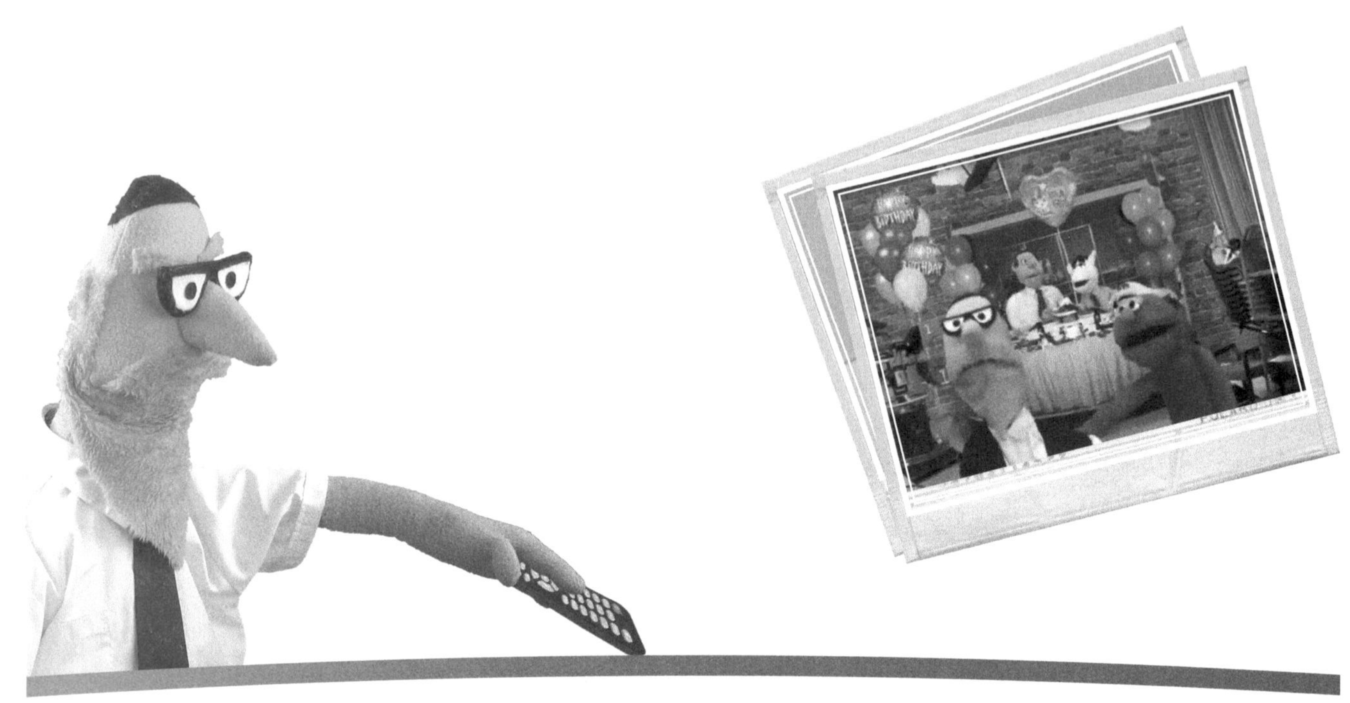

VEZOT HABRACHA

(The Last Show?)

JONO: Well, after forty some odd episodes, the Parsha Report has finally reached it's last episode. It's difficult for all of us here at the show, but we're trying to keep a positive attitude. We're even planning a surprise retirement party for the rabbi, and I think we're doing a pretty good job of keeping it under wraps.

(Cut to Jono and Rabbi Itche in the studio. Jono is holding up a giant novelty card for Rabbi Itche to sign)

JONO: Hey, rabbi, could you sign this giant novelty card?

RABBI: (As he signs) Sure, Jono, what's this for?

JONO: Oops. Nothing. (Runs off)

RABBI: (Saying out loud what he is writing) Best of luck, we'll all miss you. Signed, Rabbi.

(Cut back to Jono on the roof)

JONO: We all have our different ways of dealing with the show ending.

(Cut to Larry Goldstein in his office, studying a a huge legal book)

JONO: (Voice-over:) Larry Goldstein has been staying up all night for past 2 weeks looking for legal precedent to keep the show on the air.

LARRY: I've got it! Two words—indentured servitude. All we have to do is make Rabbi Itche Kadoozy our indentures servant, and we can keep the Parsha Report going for as long as it takes for the supreme court to explain to us that it's virtually identical to and just as illegal as slavery.

(Cut to empty Parsha Report studio)

JONO: (Voice-over:) Roy is trying to make peace with his feelings by way of ancient marshall arts he learned when he used to live in japan.

(Roy jumps down from the ceiling in full ninja attire, swinging nun-chucks)

(Cut to Jono on the roof)

JONO: G-Fish is trying to keep up his tough exterior, but we can all tell that it's getting to him too.

(Cut to G-Fish on his cell-phone)

G-FISH: Alan, I want you to get me out of this contract as soon as…yes, I know this is the last episode, but every day I continue this gig is one more kick to the stomach of my career as a serious actor. I'M CLASSICALLY TRAINED!

(Back to roof)

JONO: Then there's me. I'm still not sure exactly how to deal with the end of the Parsha Report.

(Cut to Jono in the park with a boom box)

JONO: (Voice-over:) First a held a memorial service for the show in central park.

(Jono hits play on the boom box and bagpipe music starts to play. Jono stands solemny looking down toward the ground. Cut to the ground where we see a big VHS tape labeled "Parsha Reports (Syndicated version)." Jono places a daisy on the tape.) I'm sorry to see you go, show. Although, I'm not sorry to see YOU go, stupid syndicated version of the show! You took out the best parts! (Cut to shortened version of the sit-com credits. The theme song has been shortened to "people can be so different, or so they say. Good friends, good times.")

(Back to roof)

JONO: Next I tried pooring out my emotions to a psychologist.

(Cut to Jono at Gilbert poznanski's office. Jono is laying on the couch.)

DR. G: Tell me more about that dream.

JONO: Well, after the giant humming bird landed, I got off, thanked him for the ride, and lloked around, only to find that I was in a magical cartoonland...where all the trees and lampposts talked...and owed me money. (Cut to Jono frolicking in cartoon land. Every ounce in a while trees and lampposts say "hellooooo!" and hand Jono wads of cash. Cut back to office)

DR. G: (Writing on note pad) Very interesting, go on. (Cut to note pad to reveal ridiculous doodles.)

(Back to roof)

JONO: I even tried Roy's way.

(Cut to Jono doing karate moves in the studio. Roy jumps in from ceiling in ninja suit)

JONO: AAAAAAAH!

ROY: Hey, Jono. Nice moves, but try loosening up those muscles. The strength should come from the focusing your energies, not from tensing up your muscles.

JONO: Please don't jump kick me in the throat.

(Back to roof)

JONO: Finally I resorted to drowning my sorrows in chocolate milk.

(Cut to Jono and Marvin sitting at a table with chocolate milk in front of them)

JONO: (In a chocolate milk stupor) I…I…idonowadimgonnado. Ahhhhh (Crying)

MARVIN: You done yet?

JONO: (Snaps out instantly) give me about five more minutes. (Back to stupor) I…I never told him…I never told him that I…I actually like doing the sho-o-o-ow. (Crying. Jono slumps over the table sobbing)

MARVIN: (Looks at his wrist) Isn't it time for the Rabbi's retirement party?

JONO: (Snaps out) Oh, wow. Thanks for the heads up Marvin. (Jono runs out)

MARVIN: You know, I think that kid is gonna be ok.

(Jono jumps on a chair and rolls over a table and lands on his back on the floor.)

JONO: (In severe pain) I'm ok.

(Cut to studio. The studio is decorated with balloons and streamers. Roy, Larry, Gilbert, G-Fish, and pigeon are mingling. Jono is not there)

G-FISH: (Talking on cell-phone) Well, I'd love to meet you for lunch and maybe toss some ideas around. What? Well, I'm trained primarily in opera, but I do consider myself somewhat of a octuple threat.

ROY: Shhhhh. Everybody get ready, he's coming in.

(Rabbi enters and everybody yells "SURPRIZE!")

RABBI: What? What's going on here?

ROY: Best of luck on your retirement rabbi. We'll all miss the show.

RABBI: What? Retirement? Where's Jono?

ROY: I don't know. He's been taking this pretty hard, he's probably gone off somewhere to…cope. (Looks at wrist) Oh, I gotta get to the airport. See you later, everybody, it's been great working with you.

(Cut to Jono on the roof driving his rc hummer back and forth.)

JONO: (Voice-over:) I don't know if it was the fear of the show ending that was keeping me from that party, or the confusion of trying to figure out what comes next, or the fact that Roy forgot that I requested mild salsa.

(Cut to party)

PIGEON: (Holding a tortilla chip) Oh dear. (Choked up, holding back tears or pain.) Is this extra spicy? Oh…wow. My eyes…. I'm blacking out.

(Back to roof)

JONO: (Voice-over:) But something was making this really hard for me.

RABBI: (Comes out from the stair well, onto the roof.) Jono!

JONO: Rabbi, Rabbi, Rabbi! (Laugh track) How did you find me up here?

RABBI: You always come up here to think.

JONO: Yeah, I know, but I never appeared up here before on any other episode. We never established that.

RABBI: I know, but following the continuity of this episode, and for the sake of raising the emotional stakes it just made sense to meet you up here. Look, Jono, the show's not over.

JONO: Rabbi, you don't have to do this.

RABBI: I'm not retiring. Vzot Habrachah may be the last Torah portion in the Torah, but learning the weekly Torah portion doesn't stop after that, and neither does our show. Every year on Simchat Torah, we finish the last Torah portion, and then we begin again right then and there with Parshat Bereishit—the first Torah portion.

JONO: Sooooo...We're doing the Parsha Report again this year?

RABBI: No, we've done that. It's time for something new. Just like when I learn the Torah portions again this year, I hope to learn new things I didn't know last year. The same is true with our show. There's new things to teach about, and just as soon as Roy get's back from his trip to japan, we'll start working on the next project.

(Cut to Roy in a Japanese village, surrounded by ninjas, then cut back to roof)

RABBI: Do you feel better now?

JONO: Yeah, thanks. I had a backup plan, though. I tricked everybody into signing a new contract for this year. But I guess now I don't need that. Thanks rabbi. (They hug; cut to party)

G-FISH: What do you mean you can't get me out of it? Well how was I supposed to know it was contract, it looked like a giant novelty card!

(Fade out then back in to card. The inside has printed on it, in comic sans "Wishing you the best of luck on your retirement!" In smaller letters "We, the undersigned, do hereby commit to another year of the Rabbi Itche Kadoozy Show." Around it, on the rest of the card, are all the signatures of the cast-members, including Rabbi. (Fade out)

[THE END]

WASOME!

THE QUEST FOR FISH

Show creator and writer **Dovid Taub** with **Rabbi Itche**

INTRO & BEHIND-THE-SCENES

by Dovid Taub

"The Rabbi Itche Kadoozy Show" has always been comprised of an interesting mix of genres, not just from series to series, but even within a given series or episode. It was always a comedy and always educational, but it was also sometimes a sitcom or a satirical news report or a farce. For "The Quest for Fish" I chose yet another genre, making this series a Chassidic-puppet-educational-action-adventure-comedy. I'm still petitioning the Academy Awards to add that category.

I started writing this with absolutely no clue where i was going. In Chapter 2, I introduced a "Mystery Man." He was clearly a henchman of some sort, giving updates to his boss over the phone, but I had no idea who was on the other end of that call. Eventually, though, it became clear that this was a story about identity—both personal and communal—and was the perfect vehicle to explore the journey of the Israelites from slavery in Egypt to becoming a people at Mt. Sinai.

As for the other end of that phone call—SPOILER ALERT—Geoffrey Juan Delatiste was a namc that Real Jono and I made up as teenagers in 1998. Over the years we added some background including the fact that Mr. Delatiste is a cryptozoologist.

Fast-forward a few years to me scratching my head trying to figure out who should be the antagonist in a story about a magical talking Gefilte Fish trying to reunite with the rest of his kind, and eventually Geoffrey Juan Delatiste popped into my mind.

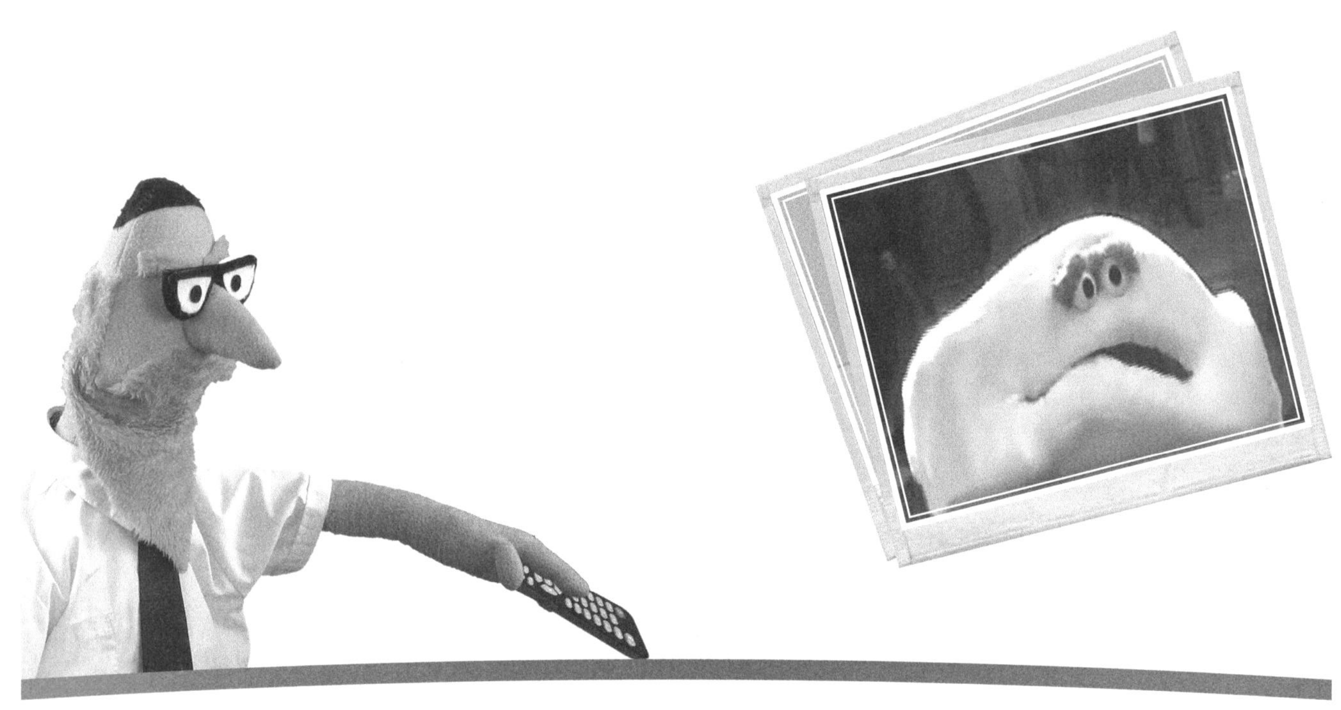

EPISODE 1: ORIGINS

SCENE: Jono and G-Fish are walking down the streets of Chinatown.

JONO: Ok, G-Fish, we've been wandering through these streets for hours and you still haven't told me what we're looking for. Not that I don't enjoy wandering through the streets—because I spend a majority of me week doing it, but...

G-FISH: I'm looking for that creepy shop you bought me from. Do you Remember it at all?

JONO: Oh yeah! I'd like to find that place again too. Aside from selling Gefilte Fish, monkey's paws, and mugwais, that spooky old guy who owned it also made a TOTALLY RADICAL smoothie!

G-FISH: Stay focused Jono. I'm trying to find more information about my past. The memories I have of my life in the ocean with my family are through the eyes of a child. I want to know more about my Gefilte Fish heritage.

JONO: Fine, but after we get that, can we get smoothies?

SCENE: We are in the office of a big movie producer in California. His big fancy office chair is facing away from us, so we only see the back of the chair, but hear the producer's voice.

PRODUCER: Goldstein, get in here.

(Ari Goldstein, a young man with sunglasses who thinks he's a big shot runs in quickly)

ARI: Hey, yeah, at your service, what's up, need me to bounce some ideas?

PRODUCER: No. You don't have ideas, you're my danish boy, don't forget that.

(Through the window next to the door we see a sad intern sitting at a desk)

INTERN: (Sadly) I tot I vas yor Danish boy.

PRODUCER: Look, you said you knew a film student who wanted an internship here, right?

ARI: Yeah, his name is Jono, he's…. friends with my dad's rabbi.

PRODUCER: Creepy. Get him on the phone.

ARI: (Pulls out his cell-phone and dials. Larry Goldstein answers and we go to split screen) Dad?

LARRY: Ari! How are you, kiddo? Ha!

ARI: Fine, thanks, Dad. Look, is Jono around?

LARRY: Actually he's in Chinatown right now helping Gefilte Fish find his roots.

ARI: (To producer) He's not there.

PRODUCER: And?

ARI: And…He's…Like not there?

PRODUCER: Then…Like, where is he Ari?!?! It's always like pulling teeth with you!

ARI: Oh…He's in Chinatown helping some Gefilte Fish find his roots.

PRODUCER: (We cut to a front view of the chair, revealing that the producer is in fact a Gefilte Fish.) A Gefilte Fish you say? (Do-do-dooooooo!)

ARI: Yeah. Oh. I'm sorry…I didn't…. I mean…Am I fired?

SCENE: Rabbi is sitting in his living room in Brooklyn, NY, writing and Jono enters)

JONO: Hey, Rabbi, Rabbi, Rabbi!

RABBI: Hi, Jono. So how did it go in china town?

JONO: We couldn't find that creepy little shop. It's like it just disappeared.

RABBI: That's Strange.

JONO: And by disappeared I mean we saw the landlord—or a member of the Chinese Triad Mafia—evict the guy from the shop and smash up any evidence that would lead us to Gefilte fish's family. But I did get a smoothie and this cool cool Chinese finger trap while we there.

RABBI: Oh, I love those things, can I see it? (Reaches out)

JONO: Eh! (Pulls it away) the Chinese finger trap is not a toy. It's highly dangerous weapon used by ancient Chinese warriors to frustrate their enemies.

RABBI: Right.

JONO: So how are you doing with the show? Have you written anything yet?

RABBI: Well, the month of Nissan is starting this week. It's a very special month for many reasons, but it also happens to be the month in

which all three of our forefathers, Abraham Isaac and Jacob, were born.

JONO: Oooh! Happy birthday!

RABBI: (Awkwardly) Thank you. So I figure I'll write about the importance of learning about our ancestors; through understanding who our forefathers were, we can better understand who we are us Jews, and why that heritage is so important.

JONO: Cool cool. Thank's for the heads up, I'll go think of something reckless and irresponsible yet strangely apropos that I can do to disrupt the show.

(G-Fish and Larry rush in excitedly)

G-FISH: Everybody, Everybodeeeeeeeeeee! I have wonderful news that I can't wait to tell you! You tell them, Larry.

LARRY: Well, my son Ari called me today.

JONO: The one who works for a producer in Hollywood?

LARRY: Yeah. Well, it turns out that the producer himself is actually a Gefilte Fish! Ha!

JONO: That's Great! Why do I care!? (…this said with the same enthusiasm as "that's great!")

RABBI: A famous movie producer that's a Gefilte Fish? Is nobody else completely baffled by this?

G-FISH: He wants me to go to Hollywood to meet with him! This may be it guys, my chance to find out more about my past!

JONO: Hooray for you! I'm going to Hollywood! Let's go pack our bags!

RABBI: I don't know. I'm supportive of G-Fish trying to find other Gefilte Fish, but I'm not sure that flying across the country to speak to a total stranger is the way to do it.

JONO: But Rabbi, G-Fish wants to learn about his Gefilte Fish heritage so he can understand who he really is. That sounds a lot like what you just said about our forefathers. (Under his breath) And I wanna go to Hollywood to get Jackie Mason to sign my scrapbook. (Show a crude scrapbook clearly made by Jono of pictures of Jackie Mason cut out and glued onto pages to look like he's hanging out with pictures and crayon drawings of Jono)

LARRY: It's true, Rabbi. When I learned about how Abraham questioned the beliefs of the society around him in order to truly understand who created the world, that meant a lot to me. Or when you taught me about how Abraham and Sarah had a special tent with doors on all sides just so they could welcome guests, that really made me think. It's only fair that we help G-Fish to have that same opportunity to learn about his Gefilte Fish heritage. Ha!

RABBI: That's an excellent point Larry. You guys are right. Let's pack our bags and get ready for the glitz and glamour of Hollywood!

CUT TO: Producer Fish and Ari walking down a truly revolting Hollywood street (Walk of fame stars, pollution, homeless people, police and/or ambulance sirens in the background, etc…) Producer hacks violently.

PRODUCER: This town's disgusting.

(Back at shul)

RABBI, JONO, G-FISH, LARRY: HOORAY!!!

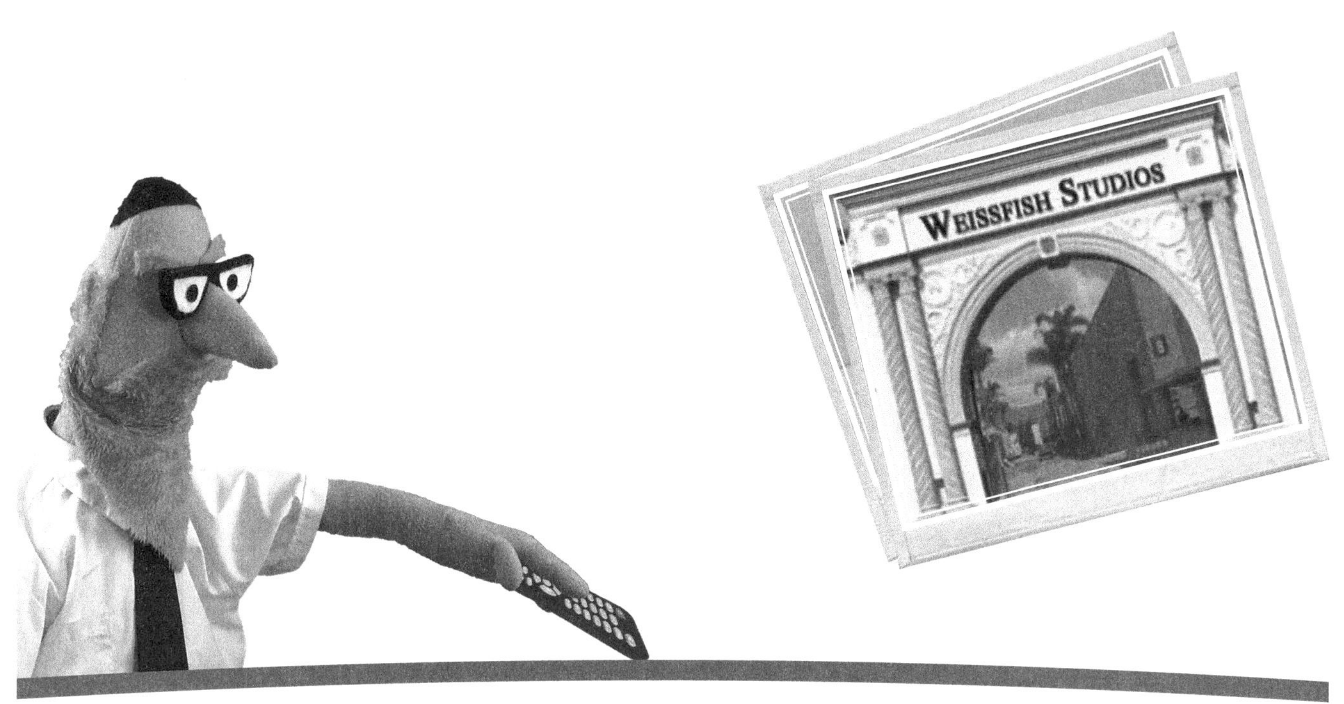

EPISODE 2: LIMITS

SCENE: Rabbi Itche, Jono, and G-Fish sit in the office of Harvey Weissfish, the movie producer.

HARVEY: It's a pleasure to have you all here. I, as you probably already know, am legendary Hollywood producing mogul Harvey Weissfish. How was your flight?

RABBI: It was…

HARVEY: Wonderful! That's wonderful to hear. Let's get straight down to business. (Look's at G-Fish) I understand you are looking for your family. Someone who can shed some light on the history and traditions of your people.

G-FISH: I'm still so shocked that I found my family so quickly.

HARVEY: Well, too bad, you haven't.

JONO: Boooo!

HARVEY: But I may be able to get you in touch with them—or at least someone who can find someone who knows a guy who can help you find a guy to find them.

JONO: Yaaaaay!

HARVEY: I met a very interesting Gefilte Fish couple in china last year while we were out there shooting a picture.

JONO: Ooh! Which one, Harvey?

HARVEY: Please, call me Mr. Weissfish. The picture was called "A foggy night in London." They wouldn't let us shoot in London, so we had to shoot in china. Slap a clock on the great wall and you'd be surprised how much in looks like big ben. It's called thinking outside the box. Try it sometime.

JONO: (Enthusiastically) I'll agree to now, but forget to later.

HARVEY: Who is this kid? I love this kid. Never change. I mean that. (Turns back to G-Fish) Now G-Fish, you told me on the phone that you were purchased from a shop in Chinatown, which means there's a good chance you, like my $140,000 rug you're dripping jelly broth all over, may have been imported from China. I'll take care of the air fare and I want you and your friends to go there tonight.

RABBI: China?!

G-FISH: This is all so much to take in. Why are you willing to do this for me? You don't even know me.

HARVEY: I don't have to know you. I was you once. I was a young Gefilte Fish searching for his past, and I want that search to be easier for you than it was for me. That and I want the movie rights to your story.

JONO: They sure act like they're related.

HARVEY: You are all acquainted with my danish boy Ari. He'll be going with you on your journey. He can get you anything you need—a cab, airplane tickets, or perhaps a bottle of spring water.

RABBI: That would be nice actually, I'll have a water.

HARVEY: Not now.

ARI: Excuse me, sir, but you didn't tell me about this. I mean, this isn't part of my Job description.

HARVEY: And it's not part of mine to listen to your ideas for computer animated movies about talking molecules. (Turns to G-Fish) You all have quite an adventure ahead of you, so you better go get yourselves ready.

(Everyone get's up to leave)

RABBI: Thank you for meeting with us, Harvey.

HARVEY: Mr. Weissfish.

JONO: It was truly an honor, sir. I'm a huge fan of your films. "A Foggy Night In Kuala Lampur" was a masterpiece. Where do you get all your original ideas?

HARVEY: Well, that's the real reason why I hired the danish boy.

ARI: Oh, wow...Thank you, sir. I knew that underneath the insults, hostility and bossiness, you were just trying to bring out my amazing, untapped potential.

HARVEY: Not you, Goldstein, the Danish boy!

(Through the doorway we see the Danish boy waving.)

DANISH BOY: I Lav yoo meester veissfeesh!

(Rabbi is on a pay phone at the Los Angeles Airport)

RABBI: Thank you so much for understanding, Faiggie.

MRS. K: You're a good man, Rabbi. I know how important this is to Gefilte Fish and I respect you for caring so much about helping other people...and fish people.

LOUD SPEAKER: Last call for flight 304 to Beijing China.

RABBI: Oh, I have to go, Faiggie. Send my love to the grandkids.

MRS. K: Safe travels, Rabbi!

(Rabbi hangs up and joins G-Fish, Jono, and Ari.)

ARI: This is absurd. It's bad enough I'm Weissfish's danish boy, but now he's hiring me out to be other people's danish boy?!

JONO: Wait, I'm confused. I thought the Danish boy was the Danish boy.

ARI: The Danish boy's not the Danish boy. I'm the Danish boy! The Danish boy is just A Danish boy!

JONO: Oohhh. Ok, now I get it. (Whispering to G-Fish) No I don't.

(Transition to a shot of the airplane flying through the sky. Cut to an interior shot of the plane.)

JONO: Ari, can you get me another bag of peanuts? Thanks. You're a prince. Never change. I mean that.

ARI: This is totally insane. Look, I understand that you guys have something important you have to do, but I'm supposed to be in Hollywood building my career! (Sadly..) Ha!

RABBI: Aside from Jono's ridiculous requests that you do not need to and should not do, doesn't it mean something to you that you're helping somebody else? That you're helping Gefilte Fish find his family?

ARI: Oh, yeah, by getting you a bottle of mineral water?

JONO: Oh, thank you danish boy, I could really go for a mineral water.

RABBI: Not now, Jono.

ARI: I don't have time to help other people right now. I should be back in California weaseling my way into the movie biz and coming up with bad ideas about robot dance contests. As soon as we land, I'm getting right back on this plane and going back.

JONO: Why do you have to get back on the plane? Why don't you just stay on the plane?

G-FISH: Well, they need to deplane everybody first, restock the pretzels, you know how it is.

PILOT: (Over the speaker) Ladies and gentlemen, this is your pilot speaking, just giving you an update. On behalf of all of us here at Dotcomairways.com we hope you're enjoying your flight. We'll be landing in Beijing in about 5 hours. In the meantime, feel free to take a look out the window at the beautiful desserts of Egypt.

RABBI: That's exactly your problem, Ari.

ARI: Egypt? My Problem is Egypt? Pfffft!

RABBI: Yes. Egypt is called Mitzraim in Hebrew. It also means "narrow places" or limitations. You are a slave in Egypt just like our ancestors were 3000 years ago. Except your "narrow place", or your limitation, is a spiritual one.

JONO: Right now my limitation is a physical one. The stewardess said I can't have a 30th bag of peanuts! But I gotta prove to G-Fish that I CAN eat my own weight in salty treats.

RABBI: Helping other people is a mitzvah, Ari, and mitzvahhs aren't always easy. Sure, some of them come naturally, or by habit, but others just seem to be going against our nature. Building up your own career is very important, but it's something you already know you're good at.

ARI: Yeah.

G-FISH: And not everyone can say they're a danish boy. Except maybe the Danish boy.

RABBI: You're not helping. The point is, by helping us with this trip you're doing something good and something completely new to you, something you haven't been able to do well, or at all before. So take the opportunity to push past that limitation and break free from your own Egypt. (Pause) Egypt? Wait…Why are flying over Egypt?!

PILOT: Ladies and Gentlemen, this is your former pilot speaking. I'm sure all of you are aware of Dotcomairways.com's outstanding record of

punctual flights as well as our truly gracious personnel…let's give them a hand, shall we? (People applause) What you probably don't know is that about 5 minutes ago Wallstreet announced that our airline was purchased in a hostile corporate take-over by a popular and extremely profitable internet search engine that searches for internet search engines. The new company is subsequently suspending all Dotcomairways.com flights indefinitely…including this one…the one you're on…effective immediately. Soooo…we're going to be landing in Egypt, because it's right below us and has become your new point of destination. (Annoyed grumbling is heard, until the plane suddenly dives down and the grumbling is replaced with shock.)

(Rabbi, Jono, G-Fish, and Ari are sitting in the airport in Egypt, two days before Passover.)

JONO: There sure are a lot of Egyptians in China.

RABBI: Jono, we're not….. (Sigh) I'm not even going to try.

JONO: I'm just kidding, I know we're not in china. (Leans over to G-Fish and whispers) actually I have no idea.

(Suddenly, the group spots a mysterious man with a sign that reads "KADOOZY")

ARI: Hey, Rabbi, that guy must be waiting for us. Let's go see what he wants.

JONO: And/or ask him for a ride to the local six flags.

(The group approaches the mystery man.)

RABBI: Excuse me, I'm Rabbi Itche Kadoozy. Are you looking for me?

MAN: (Looks at G-Fish) You are helping a Gefilte Fish on his journey. I have been sent to help you.

G-FISH: Hooray for meeeee!

MAN: But you must follow me quickly.

(Transition to the group trekking through the dessert. Eventually they stand at the entrance of a pyramid.)

MAN: This is our destination. You will find what you are looking for here.

G-FISH: My Parents? They're here?

MAN: (Pause) Maybe.

JONO: The only parent we're gonna find in there is a MUMMY! (Looking around for validation) Get it? Mummy?

(No one responds)

MAN: Hurry. Into the pyramid. But you must leave your personal belongings here. I will guard them until you come out. I must not enter the pyramid with you.

ARI: Why not? Afraid of an ancient curse?

MAN: (Sadly) No. I'm afraid of the dark.

(The group cautiously enters the pyramid and suddenly the door slams behind them. They are stuck.)

JONO: Waaa! I want my mummy!......Get it? Mummy?

EPISODE 3: OBSTACLES

SCENE: Rabbi Itche, Jono, G-Fish, and Ari are trapped inside a pyramid.

JONO: Waaa! I'm so scared! I want my....

G-FISH: You make one more mummy joke and I'll tell everybody your deep dark secret about your unmanageable fear of flowers.

JONO: Fine. But just for the record, you sort of just told everybody anyways.

ARI: This is horrible. Absolutely horrible. I can't believe we're stuck in this musty, dingy, horrible pyramid!

JONO: Could you say horrible one more time?

RABBI: What about that tunnel? (Show shot of a tunnel leading deeper into the pyramid)

G-FISH: I'll go scout it out. (G-Fish approaches the entrance to the tunnel, takes a deep breath, and looks back) Well, here I go guys. Wish me luck. (Enters tunnel.)

(Wait a few seconds while the rest of the group looks around nervously. Then…)

G-FISH: (Off screen) I SAID WISH ME LUCK!

ALL: (Very quickly and apologetically) Good luck!

(Transition to group 1 hour later. They are all much more tired and depressed. G-Fish pops out of the tunnel.)

G-FISH: It's no use. The tunnel is completely dark and it just keeps on going. There's no way of knowing if it even leads to the outside, and even if it does, who's to say we'd make it to the end?

ARI: Forget it, it's hopeless. The tunnel probably just leads deeper into the pyramid. We're doomed.

RABBI: Do you all realize what type of situation we're in here? I mean, it's a day before Passover and we're stuck in a pyramid! No matzah, no Haggadah, no bitter herbs! We're stuck in Egypt and we can't even make a Seder!

JONO: Haha. We should start calling somebody bitter herb. Preferably somebody named herb, but I guess Ari will do fine too.

(Shot of Ari just staring in Jono's direction, not amused)

G-FISH: Look, we gotta get out of here and I've got a plan. Watch and learn, people. (G-Fish moves back, pauses, takes a breath, and then screams at the top of his lungs as he charges at the door and hits with a splat.) Ow. Good thing I don't have bones. (Runs back and charges the door a second time, again with no results.)

ARI: I've got a more practical plan—give up and accept the fact that we're stuck here. Forever. Like that guy. (Cut to sarcophagus leaning in the corner) (Sadly) Ha.

JONO: Cheer up, bitter Herb, it's not that bad.

ARI: NOT THAT BAD?! ALL OF OUR STUFF IS GONE! WER'RE LOCKED INSIDE A PYRAMID! THE ONLY POSSIBLE WAY OUT IS A TUNNEL THAT LEADS TO NOWHERE! I MEAN, IT COULDN'T GET ANY WORSE IF WE TRIED! (Slams fist against wall and a rock falls on his head.) OW!

JONO: Well, Rabbi, how about you, you have a plan?

RABBI: There's not really much we can do. The only thing we can do now is pray. (Rabbi begins to recite a prayer by heart.)

JONO: With all due respect, Rabbi, that doesn't sound like doing anything. That sounds like waiting for G-d to do something. Now, if that's what it comes to, then fine, but I'm not ready to give up and pull in huge favors from The Big Guy In The Sky just yet!

RABBI: Big Guy In The Sky?

JONO: Look, I don't want this to be the first Passover night that I didn't get to sleep through a Seder! So seriously, Rabbi, hit me with the old school stuff—what did our ancestors do when they were stuck during the time of the original Passover?

RABBI: Wow, Jono, are you delirious?

JONO: Maybe, so answer quickly before I go totally nuts.

RABBI: Well…ok…let me think…(Kind of nervous about the possibility of Jono going nuts if he doesn't answer quick enough) Well, after G-d freed the Jews from Egypt, he told them to start walking towards Mount Sinai. The only problem was that there was a sea in front of them. And Pharaoh's army chasing them from behind. They were kinda stuck.

G-FISH: Hey, wait! Did anybody try this?! (Throws himself at the wall again. Pause. Another rock falls on Ari's head.)

ARI: Ow! Stop it before this whole thing caves in on us! I told you the only thing we can do now is lose all hope.

G-FISH: Lose hope…or do THIS! (Throws himself at the wall again. Pause. Another rock falls on Ari's head.)

ARI: OW!!!! WHY?!?!?!

JONO: Go on, Rabbi, complete insanity is lurking just around the corner.

RABBI: Well…basically there were four groups: those who wanted to throw themselves in the sea, those who wanted to go back to Egypt, those who wanted to fight and those who wanted to pray….

JONO: Blah blah blah and that's why we should pray. I'm gonna go go crazy now.

RABBI: No. Actually, they were all wrong.

JONO: Whuuuuu?

RABBI: G-d told them to walk towards Mount Sinai, and none of those plans matched up with that.

JONO: Whuuuuuuu?

RABBI: So while everybody was arguing, this guy by the name of Nachshon just started walking, and as soon as the water reached past his head—that's when the sea split!

JONO: Then that's what we have to do too—just start walking. It's almost Passover and we don't have any matzah and no way to make a Seder, so we can't stay here. I don't know where that tunnel leads, but it's our only chance.

G-FISH: That tunnel might lead nowhere!

JONO: And it might lead somewhere!

RABBI: Jono's right. It's our only chance.

ARI: We could do nothing.

JONO: Nothing is not an option, Bitter Herb!

G-FISH: Wait, nothing is not an option. That's a double-negative. That means everything is an option?

JONO: No, not everything, just one thing.

G-FISH: So nothing is an option besides that one thing?

JONO: No, just the one thing, going through the tunnel.

G-FISH: What?

JONO: Huh?

RABBI: Enough with the grammatical confusion! Let's just go through the tunnel!

(They enter the tunnel. A short music montage is shown of them walking through the pitch black tunnel. Eventually a small speck of light can be seen through the darkness.)

G-FISH: Look, in the distance, do you see that? It's light! We're free!

(Cut to exterior of the tunnel. It is sunny and green. A beautiful spring day)

ARI: (Emotionally) Air! Clean air! And sunlight! Beautiful natural sunlight! Oh how I missed you! I never thought I'd see…(Cell-phone rings, he flips it open) Talk to me. Yeah, I was trapped in a pyramid, didn't have good reception. It's all good in the hood now.

RABBI: And look—flowers!

JONO: Flowers?! AHHHHHHHHH! (Runs around freaking out)

G-FISH: Where are we anyways?

(A man passes by)

RABBI: Excuse me, sir!

MAN: Shalom!

RABBI: Shalom! We're in Israel!

ARI: That's great. My sister Lisa is living in Israel this year. We can call her and she can probably hook us up with a Seder! Or at least one of the other 14 people that live in her studio apartment with her can.

RABBI AND G-FISH (JONO IS STILL FREAKING OUT): Hooray!

(In the distance, the man who locked them in the pyramid, we'll call him Mr. X, is seen speaking on his cell-phone.)

MR. X: Yes sir, I see them right now. No sir, I have no idea how they got out. Yes. Yes. Of course. Next time I won't let them get away.

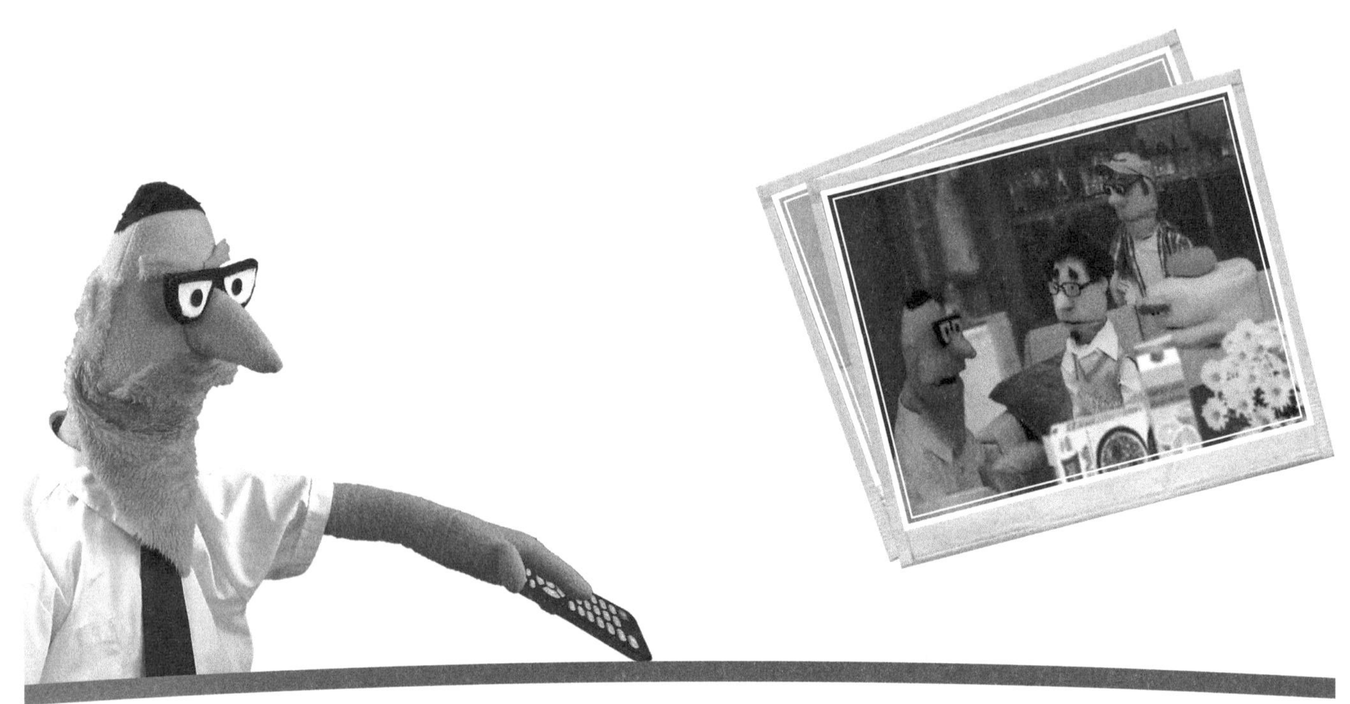

EPISODE 4: DETOURS

SCENE: Rabbi Itche, Jono, G-Fish and Ari are in Lisa Goldstein's apartment in Jerusalem. Jono is fressing slices of white bread like there's no tomorrow.

JONO: Oh bread, beautiful, fluffy, leavened bread. (Stuffs more slices in his mouth)

ARI: Jono, Passover ended a week and a half ago. Why are you still going nuts over bread?

JONO: That's between me and my bread, Ari, and I'd appreciate it if you'd respect our privacy.

(Everyone pauses and looks at Jono awkwardly.)

G-FISH: (G-Fish has been off to his own corner of the room the whole time marking off days on a calendar.) Look everybody, we've been searching for my family and the secrets of my G-Fish heritage for exactly 36 days now and we haven't made any progress. I don't know if I can wait any longer!

JONO: Me neither! I can't wait to witness the moment when G-Fish meets his family and they embrace, so I can see how exactly it is that they hug each other without arms.

ARI: Why does that intrigue you but you don't seem at all interested in how G-Fish is manipulating that marker.

(Cut to G-Fish and his calendar again. A marker is floating in front of him and exes off another calendar box.)

G-FISH: What? Can't a guy levitate a writing utensil in peace around here? (A cup floats up in front of G-Fish and he takes a sip. Everyone looks at him. He notices their stares.) WHAT?!

RABBI: You know G-Fish, your excitement about this journey reminds me of the way the Jewish people anticipated the day they would receive the Torah after G-d freed them from Egypt. They were so excited that they counted each and every day until they finally received the Torah at mount Sinai and learned what it meant to be Jewish. G-d was so pleased by this that He made it a mitzvah to for us to count the 49 days between Passover and Shavuot every year.

JONO: Ooh, 27 seconds, Rabbi. A new record! You're doing a pretty good job getting your speeches shorter.

RABBI: Thank you, Jono, I've been working on it.

(The Doorbell rings.)

JONO: Oooh!

(Doorbell rings twice)

JONO: Oooh! Oooh! It must be the pizza with extra crust I ordered!

PIZZA MAN: (Voice-over in a thick Israeli accent:) Come on, I don't hev all days.

JONO: (Looks at his bread) You'll have to excuse me, bread, but I have a pizza to attend to. (Runs to door) PIZZA PIZZA PIZAA PIZZA PIZZA PIZZA (Opens door) G-Fish!

G-FISH: 'sup.

JONO: No, I mean, the Pizza man is a G-Fish!

(Everyone moves towards or looks at the doorway. Cut to Yaniv—an Israeli G-Fish—with a stack of pizza boxes floating in front of him.)

ARI: (Calls out to Lisa who is not in the room) Lisa, G-Fish is reuniting with another member of his species, it's just the kind of sappy scene you'd be into.

LISA: (runs in with a guitar around her neck) Ooooh, I love sappy!

YANIV: (Looks at G-Fish) Ahhh, I see you also are having a G-Fish. Welcome to Israel!

G-FISH: Another G-Fish! This is amazing! This is fantastic! This is gymnastic!

RABBI: Gymnastic?

G-FISH: I dunno. It just felt like that came next. Hoo-ha! (G-Fish does a back-flip) Gymnastics!

JONO: What's your name, Israeli Pizza Delivery Fish Man?

YANIV: My names is Yaniv. Please be telling me where you are coming from.

(Transition to the group sitting around in the living room)

JONO: …so then I opened and scarfed down yet another loaf of bread and that's when you came in.

YANIV: This is very interesting story. (To G-Fish) I am afraid I cannot be helping you to finding your family, but you would like maybe to come with me to my house and I can be showing you my family and how I live as G-Fish.

G-FISH: That sounds great! Let's go right noooooooow!

(Through a window on the back wall, we see Mr. X—the Egyptian dude—poke his head up to spy on the group. Cut to exterior shot of Mr. X outside the window)

MR. X: (On phone) Yes, I see them right now. Yes of course, I will not let the fish out of my site. Yes. Yes. Yes, I will not forget to pick up your dry-cleaning.

(Transition to G-Fish and Yaniv in Yaniv's apartment.)

G-FISH: I can't tell you how wonderful it feels to be spending time with another G-Fish. I mean, I just feel so at home. So comfortable. So.... WHAT IN THE WORLD IS THAT? (Looks at a bath tub full of red goop which is sitting in the middle of the room.)

YANIV: Oh, this? It is a bath tub full of Chrain.

G-FISH: Chrain? You mean, that bath tub is full of horse radish?

YANIV: What, you never take Chrain bath before? (Jumps up and dives into the Chrain tub with a splash.) (Relaxed...) Ahhhhhh. (Then, as if Chrain were burning your sinuses...) Ahhh! Oh! Ouch! Wow! That's strong. (Relaxed again...) Ahhhhh. (SNIFF) Oh man.

G-FISH: (Turns away quickly.) Oh the horror! The unsanitary, sticky, grossitating horror.

YANIV: What is being wrong? (Splashes around and plays a bit in the Chrain.) Ohhh...that stings.

G-FISH: I can't believe you're actually enjoying that. I take 8 showers a day just to wash off my jelly broth secretions, and you are actually voluntarily swimming around in a tub full of Chrain? I don't think I can take this. Good day sir. (Exit's apartment)

(Cut to exterior of building. In the background, G-Fish exits and walks down the street. In the foreground, Mr. X is watching.)

MR. X: He is walking out of the building now. (Pause) Fine, floating, you know what I meant. (Pause) Yes, they got the mustard stain out of your shirt.

(Cut to Rabbi, Jono, Ari, and Lisa in Lisa's apartment.)

RABBI: So, any ideas as to what our next move should be?

ARI: Well we never had our passports stamped coming into this country, so we're going to have a pretty hard time getting out. Face it, we're stuck here forev...

JONO: EH!

ARI: We're stu...

JONO: MUH!

ARI: There's...

JONO: BLUH!

LISA: (She's been writing on a piece of paper) Hey guys, I just finished writing a song about G-Fish and his search for his heritage. Here, Ari, you sing the lyrics and I'll play the tune on my guitar.

ARI: WHAT? Why do I have...

JONO: GUH!

ARI: (Lets out a long, exaggerated sigh)...Hit it, sis.

(Lisa starts strumming a folky tune on here guitar.)

ARI: (Singing reluctantly) Listen, dear friends to my little song, 'bout a poor little fish who's the star of this song. (Spoken to lisa:) You rhymed song with song?

LISA: (Continues strumming the whole time) keep it going, don't break the rhythm.

ARI: (Singing) This fish had three friends with whom he did go...A Rabbi, A Jono—(Spoken:) a Jono?

LISA: Yes

ARI: (Sings) And a guy with a fro. (Spoken happily:) Hey, that's me! I'm starting to like this song!

JONO: Yawn. I'm not. Let's stop and eat bread.

(G-Fish enters)

G-FISH: Hey guys. Ready to smuggle ourselves to china?

(Everyone turns to G-Fish, shocked to see him)

RABBI: G-Fish! You're supposed to be spending time with Yaniv.

G-FISH: Yeah, well it turns out that Yaniv is a super weirdo. HE TAKES BATHS IN HORSERADISH! So I ditched him and now I'm here. Ready to smuggle ourselves to China?

RABBI: What? You ran away because a G-Fish dipped himself in Chrain? I can't believe I'm saying this, but—it actually makes perfect sense for a G-Fish to dip himself in Chrain.

G-FISH: Yeah but it's gross. Really really super weirdo gross. And besides, We've had enough distractions already. The task at hand is to go to china to find my family so I can find out what it means to be a G-Fish. Anything else is just keeping me from that goal and making me nauseous.

RABBI: I'm not so sure about that, G-Fish.

G-FISH: So you think getting stuck in a pyramid HELPED us find my family? Gee, I must have missed the part where my crazy uncle Leon was hiding in A SARCOPHAGUS!

RABBI: Remember what I told you earlier about the Jews counting down the days until they received the Torah? Well, there was a reason why they had to wait 49 days in the first place—because they weren't ready yet. They were slaves for so many years, they didn't know yet how to be responsible for their own decisions. And so those 49 days were a process through which the children of Israel prepared themselves one step at a time , so they would be ready to accept the responsibility of the ethics and values of the Torah. I guess what I'm trying to say is, if you had such a hard time getting along with another G-Fish because he did something that seems quite natural for a G-Fish to do, what do you think will happen when you meet your family and see all the G-Fish things they do.

G-FISH: Ooooooh kaaaaaaaay. You're going to have to say that again in one sentence or less.

RABBI: Maybe all these distractions are actually a process you need to go through to become ready to accept the responsibilities of being a G-Fish.

G-FISH: Awwww maaaan!

JONO: (Jono has been standing by the window, looking out.) Um, everybody? Remember that guy who locked us in the pyramid?

ALL: Yeah.

JONO: Well, he's staring at me through binoculars.

ALL: WHAT?!

RABBI: This is ridiculous!

JONO: Oooh, that's the first time you said that during this adventure.

ARI: This is horrible!

JONO: Definitely NOT the first time you've said that.

(Knock knock knock. Everyone freezes)

RABBI: (Cautiously) Who is it?

YANIV: It is me, Yaniv!

(A sigh of relief. They open the door and Yaniv enters)

G-FISH: Yaniv, I'm sorry about ditching you before…

YANIV: Forget about it. There is no time now, you are being followed by the man who locked you in the pyramid. He is working for someone who wants to stop you from reaching your goal.

JONO: How do you no so much?

YANIV: I am secret agent for secret organization that is protecting the Gefilte Fishes. I can secretly help you, but we must secretly leave very soon.

(Cut to Mr. X)

MR. X: (Into phone) Yes sir, I will go in now and capture them! (He enters the building. Cut to apartment)

G-FISH: What kind of secret organization? Is there a handshake?

JONO: Or a milk shake? Please say there's a milkshake.

YANIV: (Getting nervous) There's no milk shake.

JONO: (Holds up a loaf of bread and speaks to it) Some day we'll have a milk shake friend. Don't worry.

YANIV: The secret organization is a secret counsel of wise old Gefilte Fishes. But we must leave immediately!

(Cut to Mr. X ascending staircase)

JONO: How old is old for a G-Fish?

YANIV: Please, we must go now!

JONO: And how wise is wise for a G-Fish?

(Cut to Mr. X walking down the hallway and up to the door.)

MR. X: (To phone) I'm going in. (Kicks open door. Cut to his face. He stares. Cut to apartment. It is empty. No one is there.) It's empty! And I totally forgot your shirt somewhere. I'm so sorry.

(The gang is frantically running down an alley. Lisa is somehow playing guitar)

ARI: (Singing off a piece of paper:) Here we go running as fast as we can, From a mysterious and creepy Egyptian man. This journey is not as simple as we wish, Yes my friends it's our quest for fish. Yes, my friends, it's our quest for fiiiiiiish....

LISA: Very good Ari!

EPISODE 5: DO-OVER

SCENE: Mr. X stands in Lisa's apartment

MR. X: I'm so sorry sir. I won't let…ok, honestly I probably will let it happen again. I'm not very good at my job.

(Cut to the gang hanging from a helicopter ladder, cheering.)

JONO: Hooray! I think I'm gonna vomit!

(Transition to Gefilte Fish headquarters. It is a huge magnificent building with a sign in the front that reads "Secret Gefilte Fish Counsel". Cut to interior of headquarters. G-Fish and friends are being escorted down a long corridor filled with portraits of various Gefilte Fishes from different eras.)

GUIDE: Welcome to our headquarters gentlemen. As you probably already know from reading the giant sign on the front of the building, this is a secret organization. So please don't

tell your friends about this place, and if you do, please remind them that this is a secret.

(The group gets to the end of the corridor and enter a large, beautiful reception/waiting area. There are Gefilte Fishes passing through every so often, and in the background there is a reception desk with a Gefilte Fish answering phones and "typing" on a computer.)

GUIDE: Ok gentlemen, help yourself to a cup of jelly broth, and someone will be with you shortly. (Exits)

G-FISH: This is so amazing! I've never seen this many Gefilte Fish before!

JONO: What about when I took you to my grandparent's Seder and you flipped out and made a scene?

RABBI: I assume he means the giant talking type of Gefilte Fish.

JONO: Ohhhhhhh, gotcha. (Leans over to G-Fish and whispers…) I actually don't get it.

(Ira, an old, wise Gefilte Fish enters)

IRA: Percibal!

RABBI, JONO, ARI: Percibal?!

G-FISH: So that's what the P in Gefilte Fish is for! Already I'm learning so much about myself!

IRA: We've been expecting you. My name is Ira, and I am a member of the Gefilte Fish Counsel. We have so much to tell you, and so much for you to do.

G-FISH: Hooray for meeeee! What's next?!

IRA: Actually, you came just in time for a special Gefilte Fish Holiday. All the Gefilte fish from all over swim across the ocean to gather together with Murray, the wisest oldest Gefilte Fish on a deserted island, where they boil a giant carrot and eat it together.

G-FISH: Eh. Not interested.

RABBI: What?!

IRA: It's a very important part of the Gefilte Fish heritage.

G-FISH: I get to learn about my Gefilte Fish heritage?!

IRA: Well, no. It's not so much of an informational thing as it is a growth experience.

G-FISH: Not interested. I have a policy against growth experiences.

IRA: Well, if you change your mind, here's a map to the island. But keep it mind that the holiday begins tonight and ends at sunrise tomorrow morning.

G-FISH: Thank you. Oh, and would it be possible to get a wake up call for any time after sunrise tomorrow morning?

(Transition to G-Fish and Jono playing a board game in their quarters. There is a window behind them through which we see dozens of Gefilte Fishes diving into the water and swimming away. Jono is distracted by this spectacle.)

JONO: This is soooo cool, G-Fish. Are you sure you don't want to go?

G-FISH: I told you, I have a policy.

JONO: But this looks totally wasome!

G-FISH: Come on! What's the big deal?! I want to learn about by Gefilte Fish heritage, not participate in some cheesy boring growth experience. If I wanted that I would have gone to that motivational seminar you tried to drag me to.

(Cut to a motivational speaker)

SPEAKER: I want everybody here to give a big round of applause for yourself. Because, aside from me, YOU are the most important person in this room.

(Cut to a bunch of empty folding chairs. Jono is the only one in the audience. He applauds himself)

JONO: Yay, me!

(Back to G-Fish and Jono)

G-FISH: I'm tired of monopoly. Let's play Chicago-opoly.

(Transition to a few hours later. Outside is dark and there are only a couple of straggler fishes swimming away)

G-FISH: Ok, time for university of Texas-opoly!

(Transition to another few hours later. Jono is slumped over on the table. Outside the sun is rising.)

G-FISH: Ok, ready for Solar-System-opoly?

JONO: Please, G-Fish. I'm tired. I want to go to sleep. I don't want to play anymore opolys. What are you trying to prove?

G-FISH: Ok, big guy. I guess you can go get some shut eye. I guess I'm gonna head on over to check out the end of this growth shindig.

(Cut to the pier, or wherever it is that the Gefilte Fishes were swimming away from. Several Gefilte Fishes come swimming up as G-Fish approaches.)

FISH1: Oh man, that was awesome!

FISH2: Totally! This is why I love being a Gefilte Fish!

GFISH: Hey, guys, are things still happening at that thing?

FISH1: No way, dude. It ended like an hour ago, at sunrise. You weren't there?

GFISH: I was busy playing opolies. (Jumps into water and swims off. He swims along in the ocean for a while. As he swims, we hear "Oh man, that was awesome!" and "Totally! This is why I love being a Gefilte Fish!" echo in his head. Eventually, we see him arrive on the island. There is a beautiful palace like structure. G-Fish approaches it, and as he reaches the front entrance, Murray, the oldest wisest Gefilte fish exits and slams the door behind him.

G-FISH: I'm here! I'm ready to grow.

MURRAY: I'm sorry, Sporto, you missed it. It's all over. There's nothing left. You totally missed…

G-FISH: Yeah, I get it.

MURRAY: Good. Just making sure.

G-FISH: But can't you make an exception?

MURRAY: Sorry, sports fans, we have a policy. Now if you'll excuse me, I have a warm Chrain bath waiting for me at home.

(Transition to G-Fish swimming sadly back to headquarters. Transition to G-Fish moping in his quarters. Jono is there, and Rabbi enters enthusiastically, holding a manila envelope.)

RABBI: Good news, everybody! The Gefilte Fishes were able to work out our passport problem. Everything is taken care of, and we're ready to go to china!

(G-Fish doesn't react)

JONO: Hey, why the long face…Percibal (Snickers)

G-FISH: what's the point. I missed out on a chance to really grow as a fish. Who even cares about getting to China anymore.

RABBI: That's quite a change of attitude…Percibal. I thought you had a policy.

G-FISH: Yeah, well it turns out my policy stinks. I totally messed up and I may never have this chance again.

RABBI: Look, Percibal (Jono snickers) at the time of the original Passover, some of the Jews were unable to participate. They missed it, and there was nothing they could do about it. But they couldn't get over it, and they felt so bad that they went to Moses and begged for another chance. Moses asked G-d, and G-d gave them a second chance, a month after Passover. A second Passover. And to this day, that Holiday is a reminder that we can always have a second chance.

G-FISH: Not in this case. It's all over. Murray the wise old Gefilte Fish told me himself. In several different ways.

RABBI: Of course he did. The second chance can't just come from Murray. It has to come from you. You have to change, and make it happen.

JONO: Yeah, Percibal (Snickers)

RABBI: Gefilte Fish, I think you know what you need to do. And while he's doing that, Jono, can I trust you with getting us tickets to China?

JONO: Absolutely! (Whispers to G-Fish…) Not. Absolutely not.

(Transition to G-Fish swimming across the ocean. He is determined. He get's to the palace, and enters.)

G-FISH: Murray! I'm here!

MURRAY: Percibal. I'm surprised to see you here. I already told you that you missed everything. In fact, I'm pretty sure I paraphrased it several times to the point of being annoying.

G-FISH: I want to do this thing! This carrot thing! I want to grow!

MURRAY: But I thought you had a policy?

G-FISH: I'm suspending my policy.

MURRAY: Well, If you can suspend your policy, then I guess we can suspend ours. Come on over here, champ, I've got a carrot for you.

G-FISH: Yaaaaaaay!!!!!

(Fade and cut to Jono at the airport ticket counter. Mr. X (In a horrible disguise) stands on the other side of the counter and issues Jono tickets)

MR. X: That's 6 tickets to…(Snicker)…China (Snicker)

JONO: (Nervously) Hahaha…China. (Whispering to no one…) I don't get it.

(Jono walks away with the tickets. Mr. X takes off part of his horrible disguise and speaks into his walkie-talkie)

MR. X: Sir…I have totally redeemed myself. They won't get far this time.

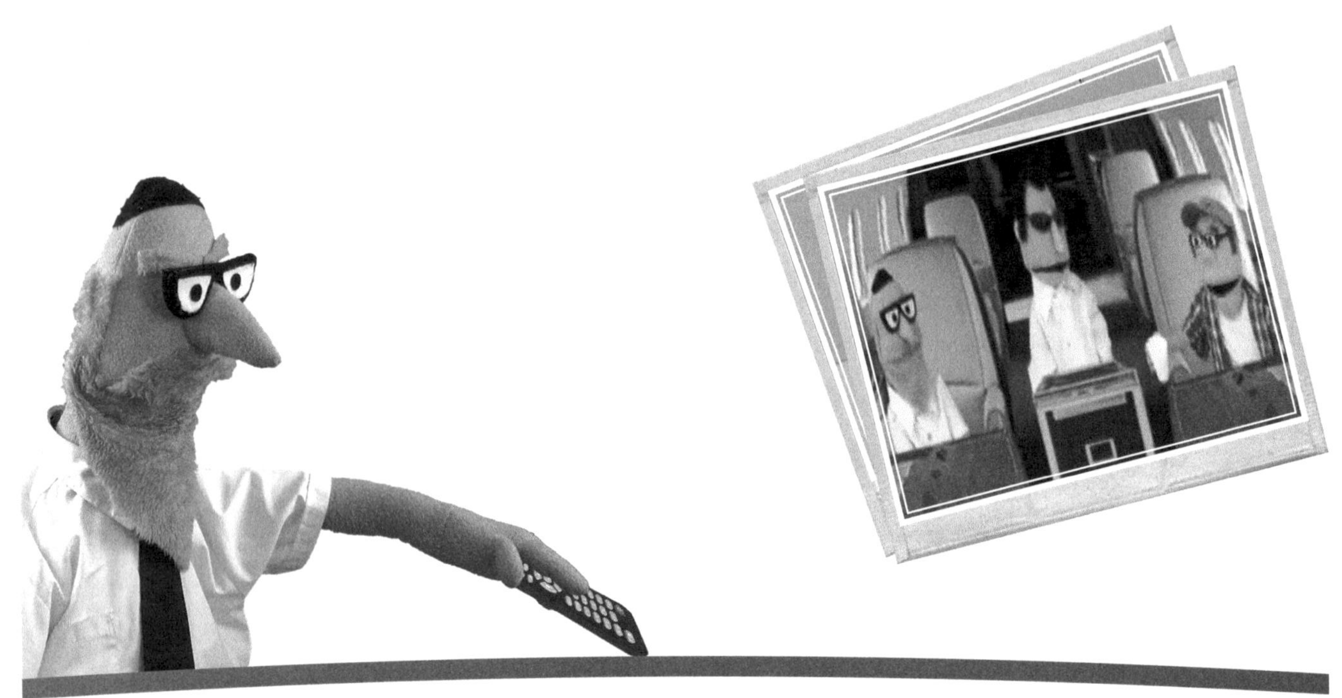

EPISODE 6: RESPECT

SCENE: Rabbi Itche, Jono, G-Fish, and Ari are on a small private jet.

G-FISH: Ahhh. Finally we're on our way to China to meet my family and discover the secrets of my G-Fish heritage.

JONO: Ummm…I'm surprised nobody thought of this before, but, why didn't we just dig a hole?

G-FISH: To china.

JONO: Yes. Dig a hole to china.

G-FISH: That's ridiculous, Jono. If we dug a hole straight through the earth, all the way to china, and then jumped in, we would get half way through and then the force of gravity would start pulling us back to the center. We'd bounce back and forth for a while until we slowed down and then just got stuck at the core of the earth FOREVER!

(Mr. X in his bad mustache disguise enters pushing a drink cart.)

MR. X: Can I interest anybody in a beverage? Tea. Coffee, or perhaps a soda?

JONO: Yes, I'll have a diet coke with lime please.

RABBI: Something isn't right here. I can't quite put my finger on it, but…

MR. X: Here you go sir.

JONO: Thank you. (Takes a sip and does a spit take.) You're right Rabbi! Something isn't right here at all! This isn't diet coke with lime! This is coke zero with actual lime juice squeezed into it!

MR. X: (Smacks his head) Oh, man! I'm worse at serving drinks than I am at trapping people in pyramids!

RABBI: WHAT?!

MR. X: (Smacks his head again) Oh, MAN! I'm worse at pretending not to be the guy who locked you in a pyramid than I am at…. Being the guy who locked you in a pyramid!

RABBI: WHAT?!

MR. X: Excuse me, I have to go. (Quickly rushes out with the drink cart.) Drink service will be temporarily suspended. Please be careful when opening the overhead compartment as lavatory smoke detectors my have lost cabin pressure during oxygen mask. (He exits)

RABBI: What is going on here?!

JONO: Ohhhhhhhh, now I get it. (To G-Fish) You're right G-Fish, we would just get stuck in the center of the earth forever.

RABBI: Focus, Jono. I'm not going to point any fingers but…YOU BOUGHT OUR TICKETS FROM THE GUY WHO LOCKED US IN THE PYRAMID?!

JONO: But he had a mustache!

RABBI: I can't believe this!

JONO: And competitive prices!

ARI: Well that's good, at least.

G-FISH: Cool it guys. I've got a theory. I think this guy was sent by Harvey Weissfish to make our story more interesting for when he makes it into a movie.

ARI: That's a terrible theory.

JONO: (Mimicking Ari in a silly voice) That's a terrible theory.

ARI: (Ignoring Jono) I think it's the guys from the Chinese mafia who smashed up the shop that Jono bought G-Fish from.

G-FISH: Oh come on, Ari. It's always the Chinese Mafia with you. My toothbrush is missing! Oh the Chinese mafia probably took it! What happened to my cell-phone reception? Oh, the Chinese mafia hijacked the satellite. Pshh.

RABBI: Maybe there's someone who is against the whole idea of G-Fish heritage.

JONO: Who, Mel Gibson?

RABBI: Do you have a better suggestion, Jono?

JONO: I think it's the same guys who faked the moon landing.

RABBI: That's absurd!

(Everybody starts yelling at each other. Cut to another part of the plane where Mr. X is talking on an Air-Phone.)

MR. X: I am so sorry sir. I gave them the wrong beverage.

(Cut to GEOFFREY JUAN DELATISTE on his cell-phone)

MR. DELATISTE: What?! So?

MR. X: Well, to make a long story short, they know they're not going to china. It's only a matter of time before they work together to devise a plan to escape, like they always do.

(Cut to the group arguing)

RABBI: That doesn't even make any sense!

JONO: You don't make any sense! He (Pointing to G-Fish) don't make any sense! That fake mustache don't make any sense! I don't make any sense! I'm scared. I want my mummy.

G-FISH: I don't see how that joke even applies here, Jono.

JONO: I don't see how you even apply here!

ARI: Will everybody just stop saying their absurd ideas and listen to my absurd ideas?

G-FISH: No!

JONO: Who made you the King of this airplane?

G-FISH: That guy!

(Cut to a weird looking guy in another seat)

WEIRD GUY: Helloooo, Your Majesty!

(Again they all speak on top of each other. Cut to Mr. X)

MR. X: What should I do?!

MR. DELATISTE: Just...(Sigh) I don't have time for this, I'm in the middle of a very important negotiation. Can I put you on hold?

MR. X: Fine, but this Air-Phone is costing me $45 a minute.

MR. DELATISTE: It's a business expense.

MR. X: Oh goodie.

MR. DELATISTE: Hang on...

(CLICK. cut to a wide shot of Geoffrey Juan Delitiste which reveals that he is talking to an elderly G-Fish couple.)

MR. DELATISTE: Look, Sidney, Gertrude, I need to have those scrolls, and I think I've made quite a generous offer.

SIDNEY: But they are sacred G-Fish artifacts which tell of our history and a very special recipe for G-Fish!

MR. DELATISTE: Which is exactly why I need them for my museum of crypto-zoology.

GERTRUDE: But we're saving them to pass down to our son Percibal!

MR. DELATISTE: I'm sorry, Mrs. Fish, but your son isn't coming. I've given you as much time as I can, but I'm going to need to have those artifacts from you in exactly 2 weeks.

(Cut to Rabbi and the rest arguing)

G-FISH: (Mimicking someone) Blah blah blah, I'm a big baby and I don't know what I'm talking about!

JONO: Stop it G-Fish, that doesn't even sound like the Rabbi.

RABBI: EVEYBODY STOP IT! This isn't getting us anywhere! Don't you see what's happening? We're so busy judging everybody else's ideas that we're not even stopping to think about what we should actually be doing!

G-FISH: I assume this would NOT be a good time to repeat all that in a silly voice. Right?

RABBI: Right. Look, Today is actually a very special day that commemorates the end of a terrible sickness that struck the students of the great Talmudic sage Rabbi Akiva. The Talmud says that the cause for this sickness was that the students weren't being respectful to each other.

JONO: Rabbi, are you threatening us with a plague? That's not cool at all. You're supposed to be the grown-up here.

RABBI: No. No I am most certainly not. I'm getting to a point. The people we're talking about here were students of one of the greatest leaders and teachers in Jewish history, and many of them were very special

people in their own right. How could they have been disrespectful to each other?

G-FISH: You started a speech you don't even know the end of?

RABBI: What? No, I was planning on answering the question myself.

G-FISH: Ohhhhh. Ok. Go ahead.

RABBI: They didn't think they were being disrespectful to each other. They just each believed so much in their own way of doing things that they felt it would be best for everyone else to think and act like them. I think what we need to do here, is respect each other's different ways of thinking, and use our unique talents to pull together and get us out of this mess!

ARI: I know how to fly a plane!

ALL: What?!

ARI: Yeah, I fly Mr. Weissfish around in his private jet all the time.

RABBI: That's great! Ari, you go take over the plane and fly us to china!

ARI: Yayyy! I'm useful again!

RABBI: Jono and G-Fish, can you guys play good cop bad cop and get some information out of that guy?

JONO: Well, Sunday night is usually boggle night and good cop bad cop is Wednesday nights, but I guess we could make an exception.

G-FISH: What are you gonna do, Rabbi? What's your special talent?

RABBI: What's my special talent?! I came up with this whole lesson.

(They stare)

RABBI: I always come up with the lessons!

(Still staring)

RABBI: (Pause) Fine, I'll go knock out the pilot. But I'm not going to do it violently, I'll do it gently, and RESPECTFULLY.

(Cut to Rabbi an Ari walking up to the pilot. They pull a curtain closed. We can no longer see them, but we can hear them.)

RABBI: Hi, I'm Rabbi Itche Kadoozy.

PILOT: Oh, hi, I'm Steve Tadesco, I've been hired to help kidnap you all.

RABBI: Nice to meet you Steve. You know, you being hired to help kidnap us reminds me of a story about my great Uncle Yaakov in Russia. Yaakov was so poor he didn't have a horse. He was walking from his shtetl in Brisketkov to his Grandmother's shtetl in Bagelrov with nothing but a chicken and a paddle ball. It was almost sundown and Yaakov needed a place to make Shabbat. The chicken suggested they camp out, but...

(The pilot starts snoring loudly)

RABBI: Well Ari, I knocked him out. Take the wheel.

(Black screen...then a loud "BOOM"—a card pops up reading: "Kidnapper's Private Jet." Somewhere in the sky outside of Israel, Jono and G-Fish approach mr. X)

G-FISH: Ok, Mr. Wise Guy, tell us who you're working for. I want answers and I want them now!

MR. X: I'm sorry, I cannot tell you.

G-FISH: LOOK, BUDDY, I've been on the force for thirty years and I'm not gonna let some smart guy kid pull one over on me!

JONO: Hey, cool it, chief. You've only got one for week till retirement, don't blow it. Why don't you let me take this for a while.

G-FISH: Fine. I'm gonna get some fresh air, but when I come back I want answers and a signed statement!

(G-Fish exits)

JONO: Don't worry about Macgillicuddy, he's a hot-head.

MR. X: Who?

JONO: He's a little bit of a loose canon, but he's a good guy.

(Rabbi slowly walks through the aisle hunched over. The sound of a body being pulled across the carpet and snoring is heard.)

JONO: So, kid, you like baseball cards?

MR. X: (Cautiously) kind of

JONO: And chocolates? All the kids your age love chocolates, right?

MR. X: Uh huh

JONO: And maybe you wanted a chocolate so much that you stole a bicycle? That sounds reasonable, right?

MR. X: I can't take this anymore! You have twisted my mind into a pretzel! You must be some type of psychological genius!

(G-Fish returns)

JONO: As a matter of fact, sir, I am (Whispers to G-Fish) Not. I am not.

MR. X: I'll tell you everything. I work for a man named Geoffrey Juan DeLatiste who is the curator of the Museum of Cryptozoology in California. (To G-Fish) There is a special artifact that belongs to your parents that he wants for his museum.

G-FISH: My parents?! They really are in china?!

JONO: WAIT! Wait…more importantly…You said something before about pretzels?

MR. X: (To Jono) Ingenious! (To G-Fish) But apparently, young G-Fish, your parents still are in China. They insist that they are waiting for you to return so they can pass this important artifact on to you, but, as you are aware, my boss has made many efforts to keep you from getting to them before he can buy it from them.

JONO: We've gotta stop this guy!

MR. X: You will never get to them in time. They are staying in a location that is so remote it can take a month to find. And they have agreed to sell Mr. DeLatiste the artifact in exactly 2 weeks.

G-FISH: Then we have to get there in less than that. Less than two weeks. Like 12 days maybe! Or perhaps 13. But no more than 14! Cuz that will be 2 weeks!

WEIRD GUY: You must hurry, Your Majesty!

JONO: Does anyone have a pretzel?

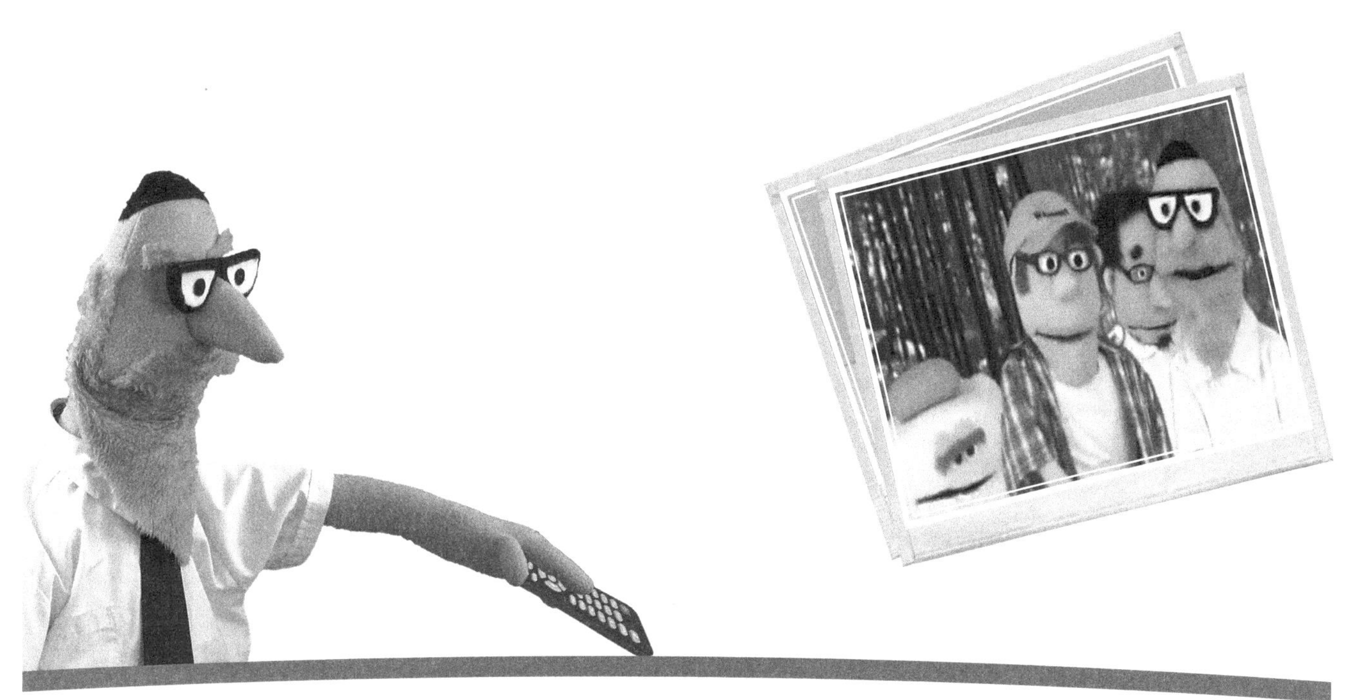

EPISODE 7: ACTION!

SCENE: Rabbi Itche and G-Fish on the private jet)

G-FISH: Rabbi, tell me honestly, do you think I'm ready for this?

RABBI: I don't know, G-Fish, you tell me.

G-FISH: I mean, I don't know if you've noticed, but after all we've been through to find my family so I can learn how to be a good G-Fish, I'm still kind of obnoxious.

RABBI: Oh, don't be so hard on yourself, Gefilte…

G-FISH: (To Jono) Hey, Jono, get your eyes off my super-cool mp3 player. You're nerding it up just by looking at it. (To Rabbi) You were saying?

RABBI: Look, G-Fish, before the Jewish people received the Torah…

The Quest for Fish

ARI: (Voice over) Attention passengers. We are ready to land in Beijing, China. Please brace yourself for a horrible lending.

RABBI: We'll finish this discussion later.

(Transition to Jono, G-Fish, and Ari hanging out on the street in china.)

G-FISH: I can't believe we're finally here! In China!

JONO: (Looking down at himself) And I can't believe I only brought one change of clothes. Grossinating.

(Rabbi comes in with a map)

RABBI: Ok guys, I talked to a fisherman who gave me this map to the G-Fish village.

ARI: Hey, Look at that!

(Cut to Mr. X holding a sign that says "Rabbi Itche Kadoozy." Rabbi and the rest walk up to him.)

RABBI: You again! What do you want?!

MR. X: You are helping a G-Fish on his journey. I can help you but you must…

JONO: Stop it. Why would we ever be tricked into trusting you again? Just stop it.

MR. X: (Ashamed) Yes sir.

(Rabbi and the rest walk away shaking their heads. Cut to the group in a boat on a river. Rabbi is holding the map and the rest look at it.)

RABBI: According to the map, there's a cave up ahead about 1 and a half kilometers into the forest.

JONO: And look here—(points at the map) it seems as though we're approaching a giant compass.

RABBI: You really don't know how a map works, do you?

JONO: Nope! I also don't know how a belt works. (Looks down) Oh, there they go.

RABBI: Anyways, (Show map as Rabbi talks) the cave is the entrance to a tunnel that leads to a chamber that opens up to a path that takes you to a rope bridge that crosses over to a mine cart track, which leads to a mountain at the edge of the Gefilte Fish village. G-Fish, Your parents are at the top of that mountain.

JONO: Hooraaaaaaay!

RABBI: But the journey is very dangerous and the tunnels and paths are protected by traps.

JONO: Boooooooo!

G-FISH: Thanks for caring so much Jono.

JONO: I do care. And I wanna get back home to my toothbrush. I haven't brushed my teeth since the morning we left.

(They all stare at Jono)

JONO: (Ashamed) The morning before the morning we left.

(They all continue to stare)

JONO: Who am I kidding? I don't miss brushing my teeth at all. (To G-Fish) I'm just really excited for you to meet your family, G-Fish… and tired of all this random weirdo crazy junk getting in the way.

RABBI: It's getting dark guys. We'll have to camp out for the night at the river bank and start out tomorrow morning.

(Transition to the group sleeping by a camp fire. Suddenly, G-Fish notices Geoffrey Juan DeLatiste standing over him in the dark.)

G-FISH: Ahhh!

GEOFFREY: Shhhhh. I'm not going to hurt you.

G-FISH: What do you want?!

GEOFFREY: I just want to talk. Here, have a drink of water.

G-FISH: Is it poisoned?

GEOFFREY: (Pause) Yes.

G-FISH: I thought you said you weren't going to hurt me.

GEOFFREY: Starting.... Now. Look, G-Fish, Percibal, whatever you call yourself, I've been keeping a close eye on you throughout your journey and I know a lot about you and how you think. And from what I can gather, you're going through a lot of trouble to get something you don't even know you want.

G-FISH: What are you talking about?! Of course I do!

GEOFFREY: You were completely disgusted by a G-Fish Chrain bath and totally uninterested in an important G-Fish ritual. And now you're about to go on a very dangerous journey to get a sacred G-Fish scroll that you know nothing about. What makes you think you're even going to understand or accept what it says? The teachings of your people need to be preserved in my museum for no one but me and some random strangers to casually glance at...not given to you so you can use them as a badminton net.

G-FISH: (In awe and wonder) How did you know I needed a new badminton net?

GEOFFREY: Just think about it, Percibal.

(Geoffrey walks off. G-Fish is confused. Transition to the group walking through the forest. Rabbi is holding the map and looking at it closely as he walks.)

RABBI: According to the map, the opening to the tunnel should be very close.

JONO: You mean, that opening to a tunnel? (Cut to a shot of the group from behind. They are standing directly in front of the tunnel.)

RABBI: (Looks up) Oh. Yeah. That's it.

JONO: Let's go! (Jono starts to walk in, and Rabbi pulls him back.)

RABBI: Jono, no!

JONO: Make up your mind, Rabbi. Maaaaaaaaaaaaaaaaa (Deep breath) aaaaaaaaaaaaaaaaaaaaaan.

RABBI: That was uncalled for. (He bends down and picks up a stick, and pokes the floor by the entrance with the stick. A big pointy metal rod shoots out across the doorway.)

JONO: Coooooool!

ARI: Cool? Cool? That could have killed us! This whole journey could have killed us. My dad's a lawyer, you know?

(They duck under the rod and enter the tunnel.)

(Show the group going through the tunnel cautiously. Eventually they reach 3 doors.)

RABBI: Everybody stop. It's very important we choose the right door. We have no idea what will happen if we open the wrong one.

G-FISH: (Floats over to a plaque type thingy on the side.) look, there's something written here.

RABBI: (Reading) Some G-Fish come in rolls, other's come in this door.

ARI: What's that supposed to mean? It's horrible.

JONO: It's a riddle, Ari. All doors to secret chambers have riddles.

RABBI: (Thinking) others come in this door....

ARI: It's too hard!

RABBI: Hang on, guys, I can get this.

JONO: Why don't we split up, and we'll each try a different door?

G-FISH: Look, there's more writing (Blows on the plaque to reveal more writing. Reads) "And by the way, if you pick the wrong door, a giant

rock will fall on your head, and it will hit you in the head, and then you'll have a smashy head.

JONO: Ouch. Nobody wants a smashy head.

RABBI: Ok, first let's think about how the doors are different…

JONO: (Looking at the left door which is slightly open) well, that one over there is ajar.

ARI: No it's not, it's a door.

RABBI: That's it! The door on the left is slightly open or ajar. Some G-Fish come in a jar!

JONO: Good work gumshoe!

RABBI: Brace yourselves, gentlemen, I'm trying the door. 1, 2, 3…(He pushes the door open to reveal a big spacious chamber with drawings of Gefilte Fishes all over the walls.

G-FISH: It's beautiful!

JONO: Look at those hieroglyphics!

(Transition to a montage of the group hiking through the forest, walking on a rope bridge, riding in a mine cart, and finally approaching the mountain. The next few lines of dialogue take place as they are still walking towards the mountain)

RABBI: This is it. The last part of your journey.

G-FISH: I don't know if I can do this, Rabbi.

RABBI: What? Why not?

G-FISH: I've been thinking, and I don't know if I even understand all this G-Fish stuff enough to be able to go up there and accept it.

(Pause)

JONO: That's your cue, Rabbi. This is where you use our personal struggles as a paper thin metaphor for the Jewish people receiving the Torah on mount Sinai.

RABBI: Am I that predictable?

JONO: Yes. But it's endearing.

RABBI: Alright then…Jono, this is where you say "Heeere we go" and start drifting off.

JONO: Oh, thanks for reminding me. (Clears his throat) Heeeere we go…

RABBI: G-Fish, when the Jewish people received the Torah at mount Sinai, they also didn't know exactly what it would say. But they knew they were Jewish and this is what they were supposed to do. So when it came time for them to accept the Torah, they said "We will do and we will listen." They accepted the responsibility to do what the Torah asked of them, before they even heard what exactly it was. All because they had faith that it's what they, as Jews, should do. G-Fish, you know that you are a G-Fish, and even if you don't understand everything right away, you can start doing it now, and continue to learn what it all means for the rest of your life. That's very much why I became a Rabbi!

G-FISH: I guess you're right, Rabbi. Let's go find my parents and claim my G-Fish identity!

RABBI: You got it, G-Fish! Let's get ready to climb this mountain!

ARI: It's gianormous!

JONO: Couldn't we just take the elevator? (Pan over to reveal an elevator imbedded in the mountain.)

RABBI: Oh. Yes. We could just take the elevator.

(Elevator doors open, the group enters and the doors close.)

EPISODE 8: HERITAGE

SCENE: Elevator doors open. Rabbi Itche, Jono, G-Fish and Ari walk out of the elevator into a beautiful mountain-top garden. Sydney and Gertrude—G-Fish's parents—are overwhelmed with Joy as they see their long lost son.

SYDENY: Son!

GERTRUDE: Percibal!

G-FISH: Mom! Dad! It's really you!

SYDNEY: Come here and give your old man a hug!

JONO: YESSS! This is it!

(G-Fish approaches his father and they embrace. How? Well, G-Fish get's "lifted" a little bit higher in the air and they revolve around each other for a couple revolutions.)

G-FISH: (Laughing a little) Ha ha. Ok. Ok, Dad, put me down. (G-Fish is lowered abruptly) It's so amazing to see you both.

GERTRUDE: I'm so happy you got here before that terrible man took the sacred G-Fish scrolls that rightfully belong to you.

SYDNEY: Come, my son, let us show you your scrolls.

(Sydney, G-Fish, and Gertrude float towards the scrolls, which are sitting on a pedestal in the middle of the garden.)

SYDNEY: Here son, read them They're yours.

(G-Fish moves closer to the scrolls and suddenly Geoffrey Juan DeLatiste shows up.)

GEOFFREY: Hold it! Everybody just step away from my scrolls, and nobody will get accidentally thrown of this mountain.

G-FISH: YOUR Scrolls?!

JONO: ACCIDENTALLY?!

GEOFFREY: That's right—MY SCROLLS! I am an EXPERT in crypto-zoology, and certainly the only person here who can possibly understand the true significance of those scrolls and use them properly. They belong to me!

G-FISH: They belong to you?! These scrolls belong to you?! (Getting really emotional and loud) You're not even a G-Fish! How could scrolls which are written to guide a G-Fish's life possibly belong to you?! Here, let's read them, shall we?! "Thou shall secrete jelly broth.!" Do you secret jelly broth?

JONO: Ewww. I hope not.

G-FISH: "Thou shall wear a carrot on your head!" Hmmm, I don't see a carrot on your head, Mr. DeLatiste! "Thou shalt not have bones!" Tell me sir, DO YOU HAVE BONES?!

JONO: OOOH! I got this one! (Bends down and pops up wearing x-ray specs.) Now let's see. (Cut to Jono's view through the x-ray specs. Cut back to Jono) Yup. He's got bones.

G-FISH: You couldn't possibly do these things!

GEOFFREY: That's the type of superficial attitude that makes you an unsuitable owner for those scrolls. To you it's just a list of "Shalls" and "Shall Nots." But to me—a man who has spent two-and-a-half years of his life and $275 tuition at the institute of cryptozoology in Venice beach California—To me, those scrolls are so much more. I see in them what you can't possibly see. I understand them far better than you fish could ever hope to. Now give me my scrolls. (Starts walking towards the scrolls)

G-FISH: (Loud and shocking) BACK OFF!

(Geoffrey freezes)

G-FISH: No matter how much you know about G-Fish heritage or cryptozoology, you are NOT the rightful owner of these scrolls. These scrolls are written so we—Gefilte Fishes like myself and my parents—can DO what they say and live by their values—in real life! Not just for some "expert" to sit and study.

RABBI: That's exactly what Moses said at Mount Sinai when the angel's claimed that they would be the more suitable recipients for the Torah….

G-FISH: Hang on, I'm not finished. These scrolls are MINE, buddy! For ME to actually DO what they say. And yes, I'll study them real close, and try to understand them the best I can, maybe not as good as you do, but what I can do is BE a G-Fish who can FOLLOW these scrolls in real life! And that's something you'll NEVER be able to do! Now get of here, sleazo, before I get REALLY angry.

(Mr. X leans over to Geoffrey and whispers in his ear.)

GEOFFRY: Fine. I'll go. But only because I've just been informed that I'm late for a meeting with bigfoot's parents. (The sound of an approaching

helicopter is heard. A Rope ladder falls down and Geoffrey and Mr. X walk away towards the ladder. Just before he starts to climb, Geoffrey turns back and shouts) You haven't heard the last of me!

(Cut to G-Fish and his parents as the helicopter is heard flying away.)

GERTRUDE: Percibal, I'm very proud of you.

G-FISH: Thank you, Mom.

SYDNEY: Here, son, take your scrolls. (The scrolls float off of the pedestal as G-Fish takes them. The three fishes are all very happy.

JONO: Well, it looks like everything ended happily ever after—with the exception of that "you haven't heard the last of me" remark, which I can only assume was supposed to leave things open ended for yet another adventure.

(Cut to a long, slow wide shot, zoomy outy thing of the whole garden and all the characters. Jono and Rabbi continue to talk as we slowly fade to black.)

RABBI: Am I going to get a chance to finish my speech about how all this reminds me of how the angels tried to argue that they were the rightful recipients of the Torah because they are spiritual and can understand the Torah better, but Moses said that the Jews were the rightful recipients because they could actually ACT on the values and commandments of the Torah?

JONO: No. I think everyone is a little too distracted. But for what it's worth, I can pretend to listen to it now.

RABBI: Works for me. Right before the Jewish people were about to receive the Torah…

(Audio fades out. Fade to black.)

[THE END]

Timeless Jewish Stories

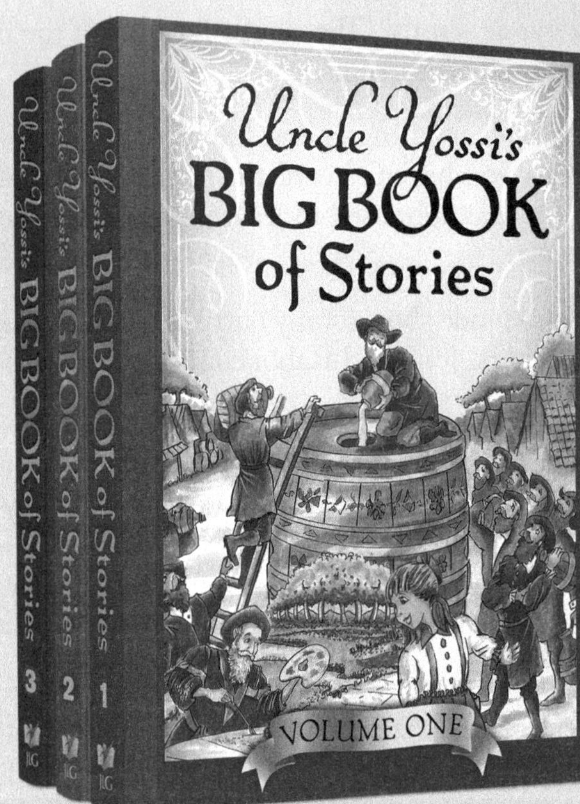

also available on

and

amazonkindle

Enjoy Over 60 Memorable Jewish Stories

www.GreatJewishTales.com

Classic Jewish Stories on Audio & Video

A fascinating audio collection of 52 stories & songs on 14 audio CDs for children of all ages and backgrounds.

(Incl. 14 CDs; Follow-along booklet; Deluxe storage case)

Four favorite stories read by master-storyteller Uncle Yossi, presented with beautiful colorful imagery from the large format Uncle Yossi storybooks.

(DVD; program time 42 minutes)

www.GreatJewishTales.com

Amazing Forgotten Jewish Stories

also available on

audible

and

amazonkindle

An exhilarating compilation of vintage Jewish stories that will leave you breathless with suspense!

www.GreatJewishTales.com

The Silly World of Chelm

also available on
audible
and
amazonkindle

Laugh and Enjoy over
150 Lovable Chelm Stories!

www.GreatJewishTales.com

MORE FUN BOOKS FOR KIDS!

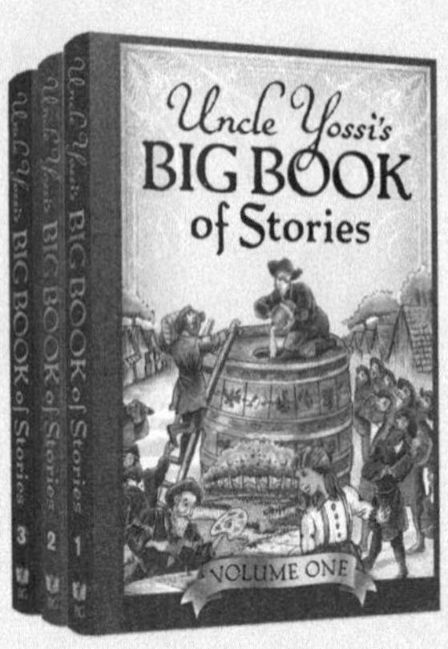

Order Today!

AT YOUR FAVORITE BOOKSTORE OR AT

amazonkindle **WWW.JEWISHLEARNINGGROUP.COM**

SEE ALL THE ORIGINAL ITCHE KADOOZY SHOWS FREE!

AT WWW.CHABAD.ORG/ITCHEKADOOZY